T0358548

INTERNATIONAL LEASING

International Leasing

Strategy and decision

SIMON S. GAO
Professor in Accounting and Finance
Napier University, Edinburgh

Routledge
Taylor & Francis Group

LONDON AND NEW YORK

Contents

Figures and tables

Acknowledgements

This book could not have been finished without the help of many people. I would like to thank Professor Dr. A.C.C. Herst and Professor Dr. M.A. van Hoepen RA for getting me started on this complex topic 'International Leasing' and for their encouragement through the years when I was their doctoral student at Erasmus University from 1987 to 1992. I would also like to thank Prof. Drs. W. Siddré, Prof. Dr. J. Spronk, Dr. W.M.L. van Bueren, Prof. H. Lunt, Prof. J. Blake, Prof. Dr. H. Peer, Dr. A.W.A. Joosen, and Drs. Frans den Adel for their comments and contribution to my PhD thesis, which forms some parts of this book.

Acknowledgements are also due to the Department of Risk and Financial Services of Glasgow Caledonian University, where I spent four years when this book was written, for providing me with various supports in terms of facilities and attending conferences and seminars.

Last but not least, special thanks to my wife Jane who has helped me persevere in the challenges of scholarly research.

1 Introduction

Internationalisation: an overview of the world leasing market

The fancy of leasing is as old as mankind. The applications of this fancy have naturally varied remarkably, based on social, legal, economic, fiscal, financial and technical circumstances prevailing in the respective civilisation and period of time. Leasing has its origins in ancient civilisations that used leasing arrangements for agricultural tools, shipping and real estate. The earliest record of leasing occurred in about 2010 B.C.[1] Those leases involved rentals of agricultural tools to farmers by the priests who were, in effect, the government officials. Land leasing has then been more common, but equipment leasing can be traced to the 1800s.

The dynamic nature of the modern leasing industry began in the 1950s in the USA when tax incentives for investment were created. In May 1952, Henry Schoenfield set up a separate corporation in the USA to handle one particular type of leasing transactions. He soon gained the confidence that leasing could be overlooked as a useful financing tool for business and decided to develop and market this technique. The company he founded with a capital of US$20,000, called the United States Leasing Corporation (now United States Leasing International, Inc.), was the first independent corporation to engage in the business of equipment leasing in the USA and still is one of the largest American leasing companies.

---

[1] Regarding the history of leasing, see Clark (1978), pp.2-13; Nevitt and Fabozzi (1988), pp.25-45.

Globally, the development of leasing accelerated in the 1960s and the 1970s in west Europe, in the 1980s in Asian and Latin American countries, varying based on the circumstance of an individual country. Expansion was primarily marked by the emergence of leasing companies to offer financing to companies within their own countries. The modern leasing industry has developed progressively since the 1960s.

Internationalisation is by now a well established fact in the world of business and finance. One of the most attractive new fields in modern finance and business is leasing. Leasing has grown enormously over the past decade: the volume level of world leasing has increased from US$63.6 billion in 1980 to US$428.08 billion in 1996 (World-Leasing-Yearbook 1998, p.2). Table 1.1 provides a general picture of the development of leasing from 1979 to 1996. Through the world, leasing has established itself as an important form of financing and expanded considerably in both developed and developing countries. Worldwide leasing provides more finance than Eurobonds, Euro-commercial paper, medium-term notes, Euronotes or international equities (World-Leasing-Yearbook 1994, p.4). In the US, leasing even provides more finance than the corporate bond and the commercial mortgage markets together.[2]

Table 1.1 Leasing business worldwide

	LEASING BUSINESS WORLDWIDE (US$ million)					
	1979	1982	1985	1992	1994	1996
North America	33,926	58,357	95,845	127,600	148,000	177,000
Asia	5,500	10,500	25,855	80,900	99,200	105,800
Europe	9,513	15,839	24,705	99,500	87,500	117,700
Australasia	3,621	4,891	3,887	4,200	5,900	7,300
Latin America	N/A	1,800	1,589	6,300	11,100	15,000
Africa	N/A	1,000	1,193	4,800	4,700	5,300
Total	52,560	92,387	153,074	323,300	356,400	428,100

Sources: World Leasing Yearbooks, 1988, 1994, 1996, 1998

During the past 35 years leasing in Western Europe has grown at a faster rate than any other form of finance. New business of leased movable equipment recorded by the members of the European Federation of Leasing

---

[2] See USA Federal Reserve Bulletin, August 1993.

Company Associations (Leaseurope) reached 90.865 million ECU in 1996, according to Leaseurope.[3]

Table 1.2 Leasing business of movables and real estate in the Leaseurope

Country	1996	1995	1994	1993	1992	1991	1990	1989	1988
Austria	2,092	2,000	1,739	1,882	1,899	2,122	2,297	2,029	1,805
Belgium	1,761	1,467	1,325	1,271	1,512	1,671	1,583	1,323	949
Bulgaria	9	19	7	N/A	10	11	125	93	75
Switzerland	2,339	2,188	1,752	530	701	948	1,105	1,089	1,013
Czech	1,334	877	817	482	416	174	N/A	N/A	N/A
Germany	22,886	21,616	19,223	19,877	19,050	16,561	13234	9,911	9,090
Denmark	889	680	630	456	485	707	780	779	500
Spain	3,738	3,234	2,744	2,558	5,120	7,170	8,588	8,933	6,314
France	9,970	9,722	8,886	9,103	11,214	13,100	22,008	22,081	18,715
UK	24,280	19,666	18,853	17,056	16,022	18,081	19,993	20,161	17,054
Greece	282	226	181	N/A	201	139	97	65	N/A
Hungary	533	301	529	490	459	N/A	N/A	N/A	N/A
Italy	8,942	8,107	6,804	6,279	9,337	13,426	15,630	8,328	5,766
Ireland	2,182	1,160	1,050	978	841	866	864	784	436
Luxembourg	162	146	124	108	167	121	172	162	60
Morocco	213	163	141	133	149	140	N/A	N/A	N/A
Norway	1,151	990	726	405	342	307	1,066	1,437	665
Netherlands	2,652	2,570	2,830	2,411	2,630	2,312	1,865	1,366	1,202
Portugal	1,280	1,061	1,101	1,422	1,557	1,288	1,151	947	688
Sweden	2,420	2,053	1,813	1,367	2,778	2,792	4,267	3,887	3,050
Finland	377	275	326	268	305	383	488	625	616
Slovakia	429	154	65	N/A	N/A	----	----	----	----
Slovenia	131	102	85	72	29	25	N/A	N/A	N/A
Russia	100	18	N/A	N/A	N/A	N/A	N/A	N/A	N/A

Leasing Business 1986-1996 (Movables and Real Estate)   ECU (million)

Table 1.2 presents the details of leasing business of movables and real estate in the Leaseurope according to the annual reports of the Leaseurope. It is estimated that equipment on lease now accounts for 15-30 per cent of all new investments in plant and equipment in European developed nations. This growth demonstrates that leasing has obtained a large share of international

---

[3] In 1996, the Leaseurope has members from 25 countries including: Austria, Belgium, Bulgaria, the Czech Republic, Denmark, Finland, France, Germany, Great Britain, Greece, Hungary, Ireland, Italy, Luxembourg, Morocco, Netherlands, Norway, Poland, Portugal, Russia, Slovak Republic, Slovenia, Spain, Sweden and Switzerland.

markets, particularly equipment and aircraft markets. Over 50 per cent of the commercial aircraft coming into services today in Europe are leased, and smaller airlines lease an even higher percentage of their planes. In the United States, the figure is over 75 per cent.

In the UK, according to the Finance & Leasing Association (which represented about 90 per cent of the UK leasing industry), assets to the value of £19,757 million at cost were acquired for leases by its members in 1996, an increase of 21.16% from 1995, which represents over 30% of all UK fixed investment in plant and equipment. In the Netherlands, the Dutch leasing market is characterised by the strong development of operating leasing in the vehicle and computer sectors.[4] In 1996, businesses in equipment leasing reached 2,641 million ECU. In the USA, equipment lease financing reached US$168.9 billion in 1996. In Japan, despite the difficult trading conditions for many of the financial sectors resulted from the Asian financial crisis, the volume of lease contracts increased 8.7% from 1995 to US$71.4 billion in 1996. For the development of leasing in other countries, see *World Leasing Yearbook* 1998.

The popularity of leasing is increasing rapidly not only in developed countries, but also in developing economies such as Brazil, China, Greece, Indonesia, Mexico, Pakistan, the Philippines, Thailand, Turkey and some African countries. Over 55 developing countries have their own leasing industries (Porter 1997). In these countries, many leasing companies have been established to modernise their credit systems and promote capital investments. Leasing activity in Asia, Latin America and Africa has remained high with enormous growth. The leasing market size of emerging countries grew by 22.2% per year from 1988 to 1995 and reached US$61 billion in 1995 (World Leasing Yearbook 1998).[5] The share of private investment through leasing more than doubled between 1988 and 1995 with leasing accounting for 4% of asset financing in Asia and Latin America in 1988 to an average of 11% in 1995 (World leasing Yearbook 1998).

Leasing in Central and East European countries like Poland, the Czech Republic, Hungary, Bulgaria, and the states of the former Soviet Union, has also been developing significantly in recent years (Gao 1995; Gao and Herbert 1996). In transferring their economies towards market economies,

---

[4] It is called operating leasing, but it involves financial service leasing.
[5] For example, South Korea had the most impressive growth with the fifth largest leasing market in the world (US16.31 billion in 1996) and the third highest worldwide leasing market penetration (26.5% in 1996).

leasing in these countries and China is not treated just as a method of financing and marketing, but also as an important mechanism for the economic reforms (see: Nikiforov and Rutgaizer 1989; Novikov 1989; Gao 1991; and Gao 1995).

International leasing which is mainly characterised as cross-border leasing was first seen in the form of an American-based leveraged lease. American lessors leased equipment (e.g., aircraft, ships, containers and oil drilling rigs) located in the United States to the users primarily outside the US., taking advantage of the availability to American lessors of investment tax credits (ITCs) and accelerated depreciation, thereby greatly reducing the cost of financing to overseas lessees. In the early 1980s, because of the availability of "double-dip" leases in the UK,[6] there was a high volume of cross-border leasing transactions by the British lessors with the American lessees. Cross-border leasing became popular in some other countries in the late 1980s and the early 1990s, when it was realised that tax incentives intended for domestic investments could also be used for aircraft and sometimes other equipment leased abroad.

International leasing has grown dramatically since the 1980s. According to Clark, the total figure for international leasing business in 1983 was about US$18 billion approximately the same size as the total domestic leasing business in Europe (Clark 1985, pp.8-9). In the UK, the international business currently represents about 20 per cent of the new plant and equipment leased by member companies of the UK Finance and Leasing Association.

International leasing has been widely used in financing infrastructure development in emerging economies - such as rail and air transport equipment, telephone and telecommunications equipment, and assets incorporated into power generation and distribution systems and other projects that have predictable revenue streams. However, international leasing has grown at slower rates than those shown by domestic leasing, due to different legislation in force in the lessee and the lessor countries, which makes the operations more risky and more expensive.

Currently, the Japanese are more involved in international leasing. Japan accounts for 17 per cent of the world leasing market, and its leasing industry has a reputation as one of the most global. Japanese leasing companies have more than 100 subsidiaries throughout the world and numerous joint ventures. Overseas subsidiary leasing, usually being considered as another type of international leasing, has developed remarkably in recent years due to more

---

[6] Chapter 9 will specially discuss double-dip leases.

expanded international joint ventures and more demand for reducing financial risks of investment. For example, Japan Leasing Corporation (JLC), which is a leading player in international operations, especially in aircraft leasing, has been paralleled by growth overseas during the last two decades. JLC established its first overseas affiliate in New York in 1971, and has since expanded its network with new subsidiaries in Hong Kong, UK, Singapore, Brazil, and many joint ventures in China and Indonesia. In addition, Japanese have developed some new forms of transactions in international leasing. For instance, "shoguns" (e.g., yen-based leases) that were innovated by the Japanese in the 1980s have since been expanding greatly in international leasing markets.

The trend in aircraft financing in recent years has been away from the traditional credit-based funding towards asset-based financing, in particular lease financing. Most airlines all over the world such as Air France, British Airways, KLM, Singapore Airlines, CAAC of China, Brazilian Airlines, Swissair and Air Portugal often make use of leasing to obtain their needs for aircraft. Typically, the growth in operating leasing for aircraft is remarkable in the last six years. In 1985, aircraft operating leasing accounted for only 3.7 per cent of commercial jet orders and has now grown to nearly one third of the market. The transactions of aircraft leasing have been completed mostly through cross-border leasing or international leveraged leasing arrangements. The growth of aircraft leasing is expected to be one of the most increasing sectors in aircraft financing in the next few years, according to the forecast of the authorities concerned. Passenger demand is expected to double by 2005 which requires around US$250 billion spent on new aircraft. More than half of the funds is expected to be obtained via leasing.

It is generally argued that the growing proportion of investment financed by leasing in many countries reflects both the gradual substitutions of leasing for other forms of finance and an increase in the overall level of investment. Now, the leasing industry is undergoing **internationalisation**: the expansion of leasing companies into countries outside their headquarters. Today, the largest ten leasing markets in the world are the USA, Japan, Germany, UK, South Korea, France, Italy, Brazil, Australia and Canada (World Leasing Yearbook 1998, p.3). Besides the rapid growth of leasing in developed countries, recent years have also seen leasing take on much more importance in countries like Botswana, Brazil, China, Greece, India, Indonesia, Mexico, the Philippines, Singapore, Venezuela, Zimbabwe and other developing countries.

Generally, the fortunes of leasing markets in the world in the early phase principally focused on tax-based leasing. However, non-tax-based leasing is now becoming more widespread. Operating leasing has been expanding considerably in most European markets. Japanese leveraged leasing has been stretching to Asian, American and European markets. Clearly, there are excellent growth prospects in those non-tax-based leasing markets that will stimulate the development of international leasing.

In the established leasing countries, brokers, consultants and packagers have additionally grown up to help participants get the best out of the deals they put through. Ancillary services are also growing, such as lease accounting and evaluation packages, asset value insurance, and to some extent also credit insurance. Noticeably, apart from national leasing associations, numerous international and regional leasing associations have been set up, such as the Leaseurope (European Federation of Equipment Leasing Company Associations, 1972), the ECLAT (European Computers Leasing and Trading Association, 1979), the Asialease (Asian Leasing Association, 1982), the FELALESE (Latin American Leasing Federation, 1983).

To conclude, leasing has become one of the largest and fastest-growing sources of capital investment establishment both in industrial nations and in developing countries. The leasing industry has since the 1980s been undergoing internationalisation. The development of international leasing is part of the process of internationalisation. The demand for international leasing from emerging economies in the 1990s has provided unprecedented and major opportunities for western lessors. But, there are many business hurdles to overcome and risks to address. International leasing brings with it complex tax, accounting, and legal issues. An international lessor must consider: business considerations unique to a particular country in which the lease transaction is done, such as restricted availability of local courts for lease enforcement procedures; foreign currency exchange risks; possible equipment export issues. This book will discuss these issues in the following chapters.

Academic challenges

International leasing has established itself as an important mode of finance through the world. However, literature in economics or finance or management in many cases gives no discussion on international leasing.

According to the American Association of Equipment Lessors, many US business school graduate courses do not incorporate leasing into their curriculum. Currently, there are only a few books about domestic leasing available which mainly concentrate on the issue of the lease vs. buy/purchase decision.

Several reasons may explain why there are so few studies on international leasing. Firstly, the lack of appropriate data on international leasing makes it difficult to undertake international leasing research as most countries do not measure leasing as an independent item in their national economic statistics. The International Monetary Fund (IMF), the World Bank and other international organisations (e.g., OECD) do not have international leasing information. Secondly, the subject of international leasing is complex as leasing itself contains many topics that are closely related to finance, marketing, investment and accounting disciplines, and many issues related to accounting, taxation and legal systems in a country. International leasing is even more complicated because different countries have different ways dealing with legal, accounting and tax problems, and have different cultural backgrounds, economic and social-political systems. As a result of the shortage of academic research, the gap between international leasing research and leasing practices is very wide. This book attempts to fill the gap.

Leasing as a new subject (or discipline) in business has numerous unsolved issues relating to its financial, accounting, legal, and taxation aspects. One of the most important areas is the strategic planning and decision making involved in international leasing. Typically, the managers of an international leasing company (ILC) who are considering entry into a new market often must make decisions under highly uncertain and changeable circumstances. The variables that have a potentially significant impact on the prospect for its success in the market typically are large in number and keep evolving over time due to continual arrival of new information and the changing of external environments. For example, a key decision that a firm's management usually faces is whether to go it alone or collaborate with a local partner in entering the new market.

In the author's opinion, many fundamental issues such as terminology, classification, characteristics, advantages and disadvantages of international leasing have not been clearly identified. Many questions are also left with respect to the financial, accounting, investment, and marketing perspectives of international leasing. For instance, evaluating foreign leasing projects an ILC is forced to confront a number of capital budgeting, financial issues that are rarely, if ever, encountered by wholly domestic leasing firms. How do a foreign lessee's tax regulations or accounting standards affect the expected profitability of a leasing project? Should management evaluate lease cash flows from the standpoint of a foreign subsidiary or the ILC, and in terms of the local currency, or from the home currency perspective? How can the interactions of investment and financing decisions involved in an international leasing project be analysed and evaluated? Should the required rate of return on international leasing be raised to reflect risks like expropriation, political risks, currency controls, and exchange rate fluctuations? Are there significant benefits to either lessors or lessees from international leasing portfolio diversification? and if so, how does this affect the value of the leasing firms?

The principal focus of this book will be on the strategic and decision-making aspects of international leasing. However, because of lack of systematic and comprehensive studies on international leasing, some other issues involved in international leasing including fundamentals and conceptual developments will also be discussed. In order to see these questions clearly, I specify the following issues involved in international leasing that will be discussed in this book. Among others they include:

- *What is leasing? How can we define the concept of leasing? What are advantages of leasing?* (Chapter 2)
- *What is international leasing? How to classify international leasing? Are there differences between domestic leasing and international leasing?* (Chapter 3)
- *What is the relationship between trade and leasing? What is counterleasing? How does leasing promote international trade?* (Chapter 4)
- *What is the role of international leasing in the world financial system? How does the global financial environment influence international leasing?* (Chapter 5)
- *What is the concept of leasing investment? What are the roles of international leasing investment? What are risks involved in international leasing investment?* (Chapter 6)
- *Why is leasing a device of international marketing? What are international leasing market segments? How can we carry out leasing marketing research and price a leasing product?* (Chapter 7)
- *What are the factors which influence strategies and decisions of international leasing?* (Chapter 8)
- *What is a double-dip lease? How to evaluate a double-dip lease?* (Chapter 9)

■ *What are strategic issues involved in international leasing from the lessee/user's point of view and how to make decisions?* (Chapter 10)
■ *What are strategic issues involved in international leasing from the lessor's perspective and how to make decisions?* (Chapter 11)
■ *What is international sale-and-leaseback? How to formulate an international sale-and-leaseback contract?* (Chapter 12)
■ *How has leasing been developed in emerging markets? What are the strategies for the leasing industries in emerging economies to be integrated with the global leasing market?* (Chapter 13)

In the post World War II, particularly in the 1950s and the 1960s, fundamental changes in both microeconomics and macroeconomics, business, financial economics and international economics began to occur. New theories, new analytical methods and new techniques resulting from econometrics, economics, statistics and other disciplines like behaviour science, sociology and psychology began to be applied to problems in finance and business economics, and the resulting transformation has been significant. For example, a number of modern theories of financial economics have been developed since the 1950s. These theories among others include:

- *Efficient Market Theory*—analysis of equilibrium behaviour of prices through time in capital markets.
- *Capital Structure Theory*—analysis of the optimal allocation of equity and debt in an imperfect capital market environment.
- *Portfolio Theory*—analysis of optimal security selection procedures for an investor's entire portfolio of securities.
- *Capital Asset Pricing Theory*—analysis of the determinants of asset pricing under conditions of uncertainty.
- *Arbitrage Theory*—analysis of the determinants of security or commodity price under a price discrepancy.
- *Option Pricing Theory*—analysis of the determinants of the prices of contingent claims such as call options and put options.
- *Agency Theory*—analysis of the control of incentive conflicts in contractual relations.

Despite that these theories are generally used at a corporate level, they may prove to be of particular importance in developing a theoretical foundation for strategic planning and decision-making in international leasing. How to apply these theories to international leasing is an extremely difficult task. Up to now few papers on this kind of topic can be found in the literature. Taking the arbitrage theory as an example, an arbitrage has traditionally been defined as the purchase of securities or commodities on one market for immediate resale on another in order to profit from a price discrepancy. In recent years arbitrage has been used to describe a broader range of activities. Tax arbitrage, for example, involves the shifting of gains or losses from one tax jurisdiction to another in order to realise profits from difference in tax rates. In a broader content, arbitrage, or risk arbitrage, has been used to describe the process which ensures that, in equilibrium, risk-adjusted return on different process exist. Obviously, arbitrage theory can be practically applied in the leasing area to ensure leasing market efficiency and to take tax, currency and risk arbitrage advantages provided by international lease financing.

The aim and structure of this book

Clearly, research on international leasing must be done to keep pace with global leasing business development. For further expanding the businesses, it is also necessary to put more efforts on the education and consultancy in international leasing which have to very much rely on research findings. Thus, there is a need for a systematic study which addresses the underlying issues involved in international leasing, taking cognisance of both the theoretical and empirical aspects.

The aims of this book are: 1) to systematically study international leasing mainly looking at its strategic and decision-making aspects; 2) to explore some international lease financing strategies and decisions to lessors and lessees; and 3) to design some models relating to international leasing evaluation and decision-making. The models will be designed with the applications of some finance theories and analytical techniques such as Net Present Value (NPV), Capital Asset Pricing Model (CAPM), Risk Ranking Technique (RRT) and others. The scope of this study, however, not only covers strategic and decision-making aspects of international leasing, but also deals with some subjects of its marketing, accounting, investment and taxation.

The book consists of 14 chapters.

Chapter 2 reviews the current literature of leasing focusing on the theoretical framework, covering concepts and advantages of leasing and presents various definitions of lease and leasing.

Chapter 3 develops the concept of international leasing with an review of the literature on concepts, types, structures and forms of international leasing. A comparison of international and domestic leasing is also given in this Chapter.

Chapter 4 discusses the relationship between trade and leasing and explores the opportunities of leasing promoting trade activities. Concept of counterleasing is proposed with a comparison with countertrade. A new form of the balance of payments inclusive of leasing transactions is suggested.

Chapter 5 analyses the global financial environment and its impact on leasing. The role of international leasing in the world financial system is discussed. The foreign exchange markets and the basic relationship are described, and measuring foreign exchange exposure and hedging strategies are also considered in this Chapter.

Chapter 6 discusses the concept of leasing investment and provides an analysis of international leasing investment with a special focus on political risks of foreign leasing investment.

Chapter 7 discusses the marketing role of leasing, international leasing market segments and marketing research. This Chapter also analyses the factors of international lease pricing and presents a pricing model.

Chapter 8 considers the general principles and techniques required for leasing analysis and decision-making, and examines the factors that influence strategies and decision-making of international leasing including cash flows, discount rate, risk, foreign exchange, inflation, taxes, import, stamp duties etc.

Chapter 9 focuses specially on the double-dip issue involved in international leasing cases by explaining the concept of double-dip and its formulation. A double-dip leasing evaluation model is developed following the Myers, Dill and Bautista framework.

Chapter 10 is concerned with strategies and decisions from the lessee's perspective, discussing why firms lease overseas, international financial leasing decision and strategies, international leasing vs. import decision and some other decisions (e.g., the lease vs. make decision, the lease payments decision and the operating leasing decision). A few decision models are proposed in this Chapter.

Chapter 11 is concerned with strategies and decisions from the lessor's perspective with a discussion of general considerations for decision-making and strategies and the development of decision-making models for international financial leasing, leveraged leasing and operating leasing.

Chapter 12 focuses on international sale-and-leaseback by addressing the issues why firms sell and leaseback, and how to structure an international sale-and-leaseback.

Chapter 13 discusses the recent development of leasing in emerging economies with a special focus on China and eastern Europe. A general comparison of the industry, markets, regulatory developments and accounting for leases among these countries is presented in this chapter.

Chapter 14 concludes the book and highlights some general areas for further research.

Reference

Clark, T.M. 1978. *Leasing*. UK: McGraw-Hill Book Company Limited.

Clark, T.M. 1985. *Leasing Finance*: Euromoney Publications.

Gao, S.S. 1991. On the establishment of new capital markets. *Shehui Kexue Yanjin - in Chinese (Social Science Study)*, no. 3: 25-8.

Gao, S.S. 1995. Leasing in Poland: privatisation, financing and current problems. *European Business Review*, no. 5: 31-40.

Gao, S.S. and W. Herbert. 1996. Leasing finance in emerging markets: an eastern European study. *Managerial Finance* 22, no. 12: 39-53.

Nevitt, P.K. and F.J. Fabozzi. 1988. *Equipment Leasing*. Homewood Illinois: Dow Jones-Irwin.

Nikiforov, L. and V. Rutgaizer. 1989. Leasing relations in the economic system of socialism. *Problems of Economics* November: 49-62.

Novikov, V. 1989. Leasing as the development of relations of socialist property. *Problems of Economics* November: 63-78.

Porter, D. 1997. The growth and development of the modern leasing industry. In *Leasing Finance*, ed. C. Boobyer. London: Euromoney Books.

World Leasing Yearbook. 1988, 1994, 1996, 1998. London: A Euromoney Publication.

2 Theory of leasing

The concept of leasing

The leasing of equipment by a lessor domiciled in one country to a lessee in the same country is referred to as domestic leasing. However, "leasing" has been defined in many different ways, focusing on its individual legal, accounting, fiscal, economic, marketing and financial aspects for different purposes. Even from the financial point of view, leasing definitions still differ considerably from each other. Some authors put emphases on financial aspects in their definitions, and others put emphases on operating aspects.

Terminologically, there are some differences between the word "lease" and the word "leasing". For example, a lease refers to a contract by which property is conveyed to a person for a specified period, usually for rent; whereas leasing means to grant possession of land, building, etc. by lease, or to take a lease of (property).[1] In other words, a lease is a contract or a formal arrangement, whereas leasing is a process of taking a lease.

The Equipment Leasing Association (ELA),[2] a well-known former leasing organisation based in London defines that "a lease is a contract between a lessor and lessee for the hire of a specific asset selected from a manufacturer or vendor of such asset by the lessee. The lessor retains ownership of the asset. The lessee has possession and use of the asset on payment of specified

---

[1] See *Collins Dictionary and Thesaurus*, published by Collins, London, 1987, p.570.
[2] The Equipment Leasing Association (ELA) and Finance Houses Association in the UK merged to become the Finance & Leasing Association (FLA) that came into effect on January 2, 1991 and most members of the ELA had crossed over to the FLA.

rentals over a period" (ELA 1976 p.1). In this definition, "the lessor retains ownership of the asset" excludes a leveraged lease. A leveraged lease is simply a lease transaction in which the lessor puts in only a portion, usually 20% to 40%, of the funds necessary to buy the equipment and a third-party lender supplies the remainder. Because the benefits available to the lessor are generally based on the entire equipment cost, the lessor's investment is said to be "leveraged" with third-party debt. In a leveraged lease a lessor raises a loan secured by the asset to be leased to finance the asset purchase price. In this case the lender may be considered to be the owner of this asset. Nunnally, *et al.* (1991) define that "a lease is a written agreement between the lessor (the owner of the property) and the lessee (the user of the property) concerning the use of and payments for the property over a specific period of time" (p.15). This definition does not cover all forms of leases because it also excludes a leveraged lease.

Wert and Henderson (1979) define that "leasing is a grant by one party (lessor) to a second party (lessee) of an interest in a property that permits the second party to use it for a period of time. Thus, leasing is a means whereby a business firm may obtain the use of a fixed asset without obtaining title to it" (pp.275-6). Clark, *et al.* (1979) argue that "leasing is a process whereby the owner of a particular asset (lessor) enters into an agreement (lease) with the user (lessee) for the latter to use the asset for a specified period of time" (p.341). Gitman (1982) considers that "leasing involves obtaining the use of specific fixed assets, such as land and equipment, without actually receiving title to it" (p.592). It is obvious that the above three definitions ignore the lease payments made by the lessee. Strictly speaking, a transaction whereby one party obtains the use of an asset from another party without charge can never be recognised as a leasing transaction.

Isom and Amembal (1982) state that "a lease is viewed as a contract between a lessor (owner of an asset) and a lessee (user of an asset) where the lessor grants the temporary possession and use of an asset to the lessee, usually for a specified period less than the asset's economic life at a fixed periodic charge (rental charge)" (p.20). Apparently, the question of why the lease period is less than "the asset's economic life" is not answered. The authors do not explain "the asset's economic life". Herst (1984) argues that "the economic life of a capital asset should be defined as that period of time during which the net present value of the cash flows generated by the asset is highest" (p.6). Normally, an asset generates cash flows during its economic life that corresponds with *the total of lease terms*. I use the phrase "the total of lease terms", because it may be a case that an asset is re-leased several times after its first short-term lease. After all, this does not indicate that a lease term in general is less than the economic life of the leased asset.

The International Accounting Standards Committee defines "a leasing transaction is a commercial arrangement whereby an equipment owner conveys the right to use the equipment in return for payment by the equipment user of a specified rental over a pre-agreed period of time" (IASC 1982).

It is quite interesting to see a different definition made by Herst (1984) in his book *Lease or Purchase——Theory and Practice*. "A lease is a loan in kind whereby a lessee promises to make a series of payments to a lessor in order to acquire the right to use an asset, usually owned by the lessor, during a period of time that corresponds with the useful life of the asset" (p.7). The attention of this definition focuses on "a loan in kind" rather than a contract. According to the author, "any lease can be looked upon as a loan in kind providing complete financing for an object" (p.5). Another feature of the definition is that a lease term corresponds with "the useful life of the asset", instead of "the economic life of the asset". The author compares the technical service life with the economic life (pp.6-7). In the real world there is uncertainty concerning the length of the useful life. Different estimates made by a lessor and a lessee lead to different lengths of the useful life. The estimate of the lessee/user who decides to lease or to buy is relevant to the useful life of an asset.

I define a "lease" as a contract essentially stipulating the separation of ownership of an asset and the right to use it; the user (lessee) will obtain the right to use the asset in exchange for promising to make a series of payments to the owner during a certain period of time that generally corresponds with the useful life of the asset. "Leasing" is a process of setting up a lease wherein the owner or lessor passes the possession and the right to use the asset to the user (lessee) in return for payments made by the user (lessee) for a certain period of time that generally corresponds with the asset useful life. According to the definitions, a lease and leasing have four main characteristics as follows:

1. Ownership of an asset is separated from the right to use the asset. The user (lessee) obtains the right to use an asset without its title held. Leasing differs from an asset purchase where the right to use and the title of the asset are simultaneously transferred from the owner to the user. Leasing also differs from hire-purchase of an asset where the right to use the asset is transferred from the owner to the user at the beginning of the contract, whereas the title is transferred at the end of the contract. In a hire-purchase contract, the user has an obligation to purchase the asset at a nominal price

at the end of the contract. Although in some countries (e.g., USA, Canada) a lease may also contain an option for the lessee to purchase the asset leased at a fair market price at the expiration of the lease, this just looks *like* a hire-purchase contract. This is because an option is not the same as an obligation. An obligation to purchase the asset at the end of a hire-purchase contract differs from an option to purchase the leased asset at the end of a lease. In addition, the price to purchase an asset at the end of a lease and the end of a hire-purchase contract is also different. The price to purchase the asset in a lease is the fair market price, whereas in a hire-purchase arrangement is the nominal price.

2. A user (lessee) has to make a series of payments to an owner or a lessor. The amount of the rental charge and the pattern (time, currency, etc.) of the payments depend on negotiations between the user and the owner. The charge can be in the form of a fixed periodic payment, or the form of a floating rate. In a high inflation country, a lessor sometimes requires the rental charge to be paid in accordance with inflation in the country. In other examples, such as in percentage leases, mineral property leases, floating rates of the lease payments are also popular.

3. The lease term is a certain period of time during which the right to use an asset is separated from its ownership. Before or after the certain period of time, the right to use the asset and ownership of the asset are united as one. Usually leasing will cease at the expiration of the certain period (the lease term), and the asset will then be returned to the owner, or an option that the lessee purchases the asset at a fair market price will be exercised.

4. The lease term generally corresponds with the useful life of the leased asset. This property makes a distinction between a lease and a rental agreement. In particular, a financial lease term directly corresponds with the useful life of the leased asset. The word "generally" used in the definition attempts to include the case of operating leasing. In operating leasing, the sum of several lease terms must correspond with the asset useful life.

Advantages of leasing

Leasing has its own operational and financial advantages in comparison with other financing tools. For example, if equipment is needed only for a limited period of time, leasing can be an effective way of acquiring its use because it eliminates the re-marketing risks an owner would have at the end of a short use period, and it also permits a more defined estimate of the effective cost of use of the equipment. Leasing removes the resale risk and allows the user to determine in advance the total effective usage cost.

In some cases, users, who lack the staff or expertise to attend to specialised asset needs, can lease the asset as a way to acquire those necessary technical or administrative services. Through service leases, users can avoid tying up time and manpower in activities that are outside of their normal operations. Financially, one of the advantages of leasing to some users is that it helps preserve their existing funds or bank lines for other uses. The absence of a down payment (sometimes 100% financing) can assist high growth rate companies in maximising their use of funds. That can be particularly attractive in periods of tight money.

Why does a firm take a lease rather than use other alternatives (e.g., buy or borrow) to obtain the use of equipment or an asset? Clark (1978), Pritchard and Hindelang (1980), Erickson (1987), Glass in Clark (1991), Riahi-Belkaoui (1998) provide some general discussions. Table 2.1 summarises the main reasons pointed out by Glass, and Pritchard and Hindelang.

Nevertheless, the reasons why leasing is chosen differ considerably from lessee to lessee. Leasing may occur whenever there are differences between firms in their tax position, so that different tax rules applied to different firms may also provide an incentive for tax transfer via leasing (Edwards and Mayer 1991, p.192). However, in order for the lessor to obtain the tax benefits associated with equipment leasing, most countries require that the lease be treated as a "true lease" for tax purposes, as opposed to a conditional sale or other secured financing arrangement. This objective can generally be satisfied if the lessor has "tax ownership" of the leased equipment under the law of its jurisdiction.

Torre (1990) discovers that under conditions where firms (insiders) have more information than investors (outsiders), leasing may offer investors an opportunity to monitor inexpensively the actions of the better informed insiders. Krishnan and Moyer (1994) argue that leasing may also have lower associated bankruptcy costs relative to secured debt, and is a preferred financial option for firms with a higher potential for financial distress or bankruptcy.

Leasing might provide the lessor to utilise non-recourse debt to finance a substantial portion of the asset cost. The debt is normally secured by, among other things, a mortgage on the asset and by an assignment of the right to receive payments under the lease. Also, depending on the structure, in some countries the lessor can utilise very favourable "leveraged lease" financial accounting treatment for the overall transaction. In some countries, it is easier for a lessor to repossess the leased asset following a lessee default because the lessor is an owner and not a mere secured lender.

Table 2.1 The advantages of leasing to a lessee

> Glass in Clark (1991), pp.31-32
>
> ....
>
> 1. Leasing provides up to 100% of the cost of the equipment;
> 2. Leasing does not tie up valuable working capital or credit lines;
> 3. Leasing offers cash flow benefits;
> 4. Leasing provides certainty;
> 5. Leasing is a sound hedge against inflation;
> 6. Leasing may be off-balance sheet;
> 7. Leasing may avoid loan covenants or capital investment restraints;
> 8. Leasing avoids dilution of share ownership;
> 9. Leasing is straightforward;
> 10. Leasing is tax efficient.
>
> ===
>
> Pritchard and Hindelang (1980), pp.4-7
>
> ....
>
> 1. Leasing offers potential savings compared to a purchase;
> 2. Leasing provides an alternative source of capital;
> 3. Leasing provides constant cost financing;
> 4. Leasing extends the length of financing;
> 5. Leasing allows more flexible cash budgeting;
> 6. Leasing conserves existing credit;
> 7. Leasing provides total financing;
> 8. Leasing may provide financing for acquisition plus related costs;
> 9. Leasing provides a hedge against inflation;
> 10. Leasing provides fast, flexible financing;
> 11. Leasing simplifies bookkeeping;[3]
> 12. Leasing provides for tax write-off of land;
> 13. Leasing reduces the risk of obsolescence;
> 14. Leasing provides trial use periods.

---

[3] This is because some leases (particularly operating leases) are off balance sheet. Under such leases bookkeeping is very simple (e.g., bookkeeping of asset depreciation is not needed).

Leasing might offer its special obsolescence value for the user. When the user of an asset is concerned that the asset may become obsolete before the end of its useful life, and, therefore, have little or no re-sale value, leasing can reduce that concern if the lessor assumes an obsolescence risk. Typically, computer and other high-tech equipment users, where new, more efficient models quickly outdate their predecessors, are faced with an obsolescence issue. Leasing might be a better option than purchase. However, because it is impossible to determine absolutely whether an asset will become obsolete, the obsolescence risk issue can cause a real dilemma in practice.

Leasing arrangement might spend less time and require less red tape than other arrangements. As a result, there are situations in which the documentation time and expense that can be saved can offset an asset lease interest rate that is higher that a loan interest rate.

Decision to lease an asset is sometimes made to avoid a user internal capital budget restrictions. For capital asset purchases above a certain amount, a manager may be required to obtain prior approval, and that approval may be difficult or impossible to obtain. If the asset is leased, it may be able to account for the rental payments as an operating expense - even though the lease represents a long-term financing similar to a capital expenditure - to get around the approval problem. In this way, it may also be able to maximise its capital budget.

Other factors (e.g., size of firm, type of industry, growth rate of firm, type of asset) may have different influences on the extent of leasing. Adams and Hardwick (1998) find that the propensity to lease is positively related to both leverage and ownership structure of UK listed companies. However, their findings provide no support for the hypothesis that companies with more growth options in their investment opportunity sets will be more likely to lease than companies with more assets-in-place.

Leasing assets can provide a hedge against inflation. An asset lease, in effect, gives the asset user the ability to acquire the asset it needs at today's prices and, then, paying for it from tomorrow's earnings. However, "this does not imply that these positive aspects of leasing will be of importance in every conceivable situation. The advantages and the disadvantages of leasing are mainly determined by the conditions of a lease contract and by the financing alternatives open to a firm's management" (Herst 1984, p.209).

It should note that the use of leasing might give up some benefits associated with the ownership of an asset. For example, when a user leases an asset, it forgoes the possibility of realising a gain if the asset appreciates in value during the lease term. Many leases give lessees the option to buy the leased asset at the lease term's end for its fair market value at that time. If the fair market value turns out to be high, the purchase price, coupled with the rent paid, can result in a very expensive deal. In such a situation, the lessee would undoubtedly have been better off if it had originally bought the asset. In addition, there is limited asset control involved in a lease. When a lease ends, so does a lessee's right to use the asset. This can create a problem for an asset user if suitable replacement asset is not readily available and the lessor refuses to re-lease or sell it to the lessee. Also, there is always the possibility that a lessor might interfere with the lessee's right to use the asset during the lease term, even though it may have no legal right to do so. Chapter 10 will discuss why firms lease overseas.

Conclusion

Leasing continues to expand as an important financing means at a healthy rate worldwide. Different definitions of leases and leasing can be found in the literature with different focuses. This chapter briefly discusses various definitions of "lease" and "leasing", and presents my own definitions of "lease" and "leasing" with its characteristics. Also, this chapter discusses the advantages and disadvantages of leasing.

A lease is a contract essentially stipulating the separation of ownership of an asset and the right to use it; the user (lessee) will obtain the right to use the asset in exchange for promising to make a series of payments to the owner during a certain period of time that generally corresponds with the useful life of the asset.

Leasing is a process of setting up a lease wherein the owner or lessor passes the possession and the right to use the asset to the user (lessee) in return for payments made by the user (lessee) for a certain period of time that generally corresponds with the asset useful life.

Leasing has its own operating and financial advantages in comparison with other financial instruments. However, these advantages are generally determined by the lease itself and the financial and tax circumstances of the lessees.

A clear understanding of the basic concept of leasing is useful to the other chapters of this book, although an in-depth discussion and debate of lease definitions is not the objective of the book. Next chapter will discuss the theory of international leasing.

Reference

Adams, M. and P. Hardwick. 1998. Determinants of the leasing decision in United Kingdom listed companies. *Applied Financial Economics* 8: 487-94.

Clark, J.J., T.J. Hindelang and R.E. Pritchard. 1979. *Capital Budgeting: Planning and Control of Capital Expenditures*. New Jersey: Prentice-Hall, Inc.

Clark, T.M. 1978. *Leasing*. UK: McGraw-Hill Book Company Limited.

Clark, T.M. 1991. *Leasing Finance*. London: Euromoney Publications.

Edwards, J.S.S. and C.P. Mayer. 1991. Leasing, taxes, and the cost of capital. *Journal of Public Economics* 44: 171-79.

ELA. 1976. *Equipment Leasing*. London: UK Equipment Leasing Association (ELA).

Erickson, S.M. 1987. *The Cross Sectional Determinants of Lease Use: a Theoretical and Empirical Study*. PhD dissertation, University of Washington.

Gitman, L.J. 1982. *Principles of Management Finance*. New York: Harper & Row.

Herst, A.C.C. 1984. *Lease or Purchase: Theory and Practice*. Massachusetts: Kluwer-Nijhoff Publishing.

IASC. 1982. *International Accounting Standards (IAS) No.17: Accounting for Leases*. International Accounting Standards Committee (IASC).

Isom, T.A. and S.P. Amembal. 1982. *The Handbook of Leasing: Techniques & Analysis*. New York: Petrocelli Books, Inc.

Krishnan, V.S. and R.C. Moyer. 1994. Bankruptcy costs and the financial leasing decision. *Financial Management* Summer: 31-42.

Nunnally, B.H., D.A. Plath and H.W. Johns. 1991. *Corporate Lease Analysis: A Guide to Concepts and Evaluation*. Westport, C.T.: Quorum Books.

Pritchard, R.E. and T.J. Hindelang. 1980. *The Lease/Buy Decision*. New York: Amacon, A Division of American Management Association.

Riahi-Belkaoui, A. 1998. *Long-Term Leasing - Accounting, Evaluation, Consequences*. Westport, CT: Quorum Books.

Torre, C.De.La. 1990. *Leasing, Information Asymmetries and Transaction Cost Economies: A Theoretical and Empirical Investigation*: PhD Dissertation, The University of Texas at Austin.

Wert, J.E. and G.V. Henderson. 1979. *Financing Business Firm*. Homewood Illinois: Ricjard Irivin, Inc.

3   Theory of international leasing

The concept of international leasing

The concept of international leasing has not been well defined. Henius (1947) defined "lend-lease", which can be considered to be the embryonic form of international leasing, as "the technique for furnishing these supplies (military supplier and civilian goods) that could best be carried out on a government-to-government basis. ... Lend-lease was a method of providing war aid" (pp.394-5). The emphasis of this definition is placed on the "government-to-government" basis, and leasing is considered to be a technique to provide "war aid" and civilian goods. According to the author, lend-lease has a definite relationship to foreign trade. However, this definition gives no indication about the financial implication of leasing. Also, the essence of leasing is not addressed.

Terpstra (1978) defines international leasing as "an important pricing-financing-marketing device for expensive equipment" (p.495). The author does not describe what international leasing actually is and how international leasing transactions take place. Nevertheless, it is worthwhile mentioning that this definition recognises the role of international leasing in pricing and marketing apart from its traditional financing function. Clark (1978) in his well-known book *Leasing*, states that "the term 'international leasing' covers two separate types of activities: cross-border or trans-national leasing and the operations of overseas subsidiaries. ... Cross-border leasing describes those leasing arrangements where the lessee and the lessor are domiciled in different countries and includes export leasing" (p.31). But later, an expanded concept of international leasing is found in his edited book *Leasing Finance*.

"International leasing, rather like international banking, encompasses several distinct functions. Two of the main types of activity—investment in overseas ventures and international co-operation among leasing companies. Cross-border business, is the focal point of international leasing" (Clark 1985, p.8). Unfortunately, the essential features of international leasing are not defined in these two books. Instead, the author mainly describes the types of international leasing transactions.

Reiners (1983) argues that "a lease is international in nature if the lessor and the lessee are domiciled in different countries, with the locations of the asset being of secondary importance" (p.4). According to the definition, the locations of a lessor and a lessee are the essential criterion for distinguishing international leasing from domestic leasing. However, the definition exclude the type of an overseas subsidiary that is another form of international leasing wherein the lessor and the lessee may locate in the same country. Meidan (1984) considers international leasing as a cross border transaction. "By international leasing is meant a transaction where the lease itself crosses a border—that is to say, where the lessor and lessee are in different countries, so that the goods are physically held under a different legal system from that under which title is held" (p.36). Meidan focuses international leasing on cross-border transactions and emphasises that the transaction of transferring the goods is carried out under a different legal system from that under which title is held.

Two Dutch authors, Beckman and Joosen (1988) in their book *Leasing van Roerend en Onroerend Goed*, discuss the term "international leasing". In their opinion, there are two types of international leasing. The first type uses international leasing in an improper sense (in *oneigenlijke zin*) and the other in a proper sense (in *de eigenlijke betekenis*). In an improper sense, international leasing is a kind of activity in which the partners (leasing company, customer or lessee, supplier of the asset), coming from different countries, first negotiate and sign a contract. After the contract is signed, the partners concerned establish a unit (a company or a subsidiary) in one country. Obviously, this kind of activity is a joint venture leasing business and/or operations of an overseas subsidiary. In a proper sense, international leasing is a lease arrangement where the partners concerned come from different countries and the asset leased is transferred through different country borders. Clearly, this refers to cross-border leasing or trans-national leasing.

In sum, the contributions made by the authors in the limited literature are shown in two aspects. One is that international leasing is considered to be not only a device of international marketing, but also an important method of international financing and investment. The other one is that international leasing covers not only cross-border leasing, but also the operations of overseas subsidiaries and export leasing. However, Pritchard and Hindelang (1980), and Isom and Amembal (1982) argue that lease transactions across international borders are generally not true leases but conditional sales contracts, since the contracts provide for the purchase of equipment at the lease termination (p.169; p.12). It is true that a contract that provides an obligation to a user for the purchase of equipment at a nominal price at the end of a contract is a conditional sales contract. However, this obligation is not part of every international lease. It is not a standard clause in leasing contracts that a lessee must have an option to purchase the leased asset at a fair market price at the termination of a lease.[1]

In my view, to define international leasing it is crucial to utilise the concept of different (national) legal systems, instead of cross-border. I define an international lease as a contract essentially stipulating the separation of ownership of an asset and the right to use it from one legal jurisdiction to another; the user (lessee) domiciled in one jurisdiction obtains the right to use the asset in exchange for promising to make a series of payments to the owner or lessor domiciled in another jurisdiction during a certain period of time that generally correspondents with the useful life of the asset. International leasing is a process of constructing an international lease wherein the use of an asset is transferred directly or indirectly from the owner or lessor in one legal jurisdiction to the user (lessee) in another without changing ownership of that asset within a certain period of time that generally corresponds with the useful life of that asset, and the user obtains the right to use that asset in exchange for paying a series of rental charges to the owner or lessor.

Essentially, there are no significant differences between international leasing and domestic leasing. But placed in an international context, leasing became more complicated because of different legal and accounting systems, multi-currency, and different social and political environments involved. For example, international leasing involves more than one legal system. In result, each transaction will involve a complex interrelationship between the laws of the jurisdiction of each of the parties to the transaction, and of the proper law of the contract. This implies the behaviours of a lessor, a lessee, a supplier, or an equity owner and a debtor are restrained not only by their own legal regulations, but also by other legal regulations concerned.

---

[1] In the UK, for example, a lease should not give a lessee an option to purchase the leased asset, otherwise it is regarded as a hire purchase arrangement.

To better understand international leasing, the following points should be emphasised:

1) The separation of ownership of an asset from the right to use it in a certain period of time is carried out under at least two legal, accounting and taxation systems.

2) Transferring a leased asset can be in a direct or an indirect form. The former refers to the process where before being leased to or used by the lessee the asset is located in the lessor's country and will be physically transferred to the lessee's country. The indirect form means that the asset is unnecessarily transferred from one country to another, because the asset owned by the lessor has already placed in the lessee country.

3) The lease term can be either the period of time during which the lessee actually uses the asset, excluding the time of transporting the asset from the lessor to the lessee, or the period of time covering both. In domestic leasing, the delivery time of an asset from the lessor to the lessee is normally very short that it can be ignored in building leasing decision models. In international leasing, however, a lease term usually includes both of them, if the delivery time is long and the delivery costs are high.[2] Therefore, the delivery time, costs of transporting and insurance are the major considerations in making international leasing decisions and planning strategies.

4) The lease term should generally correspond with the useful life of the leased asset, covering either a lease term of long-term financial leasing or the total of the lease terms of several operating leasing deals.

5) The lease payments in international leasing can be made in the form of a currency (the lessor's home currency, the lessee's home currency, or a third country currency), or of a multi-currency package, or in the form of products/services or natural resources (on a barter base).

Sometimes, international leasing in the literature is regarded only as cross-border leasing. I argue, on the one hand, that the term "cross-border" is not a precise term in describing international leasing, since the term "cross-border" is obviously related to territorial boundaries that may not perfectly reflect social and economic meanings. On the other hand,

---

[2] For example, in satellite leasing, the delivery costs of a satellite are very high in comparison with the equipment cost itself. Typically, to get a satellite in geostationary orbit, some twenty thousands miles up in space, requires the launch of the spacecraft on a rocket costing as much as the hardware it carries.

cross-border leasing is only one form of international leasing. Although "cross-border" is not an appropriate term to describe international leasing, owing to its popular use, and having a direct and simple implication, I may refer to cross-border leasing as international leasing in some cases.

In addition, it is worth while mentioning that on May 28, 1988, the Unidroit Convention on International Leasing was finally accepted in Ottawa, Canada.[3] It is a significant step towards the legal harmonisation of international leasing. The Unidroit Convention strictly defines provisions on international leasing transactions.

1.—This Convention governs a financial leasing transaction as described in paragraph 2 in which one party (the lessor),

(a) on the specifications of another party (the lessee), enters into an agreement (the supply agreement) with a third party (the supplier) under which the lessor acquires plant, capital goods or other equipment (the equipment) on terms approved by the lessee so far as they concern its interests, and

(b) enters into an agreement (the leasing agreement) with the lessee, granting to the lessee the right to use the equipment in return for the payment of rentals.

2.—The financial leasing transaction referred to in the previous paragraph is a transaction which includes the following characteristics:

(a) the lessee specifies the equipment and selects the supplier without relying primarily on the skill and judgement of the lessor;

(b) the equipment is acquired by the lessor in connection with a leasing agreement which, to the knowledge of the supplier, either has been made or is to be made between the lessor and the lessee;

(c) the rentals payable under the leasing agreement are calculated so as to take into account in particular the amortisation of the whole or a substantial part of the cost of the equipment.

---

[3] Unidroit—the International Institution for the Unification of Private Law. In order to promote the development of the world leasing industry, The Unidroit has organised professionals from different countries to prepare the draft of the Convention on International Financial leasing since 1975. The drafted convention was finally adopted in the Diplomatic Conference in Ottawa, Canada on May 28, 1988. Representatives of 55 states participated in the conference, and a dozen of international organisations, including the World Leasing Council attended this conference. The Unidroit has been signed by Ghana, Guinea, Nigeria, The Philippines, Tanzania, Morocco, France, Czechoslovakia, Finland, Italy, Belgium, USA and Panama.

3.—This Convention applies whether or not the lessee has or subsequently acquires the option to buy the equipment or to hold it on lease for a further period, and whether or not for a nominal price or rental (Art.1, Chap. I of the Convention).

A comparison between international and domestic leasing

The previous discussion indicates the differences between international leasing and domestic leasing. Apparently, a notable difference is that domestic leasing involves only one legal, accounting and taxation system, whereas international leasing involves at least two systems. Leasing in an international setting becomes more complicated, because of different legal, tax, accounting, and other environments involved. Table 3.1 presents a comparison between international and domestic leasing. Noticeably, the differences result in different financial decision models. The financial decision models of international leasing will be discussed in chapters 9, 10, and 11.

Types of international leasing

Literature review

In the literature, two types of leasing, 'cross-border leasing' and 'overseas subsidiary leasing', are distinguished. Meanwhile, the classification of finance/capital leasing and operating leasing in accounting standards is also accepted conventionally.

Meidan (1984) distinguishes four types of international leasing according to three variables (the manufacturer, the lessor and the lessee) at the level of international operations: 1) export leasing; 2) subsidiary export leasing; 3) foreign subsidiary leasing; and 4) subsidiary multinational leasing (see Figure 3.1). According to Meidan, "there are four main types of international leasing operations which might span in up to four different countries, in case the manufacturer of equipment is in a different country" (p.38). Clearly, the criterion of this classification is the location of the manufacturer, the lessor and the lessee. Following this classification, export leasing and foreign subsidiary leasing are not fundamentally different, because the location of these two types is the same (see Figure 3.1).

Table 3.1 A comparison of international and domestic leasing

	INTERNATIONAL LEASING	DOMESTIC LEASING
D E F I N I T I O N	A process of constructing an international lease wherein the use of an asset is transferred directly or indirectly from the owner or lessor in one legal jurisdiction to the user/lessee in another without changing ownership of that asset within a certain period of time that generally corresponds with the useful life of the asset and the user obtains the right to use the asset in exchange for paying the rental.	A process of constructing a lease wherein the owner or lessor passes the possession and the right to use the asset to the user (lessee) in return for payments made by the user (lessee) for a certain period of time that generally corresponds with the asset's useful life. In short, the leasing of an asset by a lessor domiciled in a country to a lessee in the same country is referred to domestic leasing.
C H A R A C T E R I S T I C S 1.	Separating ownership from the right to use an asset in a period of time is carried out under at least two legal systems.	Separating ownership from the right to use an asset in a period of time is carried out under only one legal system.
2.	Transferring an asset can be in a direct or an indirect form.	Transferring an asset is in a direct form.
3.	A lease term consists usually of the time of delivery of and of using an asset.	A lease term is usually only the time of using an asset by the lessee.
4.	Transactions affect the balance of payments and the balance of trade in both the lessee's and the lessor's countries.	No such influences.
5.	At least two accounting and fiscal systems involved.	Only one accounting and fiscal system involved.
6.	Lease payments can be in the form of a currency or a multi-currency package, or products.	Lease payments are usually in the form of a home currency.

Another problem will occur, if the classification is followed. Usually, international leasing (e.g., leveraged leasing) involves not only a manufacturer, a lessor and a lessee, but also an indenture trustee, an owner trustee, and a creditor. For example, in international aircraft leasing there are often several creditors. Meidan's classification does not take their locations into account. In addition, there are many leasing joint ventures where the lessor may locate in the same country as the manufacturer, or the lessee. In this circumstance, it is impossible to ascertain the type of those leasing transactions according to the location criterion.

Figure 3.1 Types of international leasing

International Leasing

| Export Leasing | Foreign Subsidiary Leasing |

Manufacturer / Lessor
in country A;
Lessee / User in country B

(1) Subsidiary Export Leasing	(2) Foreign Subsidiary Leasing	(3) Subsidiary Multinational Leasing
Manufacturer in country A Lessor in country A Lessee in country A User (subsidiary of lessee) in country B	Manufacturer in country A Lessor in country A Lessee (subsidiary of lessor) in country B Sublessee/User in country B	Manufacturer in country A Lessor in country A Lessor in country B Sublessee/User in country C

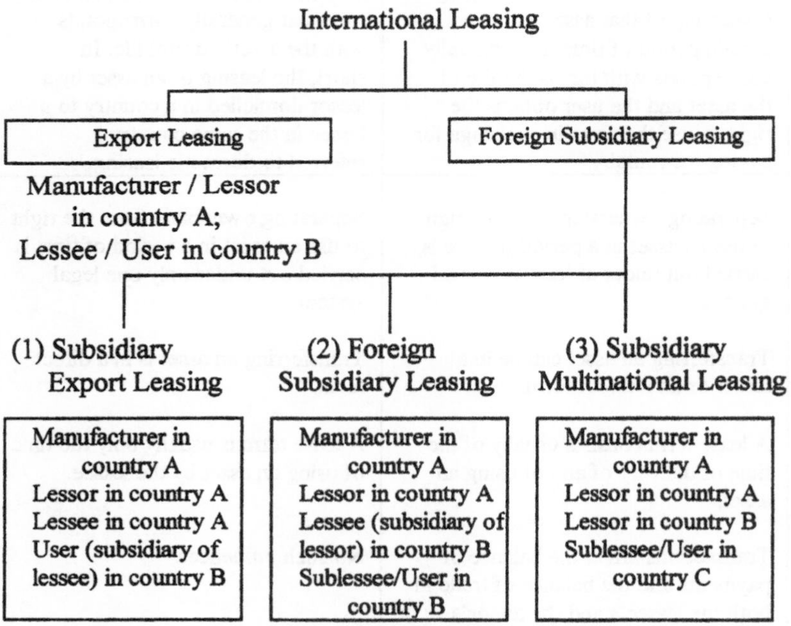

Source: Meidan, A., "Strategic Problems in International Leasing."
Management International Review, Vol.24, 1984, p.38.

Clark (1985) divides international leasing into three basic categories: investment in overseas ventures, international co-operation among leasing companies and cross-border business (p.8). The criterion of the classification is the function of international leasing. In my view, however, the difference between investment in overseas ventures and international co-operation among companies seems unclear according to this classification, since in effect international co-operation is also a kind of investment in overseas. Nagano (1988) argues that leasing has five basic functions, therefore it should be classified as: tax-oriented leasing, asset-based financing, project financing, sale-aid leasing and financing leasing. This classification differs from Clark's classification, though the same criterion (i.e., the function of leasing) is used. This classification may result in some confusions. For example, in most cases, asset-based financing leasing and project financing leasing are tax-oriented leasing. If this classification holds, it will also be difficult to distinct project financing leasing from financing leasing.

Some authors argue that a distinction must be made between a lease that is in substance if not in form, a conditional sale or hire purchase arrangement (such as a capital lease in the USA) and one that does not picture at the outset title to the leased equipment eventually passing to the lessee. The latter is a true lease and the former, a conditional sale or hire-purchase arrangement, is called a "false lease". Clearly, confusion will arise if this classification is taken, because a true lease in one country does not necessarily constitute a true lease in another.

In general, the major criteria of classifying international leasing in the literature, besides the criterion of accounting, include: 1) locations of a manufacturer, a lessor and a lessee (Meidan 1984); 2) basic functions of international leasing (Clark 1985; Nagano 1988); and 3) the substance of international leasing contracts (Pritchard and Hindelang 1980; Isom and Amembal 1982).

Criteria of classifying international leasing

To distinguish between different types of international leasing, it is necessary to find out some criteria for classification. There are many aspects that can be used as the criteria for classification. Also, it is necessary to separate a lessee's side from a lessor's side to consider the categories of leasing, since the characteristics of the demander (lessee) and the suppler (lessor) of international leasing are different. Moreover, classification should only represent general situations because different countries have different regulations governing their own leasing activities. It is impossible to cover all those leasing types or activities.

Operational motive of leasing From a lessor's point of view, leasing as an important device of finance and marketing can be used as a tool of either export to or investment in a lessee's country. The exporter of capital assets usually has the objective of providing the asset with a competitive financing package in order to get the order, and obtaining the full sale price of the asset in cash in the home currency as soon as possible. Leasing can frequently be a convenient way of meeting the objective. In this case, the motive of leasing is to promote export. It is called export leasing from the lessor's point of view. If the motive of a lessor is to invest overseas or to diversify risks, this kind of leasing can be called as investment leasing.

On the contrary, an importer usually wants to easily finance the purchase price of the asset at the lowest possible cost cover the longest possible term in the currency of choice. Leasing also meets such an objective from the importer (lessee) point of view. Leasing is often considered as an effective alternative of direct import for obtaining the use of capital assets. Under such a motive, leasing may be called import leasing. If the initial motive of a lessee is to obtain financing for the import of capital assets from a foreign lessor, leasing becomes a financing technique in this sense, and it can be called financing leasing.

Forms of leasing payments   International lease payments can be in the form of money payments, or payments in kind. Usually, a lessor in a developed country requires the lease payments in the home currency. A lessor in a less-developed country (LDC) usually expects the lease payments in a hard currency. However, a multi-currency package is often arranged in international leasing. Sometimes products produced by a lessee may be used to pay the rental. Especially, a lessee in a debt-crisis country is willing to pay the lease payments with its products. This kind of payments enables the lessee's country to eliminate foreign debts, to promote exports of its products, and to provide more opportunities for international leasing. Payments in kind instead of money payments are welcomed by thousands of companies from LDCs which are short of hard currencies. Accordingly, leasing with money payments is classified as currency leasing, leasing with payments in kind as barter leasing.

Taxation   Different countries have different tax systems. The criteria of making a lessor or a lessee owner of the leased asset for tax purposes vary from country to country. This non-homogeneous system certainly provides an opportunity for both a lessor and a lessee to take advantage of the differences in tax systems to capture tax benefits. Usually, financial leasing is often treated as tax-based leasing. A lessor with tax capacity can utilise tax incentives (e.g., accelerated depreciation allowances and investment allowances) by purchasing an asset, then leasing it to a lessee. Generally, taking advantage of taxes is one of the main purposes of using leasing instead of outright purchase or arising a loan (Tomkins, *et al.* 1979; Mayes and

Nicholas 1988; and Braund 1989). In most countries, a financial lease offers all the benefits of tax. In other countries like Germany, there are no tax advantages available to leasing. The leasing transactions in those countries are often non-tax-oriented. Accordingly, international leasing can be categorised as tax-oriented leasing and non-tax-oriented leasing.

Accounting standards In September 1982, the International Accounting Standards Committee (IASC) published International Accounting Standard No.17: Accounting for leases (IAS No.17).[4] IAS No.17 defines a lease as an agreement whereby the lessor conveys to the lessee in return for rent the right to use an asset for an agreed period of time. Two types of leases are classified under the IAS No.17, in accordance with the extent to which risks and rewards incident to ownership of a leased asset lie with the lessor or the lessee, as finance lease and operating lease. A finance lease is defined as a lease which transfers substantially all of the risks and rewards incident to ownership of an asset, whether or not the title is eventually transferred, and an operating lease which is any lease other than a finance lease. In the explanation of the IAS No.17, it suggests that since the transaction between a lessor and a lessee is based on a lease agreement common to both parties, it therefore is appropriate to use consistent definitions. Normally the two parties would classify a lease in the same way. Therefore, international leasing is categorised into capital/finance leasing and operating leasing from both the lessor's and lessee's points of view.

Number of participants In a two-country leasing case, usually only a lessor and a lessee are involved in the transaction. In such a case, the lessor who provides the whole of the purchase price for the leased asset from its own resources including any borrowing for which the lessor is principally liable, directly leases the asset to the lessee. This can be called direct leasing. All small-ticket leasing deals, and some medium-ticket leasing transactions are belong to direct leasing. The counterpart to direct leasing is leasing under which there are more than one equity owner participated in a transaction. The lessor provides only a small proportion of the capital costs from its own funds to purchase an asset for leasing. The rest of the funds required to meet the purchase price is often obtained by other financial institutions (e.g., banks,

---

[4] The IASC was founded in 1973. Some 70 countries are now represented on the IASC. Generally, compliance with international standards is not required until the standards are reflected in national standards.

insurance companies, pension funds, trusts etc.) which are generally known as debt holders. Sometimes, an indenture trustee and an owner trustee also participate in a leasing transaction. They are responsible for managing the rights and obligations of the debt and equity participants. This kind of leasing is categorised as leveraged leasing. Leveraged leasing is one of the most complex and legal sophisticated leasing transactions for financing large capital intensive equipment or assets.

From the above discussion, the major types of international leasing are listed in Table 3.2.

Table 3.2 Types of international leasing

TYPES OF INTERNATIONAL LEASING		
Criteria	*The Lessor's Viewpoint*	*The Lessee's Viewpoint*
Motives of Operation	Export Leasing	Import Leasing
	Investment Leasing	Financing Leasing
Leasing Payments	Currency Leasing	Currency Leasing
	Barter Leasing	Barter Leasing
Taxation	Tax-oriented Leasing	Tax-oriented Leasing
	Non-tax-oriented Leasing	Non-tax-oriented Leasing
Accounting Standards	Capital/Finance Leasing	Capital/Finance Leasing
	Operating Leasing	Operating Leasing
Number of Participants	Direct Leasing	Direct Leasing
	Leveraged Leasing	Leveraged Leasing

There are some other types of leasing which are classified with other standards, such as master leasing, money-over-money leasing, swap leasing, back-to-back leasing, wash leasing, wet-and-dry leasing, wrap leasing. They emerged over the last few years to meet particular tax or regulatory requirements, and financial management. However, a detailed discussion of these types of leasing is beyond this book. For some other types of leases, see (Johnson 1997).

Structures of the international leasing industry

There are literally thousands of leasing companies across the world, varying in size from thousands of dollars of assets to hundreds of millions, varying in operating from a national to an international scope, from developed countries to developing nations. In effect, the structure of the industry has changed almost as dramatically as the rate at which the industry has grown. Initially, the industry was composed primarily of third-party leasing companies, also called independent lessors. These firms purchase assets and lease them to ultimate customers from different countries, raising needed funds through equity and debt in financial markets. Recently, some leasing companies, particularly in continental Europe, are owned by a number of large banks and financial institutions; others are joint ventures between banks and commercial enterprises. In developing countries, joint ventures are the principal form. Generally, the international leasing industry can be categorised as five divisions according to its funding source, operation, structure and organisation.

Financial institution lessors   A large majority of leasing suppliers are subsidiaries and leasing departments of thousands of large commercial banks and financial institutions, called financial institution lessors. They play both an active and a passive role in the international leasing industry. Some smaller and regional banks also offer leasing services to their customers, or to their geographic trading area. Most of the large, so-called money centre banks, those operating in major metropolitan business markets, are also active in the leasing business. They offer vendor and end-user options, at transaction sizes that vary according to individual investment and marketing strategies. Leasing companies that are subsidiaries of banks usually depend on borrowing funds from their associated banks for their leasing operations. The European leasing industry is heavily dominated by the banks. In the United States, banks are the second largest segment of the leasing suppliers. In Asian countries, most leasing companies are subsidiaries of commercial banks and financial corporations. Generally, banks and financial institutions including their subsidiaries are expected to remain as significant players in financial leasing, both as advisers and providers of funds.

Independent lessors   Generally defined, an independent lessor is one that does not derive a majority portion of its business from its parent companies manufacturing or product sales. As a group this is the largest single segment of the industry in the USA, and some other countries. The independent lessors are predominantly responsible for the general acceptance of vendor-oriented leasing and finance programmes that aid in the sale of products. The independent lessors have demonstrated an ability over the years to successfully adapt to a wide variety of forces. Currently, independent lessors have more financial alternatives, such as commercial papers, asset-backed securities and bank financing, which enable them to derive a better bargain on the pricing side, and consequently be able to obtain a large share of the industry. Strategically, they have to continue to serve the needs of the business community at large by developing new products to offer directly or through creative vendor programmes.

Captives   In contrast to independents, captives are those that derive more than 50 per cent of their business from a parent company. As leasing gained widespread acceptance within the business community, and as vendor programmes gained in popularity, more and more manufacturers opted to create a leasing subsidiary to help finance their sale of products. The principal purpose of a captive lessor is to extend leasing facilities for products of the related manufacturer or supplier. A captive lessor may be a subsidiary of a manufacturer or supplier, or a joint venture with a bank or an independent lessor. A manufacturer or distributor, for example, recognises the advantages of having a captive expanding its market shares, and can utilise this technique to finance the sale of its products. Subsequently, it develops different leasing programmes. It is important for a captive lessor to have a successful captive-parent relationship that can increase revenue, improve cash flow, expand sales volume, help maintain funds and so on. The facilities offered by a captive lessor are in the nature of a sales-aid scheme, known in the US as a vendor (aid) programme. In computer leasing, most lessors are captives that promote the sales of computers manufactured mainly by their parents. However, a captive lessor does not necessarily restrict its leasing activities to related products, since the dynamic market requires the business to be more flexible. Since the competition becomes intensive, sales-aid facilities are now not solely offered by captive lessors with shareholding ties to the equipment suppliers.

Joint venture leasing companies   In the economic co-operation between east and west European countries, between developing nations and developed countries, joint venture leasing companies play a considerable role. Particularly, developing countries welcome advanced equipment, more funds and high technology from developed countries. Joint ventures are an excellent form for the establishment of a leasing company because in these countries local governments do not normally want to lose control on the companies. In developing nations, most lessors are joint ventures with prominent foreign lessors and foreign banks.

State-owned leasing companies In   some   countries   (e.g.,   China),   the government sets up some leasing companies which are treated as administrative function. These leasing companies are responsible for the allocation, leasing, and re-leasing of governmental assets to state-owned enterprises, and public organisations. For example in Russia and China, before their economic reforms, state-owned leasing companies were mainly administrative organisations under the control of the state's Materials Ministry (for example in China) or the Central Bank, which played an administrative role such as leasing assets to local state-owned enterprise, managing the leased assets, and dealing with the leased assets at the end of a lease. An important characteristic of these companies is that the main motive of their business is to allocate state-owned assets to the enterprises, based on the needs of the enterprises, not on the economic benefits/profits of leasing companies.

Forms of international leasing transactions

A direct two-country cross-border leasing transaction

A direct two-country cross-border leasing transaction is a transaction in which the lessor, domiciled in the same country as the manufacturer or the supplier of the assets to be leased, directly leases the assets to the lessee domiciled in another country, by transporting them across country borders. In such a transaction, the lessor is often a subsidiary of a manufacturer or supplier who is either a domestic firm or a MNC. Export leasing is a typical example of direct two-country cross-border leasing. In this case, the lessor is usually known as a captive lessor. A captive lessor may also be a joint venture between an independent lessor or a bank lessor and the manufacturer or supplier. First, the lessor and the lessee enter into negotiations with each other (sometimes an international broker participates in negotiations), and sign an international lease. The lessor then delivers the assets (crossing the country border) to the lessee, and the lessee pays rental charges and obtains the right to use the assets. Finally, some options may be available to the lessee depending on provisions in a contract. The basic relationship between the lessor and the lessee is shown in Figure 3.2. However, direct cross-border leasing is uncommon except in the leasing of ships and aircraft (Thompson 1990, p.291).

Figure 3.2 A direct two-country cross-border leasing transaction

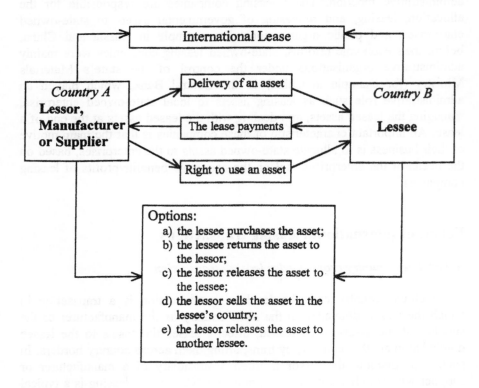

Options:
 a) the lessee purchases the asset;
 b) the lessee returns the asset to the lessor;
 c) the lessor releases the asset to the lessee;
 d) the lessor sells the asset in the lessee's country;
 e) the lessor releases the asset to another lessee.

A direct three-country international leasing transaction

Except that a lessor locates in a different country than a manufacturer or supplier, direct three-country international leasing is, for the most part, similar to direct two-country cross-border leasing. Three-country international leasing gains its name from the fact the three parties (the lessor, the lessee, and the manufacturer/supplier) are domiciled in three different countries. The basic relationship among the three parties is presented in Figure 3.3. Most three-country international leases are financial leases. The lessors are often owned by banks and financial institutions (divisions or subsidiaries). This type of transactions is often seen in aircraft leasing, ship and container leasing.

Figure 3.3 A direct three-country international leasing transaction

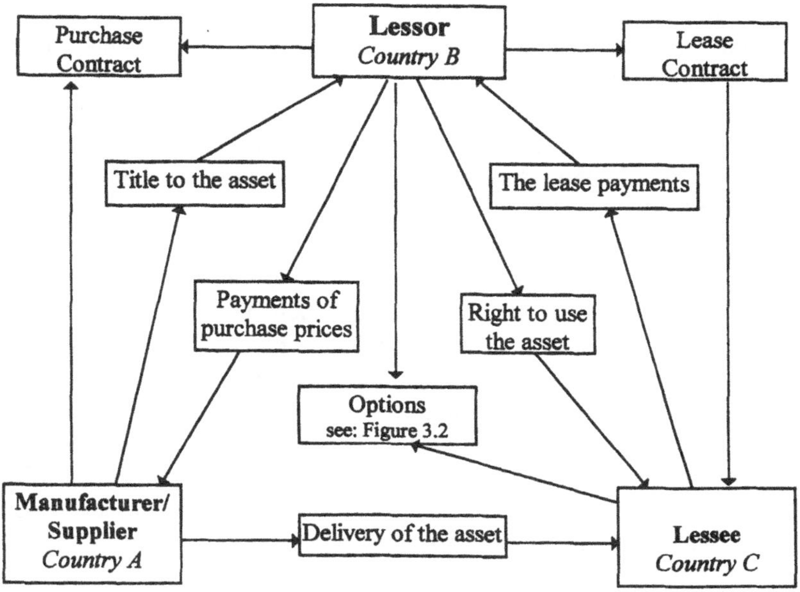

An international leveraged leasing transaction

One of the main characteristics of leveraged leasing is that a lender or loan syndicate that advances the greater part of the price of the asset to a lessor has no recourse to the lessor for repayment of the loans. Its attraction is that the equity participants (a lessor, a group of financial or other institutions acting together as the lessor) obtain the title to the leased asset by providing only a relatively small proportion of its overall costs and with the title come any related taxation incentives and government subsidiaries. These benefits are passed on to the lessee by a reduction in the lease payments and hence the implicit lease rate is often well below the current asset loan interest rate.

In international leveraged leasing, more than three parties, coming from more than two different nations, are involved in the transaction. Usually, equity participants are domiciled in different countries from the lessee. In normal financial leasing, there are only two parties (the lessor and the lessee) involved in the transaction. The difference in the number of parties involved results from the fact that in leveraged leasing the lessor puts up only a fraction of the investment cost and borrows the rest from other sources. The reason for borrowing by the lessor is the fact that leveraged leasing involves significant capital outlays. Practically, leveraged leasing represents a very complex transaction and reflects a package of agreements. The major agreements included in the package are:

1) The participation agreement: An agreement signed by all parties to the transaction. In this agreement, the commitments and obligations of each participant (the lessor, the lender, the lessee, the trustee, etc.) are set forth;

2) The trust agreement: An agreement executed by the owner participants and a corporate trustee (usually a commercial bank's corporate trust department). In such an agreement, the owner participants agree to advance their share of the equity funds and receive the lease rentals. The trustee agrees to purchase the asset on behalf of the owner participants and to hold title to the asset;

3) The indenture trust agreement: This agreement is entered into by the owner trustee and the indenture. In this agreement, the certificates of loans, its term, pattern of payments, interest rates, etc. are stipulated;

4) The lease agreement: This agreement is entered into by the lessor or sometimes the owner trustee and the lessee. In this agreement, the term of the lease, the amount of rentals, the currency, the insurance for the asset, the obligation of maintenance of the asset, etc. are set forth.

A simple structure of international leveraged leasing is profiled in Figure 3.4. International leveraged leasing is presently customary in international aircraft and ship leasing.

Figure 3.4 An international leveraged leasing relationship

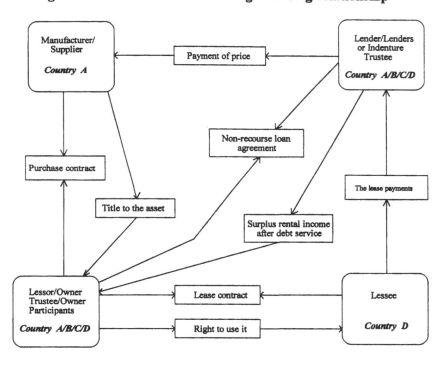

International wrap leasing transaction

Wrap leasing is a financing technique whereby short-term leasing is wrapped by long-term leasing. Wrap leasing is usually used in high-tech equipment leasing (e.g., computer leasing). The basic structure, for example, in computer leasing is as follows: a computer leasing company (the lessor in short term leasing/the wrap lessee in long term leasing) locates a user (a lessee in short term leasing) of the computer, purchases the computer and leases it to the user (the lessee in short term leasing). Before the computer is placed in service, lessor/wrap lessee sells the computer to the investor (wrap lessor) for cash and other receipts, and leases it back under a long-term lease. This transaction creates a lease-sublease situation. One leasing transaction has been wrapped in another. The investor (wrap lessor) claims the tax benefits, primarily depreciation and interest deductions. The lessor/wrap lessee gets a fee and a portion of the residual value after the termination of the wrap lease. The user/lessee can claim rental deductions and obtain the use of a computer in its business.

Wrap leasing transaction gains widespread popularity among high tax-bracket taxpayers, since it provides significant tax deferrable potential. The wrap leasing transaction can fully utilise the tax benefits associated with the ownership of the asset. More careful must be taken in international wrap leasing, since different countries treat wrap leasing differently and different nations have different tax rules. Figure 3.5 shows a simple example of international wrap leasing.

Figure 3.5 An international wrap leasing relationship

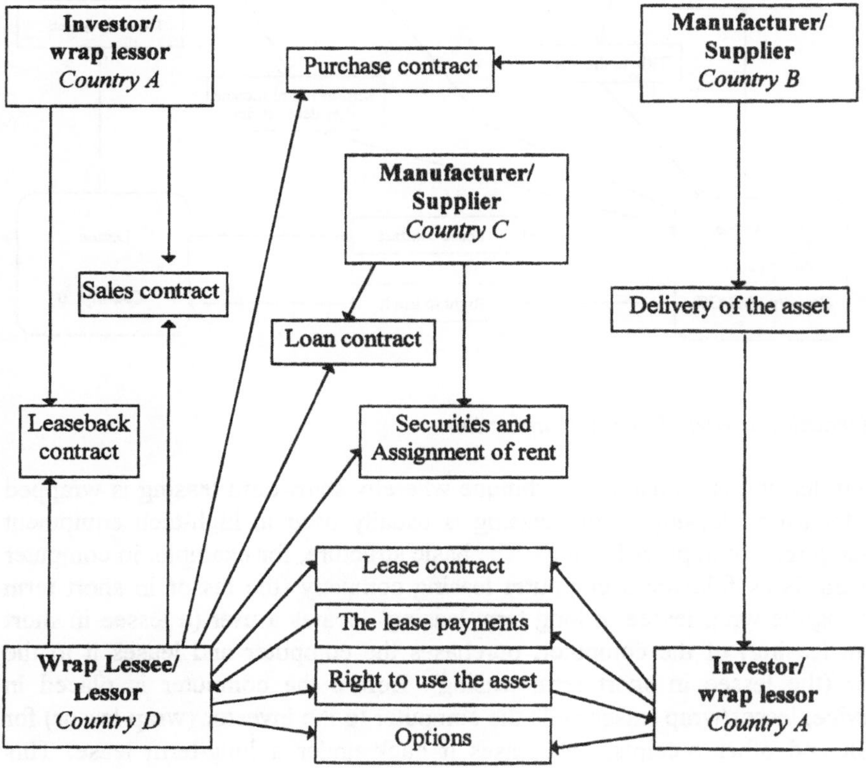

Conclusion

International leasing has not been properly defined and studied. This chapter presents a general discussion of the concepts and fundamentals of international leasing through reviewing the literature and discussing its types and structures.

An *international lease* is a contract essentially stipulating the separation of ownership of an asset and the right to use it from one legal jurisdiction to another; the user (lessee) domiciled in one jurisdiction obtains the right to use the asset in exchange for promising to make a series of payments to the owner or lessor domiciled in another jurisdiction during a certain period of time that generally correspondents with the useful life of the asset.

International leasing is a process of constructing an international lease wherein the use of an asset is transferred directly or indirectly from the owner or lessor in one legal jurisdiction to the user (lessee) in another without changing ownership of that asset within a certain period of time that generally corresponds with the useful life of that asset, and the user obtains the right to use that asset in exchange for paying a series of rental charges to the owner or lessor. There are no significant differences between international leasing and domestic leasing. But placed in an international context, leasing became more complicated.

International leasing is categorised as: export/investment leasing vs. import/financing leasing; currency leasing vs. barter leasing; tax-oriented leasing vs. non-tax-oriented leasing; direct leasing vs. leveraged leasing; capital (finance) leasing vs. operating leasing.

This chapter describes the structure of the international leasing industry and the forms of international leasing transactions. Broadly, there are five sources of lessors: financial institution lessors; independent lessors; captive lessors; joint venture lessors; governmental (state-owned) lessors.

This chapter also lists four major forms of international leasing transactions: a direct two-country cross-border leasing transaction, a direct three-country international leasing transaction, an international leveraged leasing transaction, and an international wrap leasing transaction.

Reference

Beckman, H. and A.W.A. Joosen. 1988. *Leasing Van Roerend En Enroerrnd Goed*. Leiden: H.E. Stenfert Kroses, B.V.

Braund, S.L. 1989. Leasing: review of the empirical studies. *Managerial Finance* 15, no. 1/2: 13-20.

Clark, T.M. 1978. *Leasing*. UK: McGraw-Hill Book Company Limited.

Clark, T.M. 1985. *Leasing Finance*. London: Euromoney Publications.

Henius, F. 1947. *Dictionary of Foreign Trade*. New York: Prentice-Hall, Inc.

Isom, T.A. and S.P. Amembal. 1982. *The Handbook of Leasing: Techniques & Analysis*. New York: Petrocelli Books, Inc.

Johnson, J. 1997. Types of leasing activity. In *Leasing Finance*, ed. Chris Boobyer. London: Euromoney Books, pp.17-33.

Mayes, D.C. and C.S. Nicholas. 1988. *The Economic Impact of Leasing*. London: Macmillan Press.

Meidan, A. 1984. Strategic problems in international leasing. *Management International Review* 24, no. 4: 36-47.

Nagano, O. 1988. Cross-border leasing: its current status and tasks ahead. *World Leasing Yearbook 1988*: 20.

Pritchard, R.E. and T.J. Hindelang. 1980. *The Lease/Buy Decision*. New York: Amacon, A Division of American Management Association.

Reiners, G. 1983. Leasing in an international context. In *International Finance Handbook*, ed. A.M. George and I.H. Giddy. New York: John Wiley & Sons.

Terpstra, V. 1978. *International Marketing*. Holt Rinehart and Winston.

Thompson, A. 1990. International leasing. In *Handbook of International Financial Management*, ed. M.Z. Brooke. London: Macmillan Publishers. pp. 284-292.

Tomkins, C.R., J.F. Lowe and E.J. Morgan. 1979. *An Economic Analysis of the Financial Leasing Industry*. Hampshire, England: Teakfield Limited.

4 International trade and international leasing

International trade environment and international leasing

One of the most significant economic developments since World War II is the increasing internationalisation of business. Although business has been conducted across national boundaries for many centuries, during the last few decades the business operations have extremely expanded on a global scale. Leading corporations, including many large leasing companies have increasingly turned their attention to international business in order to maintain a competitive edge in today's dynamic economic scene. Many international banks and other non-bank financial institutions have also increasingly engaged in overseas leasing business. International leasing has been used as a means to support cross-border trade.

Economic efficiency requires specialisation. The scope for specialisation goes far beyond the boundaries of any individual country. In principle, international trade takes place in accordance with economic efficiency due to comparative advantage and the economies of scale. The theory of comparative advantage is a theoretical explanation of the motive for and nature of international trade. Its fundamental assumption is that production specialisation and trade will generate higher world standards of living, if every country specialises in trade of the products in which it has a comparative production advantage. According to the theory, comparative advantage indicates which products, and in what amounts, will be traded between nations. The theoretical explanations of trade underpin the understanding of international leasing.

For example, the law of comparative advantage can provide a lessor a theoretical framework for identifying foreign lease marketing opportunities and specifying lease products. Its principles also address the topics of international pricing and a currency approach, which may be applied to pricing an international lease and selecting a currency for the lease payments. The product life-cycle theory (see: Vernon 1966; Wells 1968; Wells 1969) can be used as a timed, strategic approach to international leasing with which a lessor can forecast and determine a leased asset 'life stage'. A major contribution of the product life-cycle theory is that it accounts for foreign production decisions with export and import. Also, it acknowledges the importance of advantages in technology and marketing know-how as sources of comparative advantage.

One of the unfavourable factors in international trade is protective tariffs and import quotas. The traditional and most widely used trade device as a tax levied on trans-boundary movements of assets, is commonly called a tariff or duty. An import quota, belonging to the category of direct controls on international trade, is a quantitative restriction imposed by a government on the imports of a certain commodity. A tariff raises the price of a foreign-made asset to domestic users of that asset. The imposition of a tariff results in large domestic production of import-substitutes, in result, the global gains from trade, the level of consumer's satisfaction, the volume of imports, and the balance of foreign trade etc. will be all subject to change to some extent. As far as leasing is concerned, in most countries the leasing of foreign assets is subject to the system of tariffs or import quotas, similarly treated as the export/import of the asset. For example, in Brazil all normal import regulations also apply to import leasing.

As a result of tariffs and quotas on leasing, the prices for assets leased from foreign countries rise, compared with the prices of assets leased domestically. Consequently, this leads to more domestic leasing business of international leasing (mainly cross-border leasing) substitutes, given the market demand for assets to lease. On the other hand, the imposition of tariffs or import quotas only on leasing, will lead to more assets being directly exported/imported, less being leased, given the foreign demand for the assets and all other things being equal. However, in some countries, especially some developing countries, the leasing of foreign capital assets may not or not be fully subject to the system of tariffs or import quotas. This could be an advantage to lease foreign assets over to directly import the assets from a user's point of view.

Another unfavourable factor in international trade is countertrade. Countertrade commonly refers to a variety of unconventional international trade operations which directly or indirectly links exchanges of goods in an attempt to pass over currency transactions. The most usual countertrade arrangements are barter, counter-purchase, buy-back, and offset. Barter means a simultaneous exchange of goods of equal value. Counter-purchase is an agreement in which a supplier agrees to purchase other goods which are not related to what the supplier provided, for example, the goods not manufactured with the equipment the supplier supplied. Under a buy-back agreement, a supplier of machinery, equipment, or factories agrees to purchase goods manufactured with the equipment supplied and technology offered. Offset is an agreement in which a foreign supplier is required to assemble, purchase, or manufacture components locally. Offset is frequently negotiated in military equipment and aircraft purchase.

Similarly, I use the term "counterleasing", to refer to the phenomenon that is mostly similar to countertrade. Counterleasing refers to a variety of unconventional international leasing transactions which directly or indirectly links exchanges of the use of goods or capital assets in an attempt to pass over currency transactions. By the same token, "barter-leasing" means a simultaneous exchange through leasing each other capital assets of equal value. "Counterlease" is an agreement in which a foreign lessor agrees to lease back other, unrelated goods from the lessee's side. Lease-back refers to a process in which a foreign lessor of machinery, equipment, or factories agrees to accept the lease payments in the form of the goods manufactured with the equipment leased and technology offered. Under a lease-offset agreement, a foreign lessor who leases the main and key parts of equipment is required to assemble, purchase, or supply the components of the equipment locally, and then to receive the whole equipment at the termination of the contract.

Table 4.1 lists the arrangements in countertrade and counterleasing. Usually, the proponents of counterleasing claim that counterleasing has the advantages of conserving foreign exchange, increasing liquidity, providing credit, improving marketing, promoting exports, transferring technology, and developing the industry. Counterleasing, in my view, however, likes other leasing restrictions will increase the cost of leasing transactions and reduce competition of the leasing markets. Counterleasing may result in a nation imposing the restrictions will pay more for its import leasing and receive less for its export leasing. Even so, in reality, many developing countries are attempting to employ counterleasing because of the shortage of foreign currencies. In this case, counterleasing may relate import leasing to its corresponding export as a way of saving foreign currencies. It is argued that this view is not correct, because counterleasing in fact drains foreign currencies by increasing transaction costs and reducing competition.

Table 4.1 Major arrangements in countertrade/counterleasing

Countertrade	*Counterleasing*
Barter A simultaneous exchange of consumer goods or capital assets of equal value.	*Barter-leasing* A simultaneous exchange through leasing each other capital assets of equal value.
Counter-purchasing An agreement in which a supplier agrees to purchase unrelated other goods from the import country.	*Counterlease* An agreement in which a foreign lessor agrees to lease back other unrelated goods from the lessee's side.
Buy-back A supplier of machinery, equipment or factories agrees to purchase goods manufactured with the equipment supplied and technology offered.	*Lease-back* A foreign lessor of machinery, equipment or factories agrees to accept the lease payments in the form of the goods manufactured with the equipment leased and technology offered.
Offset Under which a foreign supplier is required to assemble, purchase, or manufacture components locally.	*Lease-offset* Under which a foreign lessor who leases the key parts of equipment is required to assemble, purchase or produce components locally, and then receive the whole equipment after the lease.

Although counterleasing is criticised for increasing transaction costs and reducing competition, the real business is expected to expand in the next century because of the increasing demand for foreign leasing in eastern Europe and other developing countries in Asia and Africa where their currencies are not convertible for foreign hard currencies, and/or lack of foreign currencies.

Since the 1960s world trade patterns have changed. The evidence of the changes is diverse. For example, developed nations trade most with each other and account for the largest share of world trade. Developing countries are becoming major producers of manufactured goods, and with supply to both developed and developing countries. The trade between the West and the East has tremendously increased since east European countries open their doors and liberate their economies. Apparently, these changes result from the diversification of products traded by individual countries and the diversification of countries that are major world traders (Cundiff and Hilger 1988, p.25). It is quite obvious that the diversification of world trade has been both a cause and a result of the significant changes in how businesses enter foreign markets. Certainly, diversification provides a significant chance for expanding international leasing. Since developing countries are becoming another major force in international trade, this in turn will give developing countries more foreign currencies to buy or to lease foreign assets they need. Also, the current trends toward financial deregulation in the US, Japan and other west European countries have created good opportunities for the development of international trade, and offered a favourable trade climate for conducting international leasing. The single currency and the single market within EU provide favourable trade environment for the member countries to develop cross-border leasing.

The trends of the deregulation, and the massive increases in the need for trade-related credit and financing worldwide, in addition of governmental interference and various export financing programmes, have created export-import markets in unprecedented depth and complexity. Moreover, international trade has historically been characterised by intense competition, and today is no exception. These circumstances could be either advantageous or disadvantageous to international lessors or lessees.

In sum, the dynamic trade environments challenge both international lessors and lessees to take new strategies and make decisions. A favourable climate of international trade will provide potential opportunities for developing international leasing, and the development of international leasing will promote the growth of international trade.

The balance of payments and international leasing

Transactions between nations are measured by an accounting system, called the balance of payments, which reveals whether a country is in surplus or deficit on trade and capital transactions with the rest of the world. For any country, the balance of payments is a systematic record of its receipts from, or payments to, other countries. The balance of payments structurally consists of the current account, capital account, and official reserves account. The current account consists of payments or receipts for goods, services, and foreign aid. Usually, the data for goods and services are broken down into two components: merchandise trade and international services. The capital account records all long- or short-term capital transfers into and out of a country. It is broken down into two subcategorises: private investment and transactions of central banks. The official reserves account measures changes in holding of gold and foreign currencies by official monetary institutions. There are various ways of expounding particular accounts of the balance of payments, but a relatively complete picture is the form of IMF (International Monetary Funds) statistics information.

The balance of payments is an effective tool for understanding a foreign country's general economic environment, and in particular for foreseeing the possible future changes in the country's currency value. When a country has persistent deficit in its trade balance with other countries, it must "use up" its reserves to pay foreigners, and thus its own reserves are threatened. The devaluation of its currency may result if other measures cannot be taken. On the other hand, persistent surplus in the trade balance can force an upward revaluation of a country's currency, thus making it more expensive for foreigners either to buy their currency and products or to lease products. Information of the balance of payments is useful to international lessors in planning strategies and making decisions.

First, the balance of payments helps forecast a potential country's leasing market capacity, and to anticipate which currency the lessee is willing to pay the lease payments if a lease is going to be negotiated. Apparently, a country that experiences a serious balance of payments deficit is not likely to either lease as much as it would or pay hard currencies if it were running a surplus.

Secondly, the balance of payments offers information on trade policies of a potential lessee's government. For example, a country that experiences a large deficit in its balance of payments is likely to strictly stipulate quotas or licences on import leasing.

Thirdly, the balance of payments provides an indication on the exchange policy of a potential lessee's government. Usually, a country that experiences a large deficit in its balance of payments is likely to place more controls on foreign exchange.

Fourth, the balance of payments is an important indicator of pressure on a country's foreign exchange rate, and of the potential for a firm leasing with that country to experience exchange risks.

Though the balance of payments may be an efficient and important instrument for both a lessor and a lessee in international leasing strategy planning and decision making, the position of leasing transactions has not been clearly located in the balance of payments, and this issue has not been discussed in the literature. Surprisingly, international leasing transactions in most nations have not been specified in the national balance of payments.[1] This is because the statistical system of leasing transactions has not been established. It may also be difficult to properly position leasing in the balance of payments as there is a lack of research on international leasing, and consequently no proper definitions and the classifications of leasing and international leasing. In practice, there are many ways of treating leasing in the balance of payments. In most cases, leasing (mainly financial leasing) is simply categorised into "international services" of the current account in the balance of payments. The reasons why leasing belongs to "international services", probably include: 1) leasing is not significant in a economy compared with other industries so that it is not necessary to value it in an independent category; and 2) it is difficult to classify leasing transactions precisely so that all leasing transactions are categorised in "services" for simplicity.

In my view, different types of leasing should be situated in different parts of the balance of payments. For example, export/import leasing should obviously be categorised in "export/import" of the current account. This is because export/import leasing leads to the same result as direct export/import. Financial leasing, being a long-term financing instrument, should be located in the "long-term capital" group of the "movement of capital and monetary gold". Similarly, operating leasing should be in the "short-term capital" group. The net rental (rental receipts minus asset costs) of leasing should be classed in the "investment income" of the current account, since international leasing from a lessor's point of view is a type of foreign investment.

---

[1] There are a few exceptions. In the UK, for example, a sub-category "Leasing: interest on overseas leasing by specialist finance leasing companies" records the interest received from overseas leasing in the balance of payments. Finance leasing is treated as if it were lending by the leasing company to a lessee to finance its purchase of the asset. In China, starting from 1987 the State Statistics Bureau began to publish information of (financial) leasing with the category "loans and lease" in the balance of payments.

Following these arguments, a reference form of the balance of payments covering international leasing transactions is recommended as in Table 4.2.

Table 4.2 A reference form of the balance of payments

Currency:
A. Current Account:
1. Merchandise:
a. Exports (incl. export leasing).
b. Imports (incl. import leasing).
c. International Services.
2. Non-monetary Gold Movement (net):
3. Foreign Travel:
4. Transportation:
a. Gross Freight.
b. Other.
5. Insurance:
6. Investment Income:
a. Direct Investment.
b. Portfolio Investment.
c. Leasing Investment.
d. Other interests.
7. Government:
8. Miscellaneous:
Total Goods and Service (1 through 8).
9. Unrequited Transfers:
Total current transactions (1 through 9).
B. Movement of Capital and Monetary Gold:
10. Long-term Capital:
a. Direct Investment.
b. Portfolio Securities: Bonds.
c. Portfolio Securities: Shares.
d. Financial leasing.
e. Amortisation.
f. Others.
11. Short-term Capital:
a. Currency, Deposits, Government Obligations.
b. Operating Leasing.
c. Others.
C. Counterpart (incl. Counterleasing) Items:
D. Others:

International leasing promoting international trade

Traditionally, international trade consists of exports: sales of home country products to foreign buyers; and imports: purchases of goods from abroad. In terms of imports, the basic purpose is to obtain the right to consume/use the goods manufactured abroad, in exchange for paying the price for this right. An importer (or an import country) has usually to finance paying the price and to try to pay the price at the lowest possible cost. Sometimes an importer not only wants to obtain the right to consume/use the assets, but also likes to acquire full services such as insurance and maintenance of the assets, as well as expertise advice. In terms of exports, the basic purpose is to sell the right to consume/use the goods manufactured home to abroad, in exchange for receiving the payments for this right. An exporter/export country has usually to offer the goods with a competitive financing package, and try to receive the full scale price for the goods in cash in terms of home currency as soon as possible. Also, in order to increase foreign orders, sometimes an exporter has to provide various types of services to foreign customers such as maintenance, insurance, replacement of assets.

International leasing, which is defined in Chapter 3 as the process of transferring the right to use a capital asset from the owner in one nation to the user in another without changing ownership of the asset, can obviously be used as a device for the importing and exporting of capital assets. This is because leasing can frequently be a convenient way of meeting the motives of both export and import.[2] Moreover, leasing can be considered as an effective alternative of direct imports for the purpose of obtaining the use of assets, when a country has more controls on the direct imports of the assets.

An important stimulus to international leasing could be the advantage to a company of using an asset through international leasing and thereby avoiding import tariffs that could sometimes be as high as the cost of the asset. Typically, to avoid export/import controls, leasing can, to some extent, take advantage of the customs clearance. For instance, in accordance with the former Soviet Customs Rules, goods and other property temporarily imported

---

[2] However, according to Reiners (1983), there are several misconceptions about export leasing: the first misconception is that export leasing does not waste anybody's time pursuing very creative lease structures if the importer is not creditworthy; the second misconception is that the lessor might be willing to write the lease at less than market rates; the third misconception is that lessors are happy to provide exporters with lease quotes because of the "do good" this generates with the exporter and because it gives the lessor firm a unique opportunity to get its name in front of the importer (pp.25-6).

in or exported out of the former USSR were not subject to customs duties, if there is an obligation of the Soviet organisation, sending or receiving these goods from abroad to make a reverse operation. This offers a chance for international leasing, especially operating leasing (Nosko 1989).

As the assets exported directly from an exporter to the customer abroad through leasing, transactions can take a number of routes. An exporter may go to a lessor (usually a large bank) in its own country, which has a subsidiary in the lessee's country and the three parties can arrange a lease in terms of the lessee's currency; An exporter may ask for a domestic lessor to find out another lessor in the customer country through a leaseclub (or a leasing association) to arrange an export leasing transaction; An exporter may transfer the business through its leasing subsidiary in its home country or the customer country; A lease itself can cross between borders from an exporter to the customer directly. Each of those routes can be fraught with its own particular problems, and the best choice will depend upon the countries and the customers involved and upon the size of the deal as well. Figure 4.1 shows the main routes of leasing promoting exports.

Leasing in some east European countries like Poland and Bulgaria, and other developing countries like Pakistan, India and China plays an important role in their foreign trade.[3] These countries have recognised the significance of international leasing and taken the device to expand their foreign trade and to modernise their economies (in China, for example, see Gao 1994). In east European countries, since equipment in many enterprises has not been changed for many years, it is of great importance to use leasing to obtain new advanced equipment for the enterprises in these countries (for the case of Poland, see Gao 1995). According to Nosko (1989), import leasing may essentially help the reconstruction of the Soviet economy and supply new equipment to the enterprises, whereas export leasing may promote the expansion of the country's export opportunities, supply the enterprises with necessary foreign currency, release their access to the international market.[4]

---

[3] For the reasons why leasing can be used in foreign trade in east European countries, see Zahalka (1983).

[4] Although the Soviet economy broke following the end of the Communist regime, this view is still correct, as far as the functions of leasing in international trade are concerned.

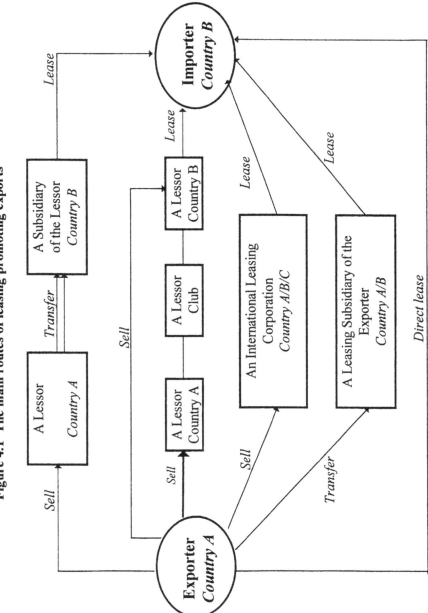

Figure 4.1 The main routes of leasing promoting exports

Conclusion

Since there is no reliable information on leasing volume worldwide, it is impossible to illustrate how and to what extent leasing has promoted international trade in the past. Despite this it may anticipate that trade through leasing will increase in the next century. The reasons are obvious: 1) leasing will be used as an alternative to import more advanced equipment to meet the demands of modernising their economies as the result of east European countries opening their doors and reforming their economies; and 2) the expanding of foreign investment and internationalisation of business will create new opportunities for equipment trading through leasing.

This chapter provides a general discussion of international trade and international leasing. One of the interesting areas which is worthwhile further exploring is counterleasing. This chapter briefly explains the concepts and different forms of counterleasing in comparison with countertrade. Also, this chapter discusses the inclusion of leasing in the balance of payments and proposes a new form of the balance of payments.

Reference

Cundiff, E.W. and T. Hilger. 1988. *Marketing in the International Environment.* Englewood Cliffs, N.J.: Prentice-Hall, Inc.

Gao, S.S. 1994. The development of lease financing in China: market, regulations, taxes and accounting. Paper presented in *The Annual Conference of the Chinese Economics Association (UK).* London.

Gao, S.S. 1995. Leasing in Poland: privatisation, financing and current problems. *European Business Review,* no. 5: 31-40.

Nosko, A.P. 1989. The introduction of leasing into the Soviet Union. Paper presented in *The Seventh World Leasing Convention.* Madrid.

Reiners, G. 1983. Leasing in an international context. In *International Finance Handbook,* ed. A.M. George and I.H. Giddy, New York: John Wiley & Sons.

Vernon, R. 1966. International investment and international trade in the product cycle. *Quarterly Journal of Economics* May: 190-207.

Wells, L.T. 1968. A product life cycle for international trade. *Journal of Marketing* July: 1-6.

Wells, L.T. 1969. Test of a product cycle model of international trade. *Quarterly Journal of Economics* February: 152-62.

Zahalka, V. 1983. Leasing in foreign trade. *Soviet and Eastern European Foreign Trade* Summer: 37-53.

5 International finance and international leasing

International financial environment and international leasing

The international financial environment is of great significance for international leasing because international finance provides services to the international leasing industry. For example, the use of a stable, widely accepted currency can reduce international leasing transaction costs. Also, the deregulation of the financial system may provide potential for developing the international leasing industry. Moreover, for either a lessor or a lessee it may be easy to maintain an optimal debt ratio, when there are more financial channels and better availability of capital.

The international financial environment is changing. The changing financial environment, according to Lessard (1988), represents in four aspects: increased international linkage of financial markets, increased financial intervention in domestic economies, exchange and interest rate instability, and resulting threats and opportunities (p.4). The change has considerable influences on international leasing. On the one hand, the current trend toward financial deregulation in developed countries has created a favourable financial environment for developing international leasing. On the other hand, many less developed countries (LDCs) have taken steps toward financial liberalisation during the past decades so that competition among financial institutions has been promoted by opening the domestic markets to foreigners and by authorising charters for new banks, leasing companies and non-bank financial intermediaries. The deregulation and the liberalisation have provided great potential for promoting the international leasing industry. However, the debt crisis of some LDCs, in particular in Latin America, Eastern Europe,

Africa and more recently South East Asia has currently caused serious financial problems obstructing the growth of international leasing. In order to control foreign debts, some countries (e.g., China, Brazil, Indonesia) have issued restrictive regulations on foreign leasing, in particular on financial leasing.[1]

It should mention that international organisations like the World Bank, the Asian Development Bank (ADB) have played an important role in developing international leasing since 1970s. Leasing has become well recognised by the World Bank, ADB and other multilateral development agencies as a useful and practical tool for accelerating development of capital markets in emerging and transitional economies. It has also been regarded as a critically important financial tool in the small and medium sized enterprise (SME) sectors of these economies. An SME that cannot qualify for a bank loan, may be able to obtain a lease, because "ownership of the asset gives the lessor strong security. ...leasing offers the advantage of ... simpler repossession procedures, because ownership of the asset is already in the lessor." (IFC 1996, p. 3.)

The International Finance Corp. (IFC), an agency of the World Bank has played an important part in introducing leasing to the LDCs since its first investment in a leasing company in 1977. The IFC has been involved in establishing and financing leasing companies in 39 countries, and from 1977 to June 1997 invested US$719.6 million in the development of leasing in LDCs (World-Leasing-Yearbook 1998). In several of those countries, such as Jordan, Peru, Sri Lanka and Thailand, the IFC participated in the formation of the first leasing ventures.[2] The ADB has supported the development of the leasing industry in Asia over the past 10 years and views lease finance as an important financing technique in the region's fledgling capital markets.

The new competitive and changing financial environment has placed important demands for the financial role of international leasing. In order to meet the demands, leasing companies have to:

---

[1] For example, "the Administrative Measures on Registering Foreign Loans" by China's State Administration of Exchange Control on November 10, 1989 requires the Chinese lessees to register the volume of financial leasing offered by foreign lessors in the administrative offices. According to the Measures, foreign financial leasing is directly treated as foreign loans which must be authorised and permitted by the certain levels of the economic committees.

[2] For example, one of the biggest leasing operations in Thailand is Thai Orient Leasing Co. which is a first joint venture leasing company established in 1978 by the IFC with other corporations.

1) provide the appropriate touchstone for evaluating both current leasing operations and strategic alternatives;
2) assess the possibility of foreign leasing investment and marketing;
3) raise the funds required for leasing assets and, in doing so, try to minimise the cost of capital;
4) minimise taxes and take advantage of different legal and taxation systems;
5) offer best services to customers; and
6) manage the risks inherent in leasing transactions.

Presently, a challenge facing lessors is to raise funds to finance the purchase of the assets as cheap as possible. One way for an independent lessor to do so is to go to financial markets. A great number of successful examples have been set, although the access to financial markets, to a large extent, depends on the regulations concerned. According to the leasing association reports, leasing companies in South Korea, for example, have tapped the local bond market with remarkable success and have also raised funds overseas. Leasing companies in Chile have been authorised to issue bonds, and to channel medium-term domestic savings. Leasing companies in India have been allowed to mobilise term deposits from the public and have raised substantial equity and debenture funds on the securities markets. However, taking deposits and issuing securities may still be prohibited in other countries.

In terms of risk management, it is crucial to a lessor to offset particular risks inherent in the firm's undertakings and/or shift them to lessees or others. Global competition increases a lessor's exposure to exchange rate volatility, but the lessor can, to a large extent, lay off this risk through hedging transactions such as currency futures, swaps, options, or foreign currency borrowing. Some aspects of exchange risks can be shifted to suppliers (manufacturers) or customers (lessees) through the choice of invoicing currencies, or the arrangement of multi-currency packages. To hedge exchange risks certainly is one of the tasks in planning international leasing strategies and making decisions.

In order to fulfil those tasks, it is essential to apply modern financial theories. Modern financial theories may provide possibilities to solve particular problems involved in international leasing. For example, an important insight of modern financial theory is market efficiency.[3] However, market efficiency *per se* is not testable (Fama 1991, p.1575). A capital

---

[3] For a detailed discussion of efficient capital markets, see Fama (1970) and Fama (1991).

market is said to be efficient when prices in the market fully reflect available information. If this condition is satisfied, market participants cannot earn abnormal profits on using available information. This classic definition, developed formally by Fama (1970), can be used to solve some theoretical issues of leasing. Is leasing an asset cheaper than buying it? According to the market efficiency theory, it is not correct to say so. Does lease capitalisation by a lessee affect its share price? It does not according to the theory. Also, according to finance theory, the allocation of risk among a supplier, a lessor and a lessee in a perfect market does not affect the value of a leasing company. The reason is that sophisticated investors, simply by holding diversified portfolios, can manage most risks just as efficiently as the company itself. In reality, however, the market is neither efficient nor perfect.[4] Therefore, many firms devote a great deal of effort to risk allocation in the form of hedging and risk sharing. For a more detailed discussion, see Barnea, *et al.* (1985), Shapiro and Titman (1985), Smith and Stulz (1985), Dolde (1993), Santomero (1995), Santomero and Babbel (1997), Oldfield and Santomero (1997). Moreover, according to Shapiro (1978), corporate international diversification as a factor may be relevant in establishing the capital structure of a Multinational Corporation (MNC). With subsidiaries in different countries, a MNC is able to diversify cash flows internationally. Such a diversification reduces overall bankruptcy risk that, in turn, enables the MNC to be more highly leveraged than a domestic firm. This argument may help an international leasing company to select its capital structure.

The foreign exchange market and relationships

Financial transactions and foreign exchange

International financial transactions, that have effects on the performance and behaviour of national economies, as well as on the decisions and welfare of firms and individuals, take place in the foreign exchange market. The foreign exchange market is the central organism that connects the monetary system of one country with those of other nations. By definition, the foreign exchange market is a market where the various national currencies can be exchanged for one another. The purpose of this market is to permit transfers of

---

[4] Fama (1991) states that the extreme version of the market efficiency hypothesis is false, because of the existence of positive information and trading costs (p.1575).

purchasing power denominated in one currency to another (i.e., to trade one currency for another). The price of one currency in terms of another is called a foreign exchange rate. In the price quotation system, an exchange rate is the price of a foreign currency in terms of domestic currency. In the volume quotation system, an exchange rate is the price of a domestic currency in terms of foreign currency.

Transactions in the foreign exchange market are accomplished on a "spot", "forward", or "swap" basis. A spot transaction requires almost immediate delivery of a foreign currency. A forward transaction requires delivery of a foreign currency at some future date. A swap transaction is the simultaneous buy and sale of a foreign currency. In turn, the foreign exchange market is constituted by the spot and the forward market together. However, the foreign exchange market is not a physical place but, instead, is a network of banks, foreign exchange brokers, and dealers. Financial markets are dispersed through the leading financial centres of the world.

The spot exchange market

In the spot market, currencies are traded for immediate delivery. The spot exchange rate is applied to the exchange of two currencies on the spot, that is, for immediate delivery. Given n currencies, $n-1$ bilateral spot exchange rates of each one vis-à-vis all the other will be defined, thus $n(n-1)$ exchange rates in total. Obviously, the exchange rate of currency i for currency j and the exchange rate of currency j for currency i are, theoretically, the reciprocal of each other.

$$F_{ij}F_{ji} = 1 \qquad\qquad [5.1]$$

Where: F_{ij} is the exchange rate of currency i for currency j; F_{ji} is the exchange rate of currency j for currency i. Sometimes, a currency cannot directly change for another one, since there is not a direct exchange rate on the list of exchange rates. Thus, it may use indirect or cross (exchange) rates. The cross rate of currency i with respect to currency j indicates how many units of currency i can be exchanged indirectly (this is, through buying and selling a third currency, say, k) for one unit of currency j. More precisely, with one unit of currency i one can buy n units of currency k in a financial centre; by selling this amount of currency k for currency j in another centre at the exchange rate F_{kj}, one obtains $F_{ik}F_{kj}$. The following relation holds:

$$F_{ij} = F_{ik}F_{kj} \qquad\qquad [5.2]$$

Consequently, by combining Eq.[5.1] and Eq.[5.2] we obtain:

$$F_{ji}F_{ik}F_{kj} = 1; \text{ or } F_{ij}F_{jk}F_{ki} = 1 \qquad\qquad [5.3]$$

Financial centres do not normally charge a commission on their currency transactions but rather profit from the spread between the buying and selling rates. Therefore quotas are always given in pairs because a dealer usually does not know whether a prospective customer is in the market to buy or to sell a foreign currency. The first rate is the buy or bid price, and the second is the sell or offer rate.

The forward exchange market

In the forward market, contracts are made to buy or sell a currency for future delivery. The forward exchange rate is applied to the agreement for a future exchange of two currencies at an agreed date (e.g., in a half year). That is, two persons sign a contract which stipulates the exchange of two currencies at a prescribed future date but at a price (the forward exchange rate) which is fixed in advance (as is the amount) at the moment of the stipulation of the contract. Forward exchange rates are normally quoted for value dates of one, two, three, six months, and one year, but actual contracts can be arranged for other monthly periods, on occasion, for periods of more than one year.

Since there exists a difference between the spot exchange rate and the forward exchange rate, it needs to know the exact amount of the divergence between the two. The divergence is usually referred to the concepts of a forward premium and a forward discount. A forward premium means that the forward exchange rate is higher than the spot exchange rate, whereas a discount means the forward exchange rate is less than the spot exchange rate. The mathematical expressions are:

$$D_v = \{[(F^s_{ij} - Ff_{ij})/Ff_{ij}](12/n)\}100\% \qquad\qquad [5.4]$$

$$D_p = \{[(Ff_{ij} - F^s_{ij})/Ff_{ij}](12/n)\}100\% \qquad\qquad [5.5]$$

Where:

D_v = a forward premium/discount as a percent per annum, under the volume quotation system;

D_p = a forward premium/discount as a percent per annum, under the price quotation system;

F^s_{ij} = the spot exchange rate of currency i for currency j;

Ff_{ij} = the forward exchange rate of currency i for currency j;

n= the number of months in a contract.

If we take the cross exchange rates (F^s_{kj}, F^s_{ki}, F^s_{jk}, F^s_{ik}, Ff_{kj}, Ff_{ki}, Ff_{jk}, Ff_{ik}) into account, then D_v and D_p are:

$$D_v = \{[(F^s_{ik}F^s_{kj} - Ff_{ik}Ff_{kj})/Ff_{ik}Ff_{kj}](12/n)\}100\%$$

$$\text{or} = \{[(Ff_{jk}Ff_{ki} - F^s_{jk}F^s_{ki})/F^s_{jk}F^s_{ki}](12/n)\}100\% \qquad [5.6]$$

Similarly,

$$D_p = \{[(Ff_{ik}Ff_{kj} - F^s_{ik}F^s_{kj})/F^s_{ik}F^s_{kj}](12/n)\}100\%$$

$$\text{or} = \{[(F^s_{jk}F^s_{ki} - Ff_{jk}Ff_{ki})/Ff_{jk}Ff_{ki}](12/n)\}100\% \qquad [5.7]$$

The main function of the forward exchange market is to allow economic agents to cover themselves against the exchange risk caused by possible future variations in a spot exchange rate. If, the spot exchange rate was permanently and rigidly fixed, an agent (a lessee or a lessor) who has to make or receive future payments in a foreign currency does not incur any exchange risks, because the agent already knows how much he/she will pay or receive in terms of its own national currency. But when exchange rates are bound to change all the time, exchange risks arise. Let us take an international leasing transaction between a German lessor and an Australian lessee as an example. From the viewpoint of the lessee who has to make future lease payments (say in Deutsche mark) to the German lessor, the risk is that the exchange rate will have depreciated at the time of the payments. In this case the lessee will have to pay out a greater amount of Australian dollars to purchase the required amount of Deutsche marks. Likewise, from the viewpoint of the lessor who will receive future lease payments (say in Australian dollar), the risk is that the exchange rate will have appreciated at the time of payments. In this case the lessor will get a small amount of Deutsche marks from the sale of the given amount of Australian dollars. One strategy to cover against the foreign exchange risks for either the lessor or the lessee is through the forward exchange market. The lessee who has to make the lease payments in Deutsche mark at a known future date can purchase the necessary amount of Deutsche mark forward, since the forward exchange rate is fixed now, the future change of the spot exchange rate is irrelevant to the lessee. Similarly, the lessor who has to receive the lease payments in Australian dollar at a known future date can sell the given amount of Australian dollar forward. In order to take effective measures to handle the exchange risk, some fundamental relationships among the spot exchange rate, forward exchange rate, interest rate and inflation rate must be familiarised.

The fundamental relationships

International financial theories have already explained the relationships between the spot exchange rates, forward exchange rates, interest rates and inflation rates (see Figure 5.1).

The relationships are described as follows:

The interest rate parity theory (C in Figure 5.1). The currency of a country with a lower nominal interest rate should be at a premium in terms of the currency of a higher nominal interest rate country. Specifically, in an efficient market with no transaction costs, the interest differential should be (approximately) equal to the forward differential. That is:

$$(1 + I_i)/(1 + I_j) = Ff_{ij}/F^s_{ij}$$ [5.8]

Where: I_i and I_j are the nominal interest rates of country i and country j respectively.

The expectation theory of forward rates (D in Figure 5.1). The theory states that the forward premium or discount is equal to the expected change in the spot rates. That is, on the average the forward rate is equal to the future spot rate. The relationship is:

Figure 5.1 Relationships among spot exchange rates, forward rates, interest rates and inflation rates

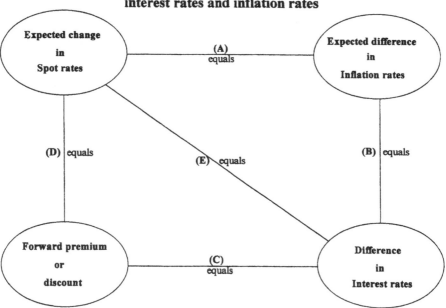

$$Ff_{ij}/F^s_{ij} = E(F^s_{ij})/F^s_{ij} \qquad\qquad [5.9]$$

Where: $E(F^s_{ij})$ is the expected change in the spot exchange rate of currency *i* for currency *j*. However, in reality, it would be unrealistic to expect a perfect correlation between the forward and future spot rates since the future spot rate will be affected by a variety of events, such as political instability, an oil crisis, a debt crisis.

The theory of purchasing power parity (A in Figure 5.1). This theory (or law) implies that the differential inflation rate is always identical to the change in the exchange rate. That is:

$$E(1 + H_i)/E(1 + H_j) = E(F^s_{ij})/F^s_{ij} \qquad\qquad [5.10]$$

Where: $E(1+H_i)/E(1+H_j)$ is the expected differences in inflation rates between country *i* and country *j*. A justification for this theory is that if a country experiences inflation rates higher than those of its main trading partners, its exports of goods and services will become less competitive with comparable products produced elsewhere. Imports from abroad will also become more price competitive with higher-priced domestic products. The resulting deficit in the national balance of trade will put downward pressure on its spot exchange rate. This downward pressure will disappear when the nation's currency has depreciated relative to its foreign competitor's currencies by the inflation differential. The general conclusion from many empirical tests of the theory is that the theory holds up well over the very long run but not as well for shorter time periods.

The Fisher effect and international Fisher effect (B and E in Figure 5.1). The Fisher effect, named after economist Irving Fisher, states that a nominal interest rate in each country is equal to the required real rate of return to the investor plus the expected rate of inflation. In other words, the difference in interest rates should be equals to the expected difference in inflation rates. That is:

$$(1 + I_i)/(1 + I_j) = E(1 + H_i)/E(1 + H_j) \qquad [5.11]$$

The international Fisher effect holds that the spot exchange rate should change in an equal but opposite direction to the difference in interest rates between two countries.

Measuring foreign exchange exposure and hedging strategies

Foreign exchange exposure is a measure of the potential for a firm's profitability, net cash flow, and market value to change because of the changes in exchange rates. An important task of financiers in international leasing is to measure foreign exchange exposure and to manage risks inherent in international transactions so as to maximise the net cash flow, and market value of a firm. There are three main types of foreign exchange exposures: translation (or accounting), transaction and economic exposure. Translation exposure measures potential accounting-based changes in a firm's consolidated financial statements that result from a change in exchange rates. Transaction exposure measures changes in the value of outstanding obligations incurred prior to an exchange rate change, but not expected to be settled until after the exchange rate changes. Transaction exposure typically arises when payments must be made or received in a foreign currency. The two most common methods to neutralise transaction exposures are a forward market hedge and a money market hedge. In recent years, an option market hedge has become another alternative for some types of exchange exposure. Economic exposure measures the change in expected cash flows due to unexpected changes in exchange rates.

Taking the Australian lessee and the German lessor in the previous case as an example, the main opportunities to hedge the foreign exchange risks are presented in Table 5.1. Moreover, a time deposit by a lessee may be an additional method to minimise the consequences of foreign exchange fluctuations. In some transactions, a lessee may be prepared to place on deposit, at the inception of the transaction with the lessor, an associated bank of the lessor or a third party, a sum in the denominated currency of the obligation that would then generate sufficient income so that the principal amount and interest would retire the rental obligation. An alternative to a time deposit may be the purchase and pledge of governmental securities with corresponding maturity. In either case, it would be a fairly special situation since it pre-supposes that the lessee is prepared to incur a substantial amount of initial expenditure.

However, the function of hedging exposure was questioned by Reiners (1983). According to the author, the attempts to solve the exchange exposure through long-dated forward exchange contracts will fail. The reason is the practical difficulties in closing a lease and currency hedge simultaneously. In fact, a lessee wants to know the cost of a lease in advance, but the foreign exchange relationship tends to change quickly and no lessee wants to commit to the currency hedge without being certain that the lease can be closed on the anticipated terms and conditions. Conversely, no lessee is willing to sign a lease without knowing whether an acceptable currency hedge can be arranged. The author takes the dollar/pound exchange as an example. "Forward exchange contracts for dollar/pound exposures are not readily available for terms in excess of five years, certainly not for large amounts and as many as 60 quarterly rental payments with different maturities. Therefore, the idea of hedging the dollar/pound exposure in the forward exchange markets was discarded as impractical. Other solutions, such as purchase by the lessee of a portfolio of the UK government securities (gilts) matching each future rental obligation under the lease, were also not practical, both because gilts in the right amounts and for the right maturities are not always available and, more important, because of the doubling-up effect such a solution would have on the lessee's balance sheet"(p.14).

Table 5.1 The opportunities to hedge foreign exchange risks

The Australian lessee	*The German lessor*
1. To buy the foreign currency forward. In this case, the lessee will not have to spend a single cent now, because the settlement of the forward contract will be made at the prescribed future date.	1. To sell the foreign currency forward. In this case, the lessor will not receive a cent now, because the settlement of the forward contract will be made at the prescribed future date.
2. To pay immediately. That is to purchase the foreign currency spot and to settle the debt in advance.	2. To allow a discount to the lessee so as to obtain an advance payment and immediately sell the foreign currency spot.
3. To buy the foreign currency spot immediately, invest it in Germany from now till the maturity of the lease payments and make the payments at the maturity.	3. To discount the credit with a bank and immediately sell the foreign exchange spot.
4. To purchase a call option on European Options Exchange having the same expiration date as the lease.	4. To purchase a put option on European Options Exchange having the same expiration date as the lease.

Generally speaking, the products of international financial markets are often difficult to be used in international leasing currency risk hedging. This is because: 1) international leasing, especially financial leasing is usually a long term transaction; 2) there are possibilities of the early termination of a lease, and the termination may result in potential breakage costs; 3) the costs of some hedging methods are too high to practice economically. However, hedging strategies can properly be used in covering against exchange exposure in international leasing transactions, provided that international financial markets are more deregulated and more flexible, and a favourable environment has been established.

When several currencies are involved, evaluating and managing foreign exchange risks becomes more difficult. A portfolio perspective may aid in this process. It is a well-known proposition of portfolio theory that, as long as returns on individual components of a portfolio are not perfectly positively corrected, a change in value should be relatively smaller for the overall portfolio than for a weighted average of the individual components. Because currency movements are less than perfectly correlated, the total variability of risk of a currency exposure portfolio should be less than the sum of the individual variability of each currency considered in isolation. This can probably explain why some international lessors prefer to use a multi-currency package rather than a single foreign currency to quote the lease payments. However, to evaluate these alternatives one must examine their costs and benefits. One point that should be mentioned is that the introduction of foreign exchange contracts into international leasing may give rise to special tax considerations, since their tax treatment may not be what is expected. Such considerations may have an important influence on planning strategies and making decisions of international leasing to both the lessor and the lessee.

Conclusion

The internationalisation of capital markets is reflected in the large flows of capital cross border and in the deregulation of financial systems in the developed countries and liberalisation of the financial services in emerging economies. The foreign exchange market has become a reflection of the activity in international capital markets. International leasing is influenced by the change of global financial environments. The increasing globalisation of leasing activities is reflected in the changes of strategies of leasing companies in their operation and managing financial and foreign exchange risk. This chapter examines the relationship between international finance and international leasing with a special focus on the international finance environment, the foreign exchange market and hedge strategies.

Reference

Barnea, A., R.A. Haugen and L.W. Senbet. 1985. Management of corporate risk. *Advances in Financial Planning and Forecasting, No. 1.* JAI Press.

Dolde, W. 1993. Use of foreign exchange and interest rate risk management in large firms. Working Paper No.93-042. Department of Finance, University of Connecticut.

Fama, E.F. 1970. Efficient capital markets: a review of theory and empirical work. *Journal of Finance* 25: 383-417.

Fama, E.F. 1991. Efficient capital market: II. *Journal of Finance* December: 1575-1617.

IFC. 1996. *Leasing in Emerging Markets.* New York: The International Finance Corp.

Lessard, D.R. 1988. Finance and global competition: exploiting financial scope and coping with volatile exchange rates. In *New Developments in International Finance*, ed. J.M. Stern and D.H. Chew. New York: Basil Blackwell Inc., pp.3-26.

Oldfield, G.S. and A.M. Santomero. 1997. Risk management in financial institutions. *Sloan Management Review* Fall: 33-46.

Reiners, G. 1983. Leasing in an international context. In *International Finance Handbook*, ed. A.M. George and I.H. Giddy. New York: John Wiley & Sons.

Santomero, A.M. 1995. Financial risk management: the whys and hows. *Journal of Financial Markets, Institutions and Investment* 4, no. 5: 1-14.

Santomero, A.M. and D.F. Babbel. 1997. Financial risk management by insurers: an analysis of the process. *The Journal of Risk and Insurance* 64, no. 2: 231-270.

Shapiro, A. and S. Titman. 1985. An integrated approach to corporate risk management. *Midland Corporate Finance Journal* 3, no. 2: 41-56.

Shapiro, A.C. 1978. Financial structure and the cost of capital in the multinational corporate. *Journal of Financial and Quantitative Analysis* June: 211-66.

Smith, C.W. and R.M. Stulz. 1985. The determinants of firms' hedging policies. *Journal of Financial and Quantitative Analysis* December: 391-405.

World-Leasing-Yearbook. 1998. London: A Euromoney Publication.

6 International leasing investment

International leasing investment

Of the strategies and decisions financial managers must make, none is likely to have more impact than the decision to invest capital overseas, since this decision involves large and extended commitments of money and management time. The evaluation of foreign investment opportunities is subject to a complicated set of economic, political, legal and strategic considerations. Country risk, for example, being defined as the elements of risk inherent in doing business in the economical, social and political environment of another country, is a major factor influencing foreign investment decisions. It is no doubt that international investment is one important and dynamic international business activity today.

Foreign investment broadly falls into three categories: portfolio investment, direct investment and leasing investment.[1] Investment in financial assets (e.g., stocks, bonds and commercial papers) is usually called portfolio investment. International portfolio investment is the purchase of foreign securities (stocks, bonds, commercial papers etc.) in order to earn a return in the form of interests, dividends, or capital gains. Under portfolio investment, the investors do not actively participate in managing the firm they that have invested. The period of portfolio investment can be long (e.g., many decades) or short (e.g., only a few days, weeks or months), as such securities are bought and sold in

---

[1] However, leasing investment has not been recognised in the literature. In this section and the section that follows, we will emphasise international leasing investment.

response to the different investors' needs and assessments of future changes in the security prices.

Direct investment involves the acquisition by domestic companies of foreign-based operating facilities (e.g., factories, warehouses, plants, hotels, financial companies). The investors buy specific tangible assets so that they produce either goods or services outside their home countries. Direct investment differs from portfolio investment in that the former is an equity holding substantial enough to bring with it a degree of control in the company. For instance, the outright purchase of more than 50% of a foreign company is a direct investment. A direct investment usually involves a long-term life period and considerable funds. The eclectic paradigm (e.g., Dunning 1988) implicitly states that foreign direct investment (FDI) occurs when its expected net present value is both positive and greater than those of alternative modes of investments. Options theory (e.g., Myers 1977; Brennan and Schwartz 1985; Bowman and Hurry 1993; Kogut and Kulatilaka 1994) argues that an investment today buys options to invest later, and the analysis of such an investment must account for the value of these options. Therefore, projects that have negative NPVs on a stand-alone basis may have positive NPVs once the value of options purchased are included. Rivoli and Salorio (1996) believe that ownership advantages increase the likelihood of FDI is an oversimplification. They argue that ownership advantages may be necessary for profitable FDI, but they are not sufficient for investment to occur even in the presence of both internalisation and location advantages (p.347).

I would like to use the term "foreign leasing investment (FLI)" to refer to a situation that an investor leases the assets to a foreign firm, institution, or governmental organisation in order to earn a return in the form of net rentals or other forms of capital gains. A typical FLI is as follows: the lessor (investor) provides the whole funds of purchasing assets and leases the assets to a foreign company, and the lessor is at risk for the entire cost of the assets and for the other possible losses. Figure 6.1 that shows a comparison between portfolio, direct, and leasing investment makes it clear that leasing investment places between portfolio investment and direct investments, as far as investment term and management involvement are concerned. This is because under leasing investment, the investors do not fully participate in the management of a firm invested, but have some influences on management of the firm, in particular on management of the assets leased, since they are the legal owners of the assets.

Although leasing investment has not been recognised in the literature, leasing has played a certain role in international investment. Investment in equipment through the mechanism of leasing was US$428.08 billion in 1996. The advantages of leasing may be one important reason to use leasing investment rather than other investments. Some academicians have tried to find out the relationships between leasing and investment. For instance, Mayes and Nicholas (1988) conclude that leasing has not only increased the level of investment rather than merely displacing other forms of finance, but has also acted as a counter-cyclical influence in the economy during a period of recession (p.87). According to Clark (1985), "every dollar used by leasing companies in their businesses is spent on productive plant and equipment. By channelling all their funds directly into new equipment, leasing companies avoid the leakage problem, faced by banks and other types of financial institution, of funds being diverted by borrowers to non-priority uses" (p.128).

Figure 6.1 Leasing investment position

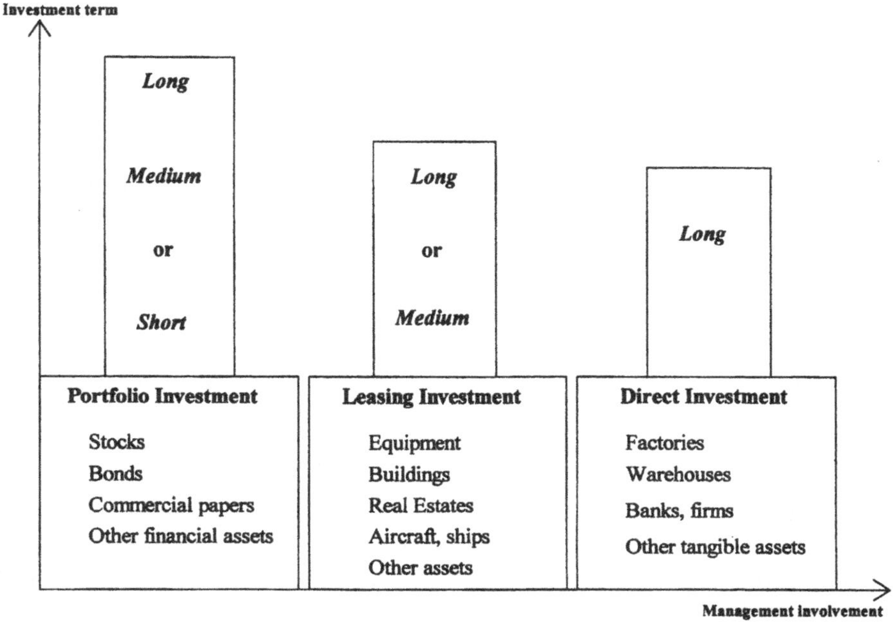

However, a FLI decision results from a complex process that differs in many aspects from that governing a domestic leasing investment decision. Besides the consideration of diversifying the risks, FLIs are usually motivated by a wider and more complicated set of strategic, behavioural, economic, managerial, and legal considerations. In most cases, the balance between the expected return and risk is very difficult to determine. The investigation process is often longer, more costly, and yields less information on which to evaluate opportunities.

The motives for portfolio investment are easily seen in terms of the risk and return concepts. In a general sense, such a concern with the firm's return subject to risk considerations may be thought to motivate all investment decisions, including direct investment and leasing investment. However, most of the literature have explored more specific motives for desiring domestic ownership of foreign production facilities. As reviewed by Giorgio (1973), theories of direct foreign investment typically explain the incentive for such investment in terms of some imperfections in free market conditions. For example, the product and factor market imperfections open the door to direct foreign investment. In addition, surveys and case studies of international firms indicate that the motivations of direct foreign investment are based on strategic considerations of five major types: 1) market seekers, 2) raw material seekers, 3) production sufficiency seekers, 4) knowledge seekers, and 5) political safety seekers.

From a financial point of view, international diversification of risks may be one of the main motivations for foreign portfolio, direct and leasing investment. A diversification can take place either through involvement in different product lines within a single country or through production of the same product line in different countries. Also a diversification can take place through investment in different categories: portfolio investment, direct investment and leasing investment.

To sum up, the greater increase in foreign investment (either portfolio or direct investment) provides a great potential for international leasing. The reason is very obvious. Large-scale investment in the infrastructure, manufacturing, airline and extraction industries creates an enormous demand for financial resources. A good part of these resources is, in turn, used to lease machinery, equipment, and industrial plants from abroad. But, the greater increase in either portfolio investment or direct investment may have a negative effect on international leasing. That is because more funds are available to the purchase of capital assets, less to the leasing of them. As international economic conditions improve, and taxation policies favouring investments are introduced, leasing is expected to be increasingly realised as a means of investments in equipment and facilities, and will therefore gain its greater expansion in the future.

Political risks of foreign leasing investment (FLI)

Understanding, predicting, and minimising exposure to international risks are an important part of international leasing analysis. When investment through leasing in foreign countries, the investor (lessor) may face: 1) international financial risks; 2) political risks (e.g., the loss of ownership of a leased asset); or 3) international regulatory risks associated with changes in tax laws, customs rules, commercial codes, or accounting standards. Therefore, risk analysis becomes an integral part of strategic planning and decision making for FLIs. Werner, *et al.* (1996) review different measures of risk.

This section is only concerned with political risks. Other studies such as Ashraful (1985), Mascarenhas and Sand (1985), Cosset and Roy (1991), Miller (1992), Dolde (1993), Werner, *et al.* (1996), Chow, *et al.* (1997) have already explored other risks involved in overseas investments. Political risks may be stated in a simple way as business risks brought about by political sources or environments (Friedmann and Kim 1988, p.64). But, developing a system to measure and analyse political risks reliably and validly becomes a difficult task, because of the variety and lack of consensus in terms of definitions, categorisations of political risk events, and conceptual approaches, as well as the shortage of information.

The relevance of political risks to international leasing can be perceived in two different ways: first, from a conceptual and general perspective, one should note that the fundamentals of international leasing are not different from those of domestic leasing. Though, the fundamentals of domestic and international leasing are the same, international leasing creates specific sets of new opportunities and problems derived from the fact that international leasing is carried out in a number of new environments. Each environment has a distinct set of realities. Political risks are a direct outcome of the political realities faced by either a lessor or a lessee. For example, the invasion of Kuwait in August 1990 brought real political risks to foreign lessors involved in both Kuwait and Iraq. A second way is to focus more precisely on some particular international leasing issues and to illustrate a variety of ways in which political risks modify international leasing strategies and decisions. For example, the lessor's ownership right of a leased asset involved in international leasing may be altered by the change of laws concerned. In such a case, the lessor may not be able to enforce his/her claims against the foreign lessee, who may be fully or partly discharged from the contractual obligations.

Political risks have direct impacts on the evaluation of leasing investment. All else being equal, investors prefer to invest in a country with stable currency, healthy economy, minimal chance of expropriation, and less possibility of lease rentals repatriation restrictions. However, no country is "risk free", and no country is always regarded as less risky. Therefore, investors must devote resources to study the political environment of a potential country to invest, and to evaluate the consequences of various political risks of potential investments. In general, an investor can use either of the two methods below to incorporate the foreign political risks in evaluating the possibilities of foreign investment:

1. *Raising the required rate of return on the investment.* Higher political risk requires the higher required rate of return; or alternatively, adjusting cash flows. Higher political risk results in more cash outflows (e.g., a premium for overseas political risk insurance);

2. *Shortening the period of payback.* Higher political risk requires the period of payback to be shorter.

Management of political risk refers to steps taken by firms to anticipate political events, to protect against loss (or to attempt to gain) from such events, or lastly to attempt to recover as much compensation after an adverse political event as possible. There are several ways to reduce political risks. One is to make a pre-arrangement between the host government and an ILC concerning the treatment of leasing transactions. Such an agreement is known as a concession agreement. This approach is valid only as long as both parties act in good faith. The second alternative is to create a joint venture funding the leased assets or a partnership. Such a joint venture or partnership may reduce the likelihood of foreign political interference. The third approach is to try to raise capital of a foreign leasing investment from the host and other governments, international development agencies, overseas banks, and from customers. This approach can, to a larger extent, reduce the likelihood of expropriation, because any expropriation threat is likely to upset relations with customers, banks, and governments worldwide. The fourth way to manage political risks is to buy insurance on political risks. To insure leased assets and other operations is the easiest way to manage political risk. The coverage includes convertibility, war, civil disturbance, expropriation and breach of contract etc. Recently, many countries offer political risk insurance to investors. However, the premiums of such insurance may be very high, in particular in wartime. For example, during the Gulf crisis, insurance premiums on aircraft, ships were about several times higher than those before August 2, 1990. Table 6.1 presents the offering of political insurance in 1997 by private sectors, bilateral risk insurers, the Multilateral Investment Guarantee Agency (MIGA) and World Bank.

World financial markets have witnessed profound changes over the last few decades. This has included the strong growth of private capital flows to developing countries. Net long-term private flows rose from US4.38 billion in 1980 (46 per cent of total flows) to an estimated US$ 256 billion in 1997 (85 per cent of total flows). The composition of these private flows has seen a marked change over the last two decades. While earlier flows were composed largely of commercial bank debt flowing to the public sector, recent years have witnessed a sharp increase in the level of private sector portfolio flows and direct investment, both of which had contributed little during the 1980s (Stern and Lankes 1998). There is also similar pattern from international leasing investment.

Table 6.1 Offering of political risk insurance in 1997

Supplier	Private market	Bi - Insurers	MIGA	World Bank
Coverage Maturity Amount per project	W, E, C, B up to 10 years > US$ 1 bn.	W, E, C, B about 15 years US$ 250 mn.	W, E, C about 15 years <US$ 50 mn.	W, E, C, B 15-20 years n.a.
Notes: W = war risk; E = expropriation; C = currency convertibility; B = breach of contract. Source: Klein (1998).				

The level and quality of FLIs depends crucially on perceptions of risks and returns. These, in turn, depend not only on basic endowments and opportunities, but also on the ability to respond to opportunities in an effective, market-oriented fashion, or more generally, the 'investment climate' in potential lessee countries. The investment climate includes macroeconomic stability, structural reform and the institutional infrastructure which underpins the market economy (financial institutions, reliable business practices, legal and regulatory framework, tax and accounting system etc.). It also includes political stability and consistent, transparent, responsible and 'market friendly' behavior from the local authorities. Equally important is the development of human capital and of physical infrastructure, both of which are vital ingredients for the success of investments. Clearly, assessment of the climate is vital to international leasing investment, and the assessment has to be based on the individual country case.

Conclusion

Growing liberalisation, integration and competition in world economies since the post-war period have been responsible for the increasing engagement of firms in overseas leasing investment activities. In fact, leasing has been one of the fastest growing economic activities, consistently exceeding the rate of growth in world economic output over the past two decades. Consequently, the contribution of leasing to total world investment activity has increased considerably in recent times, and currently accounts for over 25% of capital investment in the developed world. Clearly, leasing plays a vital role in global investment and its importance is expected to grow further as markets become more globalised.

Reference

Ashraful, H. M. 1985. *Developing a Model for Evaluating Country Risk in International Lending Using Discriminant Analysis.* PhD Dissertation, Mississippi State University.

Bowman, E.H. and D. Hurry. 1993. Strategy through the options lens: An integrated view of resource investments and the incremental choice process. *Academy of Management Review* 18, no. 4: 760-82.

Brennan, M.J. and E.S. Schwartz. 1985. Evaluating natural resource investments. *Journal of Business* 58, no. 2: 135-57.

Chow, E.H., W.Y. Lee and M.E. Solt. 1997. The economic exposure of U.S. multinational firms. *The Journal of Financial Research* 20, no. 2: 191-210.

Clark, T.M. 1985. *Leasing Finance.* London: Euromoney Publications.

Cosset, J.C. and J. Roy. 1991. The determinants of country risk ratings. *Journal of International Business Studies*: 135-142.

Dolde, W. 1993. Use of foreign exchange and interest rate risk management in large firms. *Working Paper*, No.93-042 Department of Finance, University of Connecticut.

Dunning, J.H. 1988. The eclectic paradigm of international production: a restatement and some possible extensions. *Journal of International Business Studies* 19, no. 1: 1-31.

Friedmann, R. and J. Kim. 1988. Political risk and international marketing. *Columbia Journal of World Business* Winter: 63-74.

Giorgio, R. 1973. Theories of the determinants of direct foreign investment. *IMF Staff Papers* July: 471-98.

Klein, M. 1998. One hundred years after Bretton Woods: A future history of the World Bank Group. *The EIB Papers* 3, no. 2: 31-58.

Kogut, B. and N. Kulatilaka. 1994. Options thinking and platform investment: Investing in opportunity. *California Management Review* 36, no. 2: 52-71.

Mascarenhas, B. and O.C. Sand. 1985. Country risk assessment systems in banks: patterns and performance. *Journal of International Business Studies*: 19-35.

Mayes, D.C. and C.S. Nicholas. 1988. *The Economic Impact of Leasing.* London: Macmillan Press.

Miller, K.D. 1992. A framework for integrated risk management in international business. *Journal of International Business Studies*: 311-331.

Myers, S. 1977. Determinants of corporate borrowing. *Journal of Financial Economics* 5, no. 2: 147-75.

Rivoli, P. and E. Salorio. 1996. Foreign direct investment and investment under uncertainty. *Journal of International Business Studies* 27, no. 2: 335-57.

Stern, N.H. and H.P. Lankes. 1998. Making the most of markets: The role of IFIs. *EIB Papers* 3, no. 2: 103-14.

Werner, S., L.E. Brouthers and K.D. Brouthers. 1996. International risk and perceived environmental uncertainty: the dimensionality and internal consistency of Miller's measure. *Journal of International Business Studies* 27, no. 3: 571-87.

7   Leasing as a device of international marketing

Leasing as a device of international marketing

It is very interesting to recall the statement made by McNeill (1944) a half century ago: "There is danger...that adequate attention may not be given to one marketing device, not customarily considered, which is particularly useful in the distribution of many kinds of equipment: the lease or rental agreement" (p.415). Since then, leasing as an important device of marketing has been recognised in the literature (among others, Anderson and Lazer 1978; Anderson and Bird 1980; Chisnall 1985; Wagner and Hall 1991; and Desai and Purohit 1998).

Why is leasing an important device of marketing? Obviously, leasing has the characteristic of combining financing and marketing. Leasing not only distributes assets to customers, but also provides customers financing services. The advantage of this characteristic is to increase the additional purchasing capacity of customers, especially the customers who currently face a financing constraint. Leasing can help customers obtain more favourable financing sources, conserve customers' working capital, and give the customers more flexibility. Also, leasing can help customers protect themselves against loss from obsolescence of assets, especially of high-tech assets. This is why many users of high-tech assets (e.g., computers, satellites) frequently prefer to lease rather than to buy them. Moreover, leasing can open up new opportunities for marketing assets, in particular aircraft, ships, satellites and big office equipment. For example, the outright purchase of £1 million of office equipment could be prohibitive for a small, financially constrained business. However, if this same equipment could be leased by that business for around £200,000 per year over a five-year period, that business might be a viable marketing prospect. Also leasing may allow a company, in particular a manufacturing lessor firm to penetrate markets that might otherwise not exist for the company's products. In addition, leasing may be used as a determinant of product pricing strategies. Under which, more pricing competition can be gained since leasing assets may take advantage of taxation, and acquire some additional subsidies. Recently, about 28-30 per cent of all capital goods are leased in the US, with eight out of ten companies involved in leasing.

Leasing as an international marketing strategy is likely to represent an increasing proportion of the income from export activities to industrial firms (Chisnall 1985, p.265). The balance of payments problems have forced some countries to prohibit the purchase and import of capital assets into their markets; exception may be given to the leasing of the assets. Also, the future services offered by the lessor of leased equipment (in particular high-tech equipment) may be a major benefit to the firms in LDCs, because of the shortage of trained personnel and of spare parts. The fact that leasing has frequently been able to fill a gap between financing and marketing, and enabled lessees to rely less on overdraft and other short-term funds for financing the long-term use of equipment, may also be a major benefit to the firms in LDCs to use leasing rather than other methods.

As discussed previously, leasing has played an important part in international trade activities both of import and export. For example, one of the major international trade activities of the former Soviet Union is equipment leasing. The Russians view leasing not only as a potential source of hard currency, but also as a way of attracting customers who would be reluctant to buy an unfamiliar product (Meyer 1977).

For any marketing manager who wants to market capital assets abroad, leasing can be an alternative of selling those assets to potential foreign customers. In general, there are four possible ways for capital assets to be leased to foreign customers:

1. A company itself can carry out a cross-border lease with foreign customers. In this case, the company must carry the financing and work out the lease arrangements itself;

2. A company (in particular a large manufacturer) can form credit subsidiaries (either in home country or overseas) to provide leasing for their foreign customers;[1]
3. A company can ask for financial institutions which have subsidiaries doing leasing business to lease capital assets to foreign customers;
4. A company can lease its products through a specialised international leasing company to their foreign customers.

Nevertheless, to choose a way for marketing capital assets abroad, the marketing managers must compare the costs/profits of leasing with the costs/profits of sales outright. From a customer point of view, the cost is a key factor influencing the choice between leasing and buy alternatives.

International leasing market segments and marketing research

International leasing market segments

Market analysis and market understanding can best be achieved by segmenting the entire market into parts and groups. Market segmentation can encourage an ILC to concentrate on the most important market segments, and to design marketing strategies, methods and products that can penetrate those market segments. Segmentation simplifies the establishment of marketing objectives. According to the leasing industry, the leasing market can be divided into several segments (see Figure 7.1). In general, the leasing market provides a range of leasing facilities to small, medium and large industrial and commercial equipment users. Over the past decade, leasing companies have gradually enlarged their markets, and any item of equipment with a commercial purpose can now be leased. Traditionally, aircraft, transportation and office equipment have been the most favoured assets for international leasing. In many markets, commercial vehicles, agricultural equipment, motor cars and ships have recently shared the leasing limelight with aircraft, office and transportation equipment. In Europe, commercial vehicle leasing is the mainstay of the business, whereas office and computer equipment leasing is the predominate of the business in Asia. Currently, medical equipment and

---

[1] Many international manufacturers own such subsidiaries, for example, the General Motors.

satellite leasing is worldwide gaining an increasing popularity in leasing business.

Figure 7.1 The leasing market segments

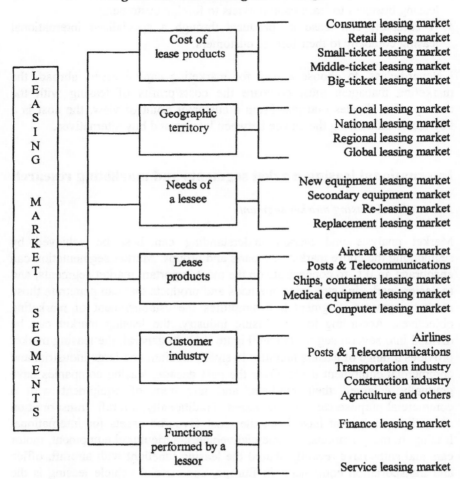

To design and to enter a foreign leasing market, it is crucial for an ILC to plan a market strategy. In doing so, it should be aware that there are two dangers when entering a foreign leasing market. One danger is to try to offer a wide variety of lease products to all market segments. This is because if doing so, it is very difficult to get all resources to serve all the market segments and to offer best service to customers. In fact, leasing companies are no longer able to cover all markets, and to provide facilities for all types of equipment. Currently, the number of specialist leasing companies is substantially increasing in many parts of the world. Another danger is to try to design a very narrow market segment, called "super-specialised market segment". This is because the market is too narrow to attract many customers, and too narrow to be flexible. Therefore it is wise to adopt a market strategy that is somewhere between these two extremes.

International leasing marketing research

The role of leasing marketing research is equally important in both domestic and international leasing. Leasing marketing research is the systematic gathering, recording, and analysing of data about leasing marketing problems. The purpose of marketing research is to facilitate decision making. The leasing marketing research process is a systematic procedure linking together the marketing researcher, the marketing decision maker, and the source of relevant information concerning a lease project. Figure 7.2 shows the leasing marketing research process. The four major components: lease problem definition, project strategy, information analysis, and decision making, are each composed of several stages. Generally speaking, international leasing marketing research is not different from the general leasing marketing research. The differences in international environments, however, make international leasing marketing research more difficult. Particularly, it is not easy to obtain reliable information for the research.

Three issues should be mentioned in collecting and analysing information related to international leasing. First, collecting information about foreign leasing markets sometimes appears to be terribly costly and time consuming. Second, lease information collected in one market may prove to be inadequate or even deceptive when applied to a new foreign leasing market. Third, leasing information collected from one source may widely differ from the other sources. Thus, it is necessary to further analyse leasing information.

Information about leasing marketing research can be categorised in two classes (see Figure 7.3). One is the general information about a potential lessee's country, including its political, legal, economic, accounting, taxation, technological and competitive situations. The other is the specific information about competitors, the potential lessee, the lease structure and pricing, and the market segments.

Figure 7.2 The leasing marketing research process

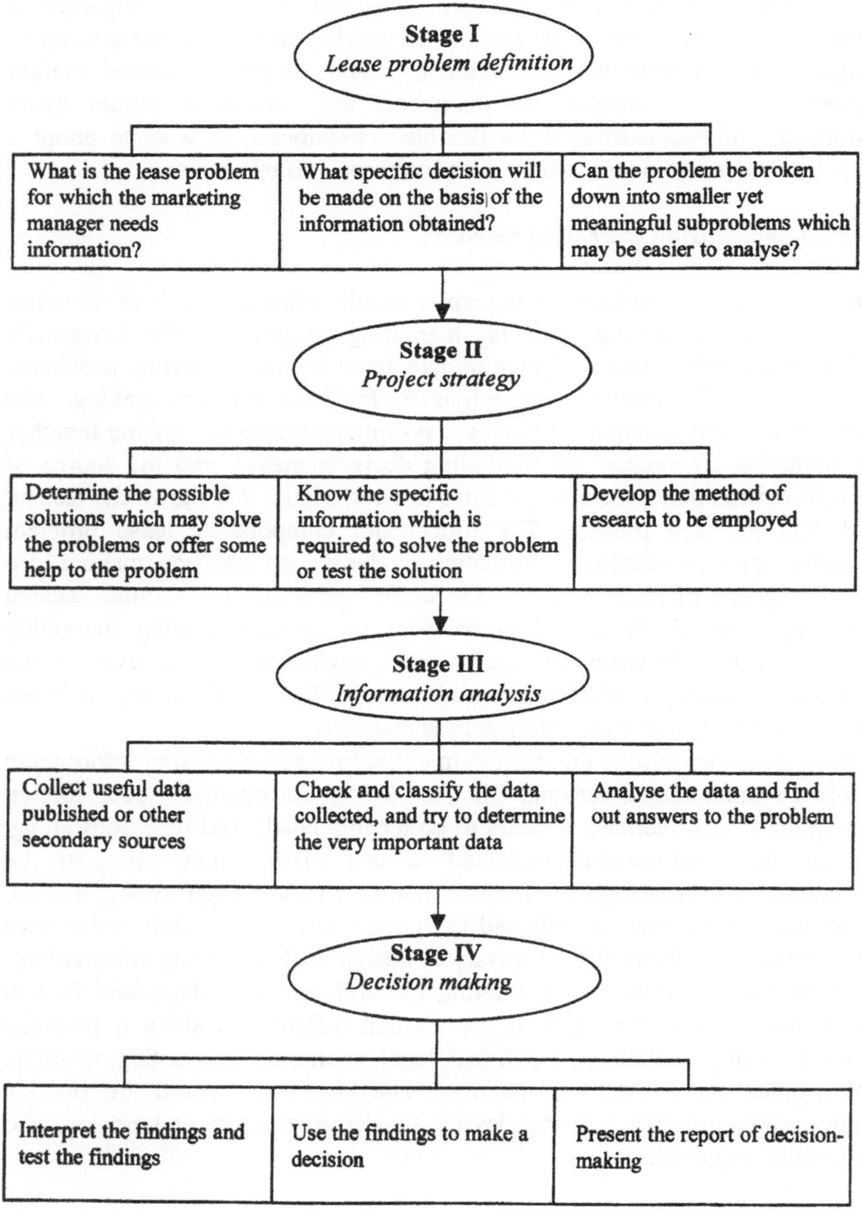

| Stage I | |
| *Lease problem definition* | |

| What is the lease problem for which the marketing manager needs information? | What specific decision will be made on the basis of the information obtained? | Can the problem be broken down into smaller yet meaningful subproblems which may be easier to analyse? |

Stage II
Project strategy

| Determine the possible solutions which may solve the problems or offer some help to the problem | Know the specific information which is required to solve the problem or test the solution | Develop the method of research to be employed |

Stage III
Information analysis

| Collect useful data published or other secondary sources | Check and classify the data collected, and try to determine the very important data | Analyse the data and find out answers to the problem |

Stage IV
Decision making

| Interpret the findings and test the findings | Use the findings to make a decision | Present the report of decision-making |

Nevertheless, any individual leasing marketing research should be based on the real circumstances involved in the market with utilising the full scope of managerial and marketing expertise ranging from legal to accounting, financial to taxation, engineering to product management. Each of these functional areas may contribute its ideas to the research.

Figure 7.3 Leasing marketing research information

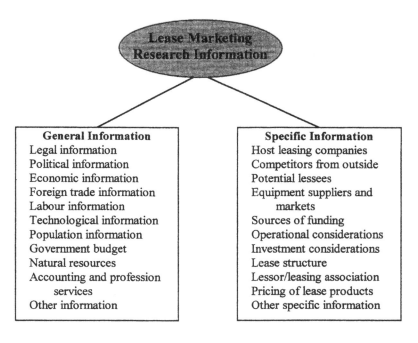

International lease pricing
========

Factors of international lease pricing

The pricing of lease products is critical to the success of an ILC. The setting of the prices of products leased overseas (or the determination of the lease payments) is complicated by factors such as possibly higher expense arising from transportation costs, duties, intermediary margins and risk. The lease payments must not only be sufficiently competitive and economically viable to attract new business, but also provide sufficient returns to the lessor's shareholders. Also, the rentals must compare favourably with rates of return available to the company or its parent company from other uses of funding and tax shelter resources. Risk has to be fully taken into account. One most important step in pricing is to measure the cost of funds. The key to a successful leasing company is the ability to obtain funds as cheap as possible.

There are many factors which have to be considered in pricing a lease product. Table 7.1 summarises some major factors concerned in pricing a lease product. Generally, in calculating rentals an ILC needs to take all the cash flows and foreign exchange rate changes into account, and to determine what mark-up on the cost of the funds is required to achieve the target profit margin. In a world of increasing competition, government regulations, and widely fluctuating exchange rates, international leasing marketers must spend increasing amounts of time to design pricing policy and plan pricing strategy. Of course, pricing lease products cannot be isolated from other decisions such as the financing decision and the tax decision. In principle, the pricing decision for a particular target leasing market should follow the overall objective of the firm. For an international manufacturing lessor, the price of leasing its products overseas should be directly compared with the price of selling them outright. It is important to determine the balance between the lease rental and the selling price. One approach is to set the lease rental and selling price so that they generate the same rate of return over the product's useful economic life. Alternatively, the rates may be set so as to encourage either leasing or selling, depending upon the desired outcomes and market conditions. High lease rental may encourage outright purchase of customers and low lease rental may encourage leasing. Many marketing strategies have derived from this relation. For instance, one strategy is to cut the price of assets but left the lease rates unchanged. Such a strategy would encourage customers to purchase the assets they currently lease.

According to Loewenstein and McClure (1986), the agency cost is an important factor that can influence lease pricing. The agency cost is the cost associated with maintenance and monitoring services, the search for secondary users, and the uncertainty about an asset's residual value. The agency cost advantage of a leasing contract over a sale contract results from the producer firm's comparative advantage in holding claim to the residual value of the asset. An asset-producing firm will find it advantageous to lease, rather than to sell, if: 1) it can easily monitor the condition of the asset following use; 2) it has better information than the user does about market conditions and technological change; 3) its product can be used in only predictable ways; 4) it has no established service reputation; 5) it can maintain the asset at a lower cost than the user can, or 6) it can re-establish the leasing market, and resell the asset at a lower cost than the user can.

Table 7.1 Major factors of pricing a lease product

1. The cost of capital;
2. The cost of the assets to be leased;
3. The expected residual value of leased assets;
4. The cost of transporting assets to the customer;
5. The cost of insuring assets and other insurance;
6. The cost of installation and disposition of the assets;
7. The servicing cost during the lease;
8. The special expense attributable to the transaction, such as advertising expense, expense of training staff for the lessee, and the agency cost;
9. The cost of duties and other fees for customs;
10. The home-country income tax liability;
11. The foreign-country income tax liability;
12. The home-country tax shelter and investment incentives;
13. The foreign-country tax shelter and other investment incentives;
14. The foreign exchange rates and the possibility of hedging against foreign exchange risks;
15. Asset risk;
16. The timing of the delivery of the leased assets;
17. The timing of actual receipt of cash flows attributable to tax benefits;
18. The impacts of the transaction on the firm's other business;
19. Political risk and other risk or loss reserve attributable to the transaction;
20. Other legal, accounting, tax considerations.

Steps of international lease pricing

From a lessor's point of view, lease pricing, in particular financial lease pricing, is essentially directed to computing interest rates implicitly involved in the lease so as to help a comparison with other lease proposals and lending opportunities. The factors listed in Table 7.1 should be fully considered and measured if possible. The majority of leases provide for level rental payments over the lease term. Normally, the periodic payments are calculated in the same way as annuity or mortgage repayments. The model designed to calculate lease rentals is based on the following steps:[2]

---

[2] In this model I do not specify discount rates for computing present values. It is only assumed that the interest rate is used to discount all cash flow streams as the intention

1. To determine the variables:
    1) To determine the present value expressed in the home currency of leased asset costs (A_0), mainly covering the costs of funds, transportation, installation of the asset, and other indirect costs and fees;
    2) To determine the interest rate per period (i). In real cases, such a determination should specifically consider the risk and the expected return on the investment of the asset;
    3) To determine the residual value of the asset leased at the end of the lease term, expressed in either the home currency (V_h) or a foreign currency (V_f);
    4) To determine the lease term (n);
    5) To determine the foreign exchange rate (either a spot exchange rate F^s_{ij} or a forward exchange rate F^f_{ij}).

2. To calculate the rental factor (RF), for either rental payable in arrears or in advance:
    1) In arrears:

$$RF = \frac{1 - [1/(1+i)^n]}{i} \qquad\qquad [7.1]$$

    2) In advance:

$$RF = \frac{1 - [1/(1+i)^{n-m}]}{i} + m \qquad\qquad [7.2]$$

Where: m is the number of rentals payable in advance for deposits.

3. To calculate the present value of residual value of the leased asset after n period. The present value can be expressed in either the home currency $PV(V^h)$ or a foreign currency $PV(V^f)$.

---

here is to show the steps of computing lease rentals rather than the determinants of the rentals. Chapters 10 and 11 will specifically consider discount rates associated with different risks involved in the models.

1) In the home currency:

$$PV(V^h) = \frac{V^h}{(1+i)^n} \; ; \; or = \frac{V^f F f_{ji}}{(1+i)^n} \qquad [7.3]$$

2) In a foreign currency:

$$PV(V^f) = \frac{V^f}{(1+i)^n} \; ; \; or = \frac{V^h F f_{ij}}{(1+i)^n} \qquad [7.4]$$

4. To calculate the rental amount, expressed either in the home currency (LP^h) or in a foreign currency (LP^f).

1) In the home currency:

$$LPh = \frac{A_0 - PV(V^h)}{RF} \qquad [7.5]$$

2) In a foreign currency:

$$LPf = \frac{A_0 F^s_{ij} - PV(V^f)}{RF} \qquad [7.6]$$

In sum, rentals can be calculated with any formula in Figure 7.4.

Conclusion

Broadly speaking, international leasing is not just an alternative to international finance, but also international marketing. This chapter mainly discusses leasing as an important device of international marketing. Also, this chapter discusses leasing marketing research. Leasing marketing research is the systematic gathering, recording, and analysing of data about leasing marketing problems, and it facilitates leasing decision making. Leasing marketing research broadly covers four stages: problem definition, project strategy, information analysis, and decision making. Nevertheless, lease decision-making also depends on a number of internal factors (or micro environments), decision theories and techniques, and tax and accounting treatments. These issues will be discussed in the next chapter. International lease pricing is also discussed in this Chapter, providing a general description of rental calculation formulas and steps.

Figure 7.4 Rental calculation formulas

<table>
<tr><td colspan="2">A. Rentals are calculated in arrears:</td></tr>
<tr><td>In the home currency:</td><td>In a foreign currency:</td></tr>
<tr>
<td>$$LP_h = \frac{i[A_0(1+i)^n - V^h]}{(1+i)^n - 1}$$</td>
<td>$$LP_f = \frac{i[A_0 F^s_{ij}(1+i)^n - V^f]}{(1+i)^n - 1}$$</td>
</tr>
<tr>
<td>$$LP_h = \frac{i[A_0(1+i)^n - V^f F_{fi}]}{(1+i)^n - 1}$$</td>
<td>$$LP_f = \frac{i[A_0 F^s_{ij}(1+i)^n - V^h F_{fij}]}{(1+i)^n - 1}$$</td>
</tr>
<tr><td colspan="2">B. Rentals are calculated in advance:</td></tr>
<tr><td>In the home currency:</td><td>In a foreign currency:</td></tr>
<tr>
<td>$$LP_h = \frac{i[A_0(1+i)^{n-m} - V^h]}{(1+i)^{n-m}(1+mi) - 1}$$</td>
<td>$$LP_f = \frac{i[A_0 F^s_{ij}(1+i)^{n-m} - V^f]}{(1+i)^{n-m}(1+mi) - 1}$$</td>
</tr>
<tr>
<td>$$LP_h = \frac{I[A_0(1+i)^{n-m} - V^f F_{fi}]}{(1+i)^{n-m}(1+mi) - 1}$$</td>
<td>$$LP_f = \frac{i[A_0 F^s_{ij}(1+i)^{n-m} - V^h F_{fij}]}{(1+i)^{n-m}(1+mi) - 1}$$</td>
</tr>
</table>

Reference

Anderson, P.F. and M.M. Bird. 1980. Marketing to the industrial lease buyer. *Industrial Marketing Management* 9: 111-6.

Anderson, P.F. and W. Lazer. 1978. Industrial lease marketing. *Journal of Marketing* January: 71-9.

Chisnall, P.M. 1985. *Strategic Industrial Marketing*. London: Prentice Hall International.

Desai, P. and D. Purohit. 1998. Leasing and selling: optimal marketing strategies for a durable goods firm. *Management Science* 44, no. 11: S19-34.

Loewenstein, M.A. and J.E. McClure. 1986. Managing the lease-sell decision. *Sloan Management Review* Spring: 77-82.

McNeill, R.B. 1944. The lease as a marketing tool. *Harvard Business Review* Summer.

Meyer, H.E. 1977. The communist internationale has a capitalist accent. *Fortune* February: 134-42.

Wagner, W.B. and P.K. Hall. 1991. Equipment lease accounting in industrial marketing strategy. *Industrial Marketing Management* November: 305-10.

8 International leasing analysis: principles, techniques and factors

Why do we consider principles, techniques and factors

This chapter will focus attention on the environments, principles, techniques and factors involved in international leasing analysis. As well known, the environments can be viewed from two different perspectives: the micro view or the macro view. From the micro point of view, a firm's ability to compete within a market, specific accounting rules and tax treatments, a customer credit standing etc. are the elements of the environment, which must be considered individually. From the macro point of view, economic policies, political systems, cultural backgrounds, legal regulations etc. are the main elements of the environment. Specifically, the environments to be considered in international leasing, from a lessor's point of view, refer to a potential lessee's country environments including economic, political, cultural, legal, accounting, competitive, technological and other environments.

In principle, the primary distinction between international business and national (domestic) business lies in the differences of their environments. In turn, the environmental differences lead to behavioural, managerial and strategy and decision differences. Although the objective of a firm may remain the same, its structure and organisation, strategies, policies and operating practices experience a great number of adjustments or even complete revisions, when the firm expands its operations or transactions beyond its home country.

Meanwhile, the environments are dynamic. The emergence of global competition has given rise to fundamental changes in the international economic environment since the 1980s. One evidence is the national economy of an individual country has been tightly linked into an integrated world economy. At the same time, almost all governments are using or (increasingly) using various approaches in pursuit of various goals (e.g., cutting budget deficit, lowering inflation, lessening foreign debt burden) of an individual country, with the result that the world economy has become more volatile. Consequently, the dynamic environments cause the changing of international leasing all the time, and increase the difficulties of its strategy planning and decision making. On the other hand, the micro environments of a lessor or a lessee, such as financial position, operation performance, credit standing, capital structure etc. are also constantly changing, resulted partly from the change of the macro environments.

Thus, studying the environments is the first step in planning strategies and making decisions. Apparently, a lessor who plans to enter a foreign leasing market needs to fully understand the foreign market. A fundamental task is to carry out the environment research. In reality, since there are many potential pitfalls for doing business abroad, in bankruptcy law for example, the evaluation of a potential foreign lessee's credit standing is even more vital than a domestic lessee's assessment. In Poland, for example, it is extremely difficult to find out the credit worthiness of lessees because Polish firms are not used to disclosing information on profits and income (Gao 1995).

Moreover, there may be legal, tax or foreign exchange control obstacles that rule out either domestic or international leasing transactions, or which discriminate against leasing. For example, under the Japanese bank law, Japanese banks are not permitted to directly engage in leasing operations as lessors; Belgium bank law prevents commercial banks from participating directly in the activities of automotive leasing; Sweden prohibits the direct participation of banks in leasing activities.

This chapter is organised as follows. The following section will analyse some general principles, rules, and requirements for strategy-planning and decision-making in international leasing. Section 3 will in detail analyse the factors that influence international leasing strategies and decisions, including cash flows, discount rates, risk factors, foreign exchange rates and risks, inflation, taxes and other factors. The final section will present a conclusion.

Basic principles and requirements

Strategic-planning is the road map for survival, it helps find out where firms should be going and how to get there. Without strategic-planning and decision-making, the performance of an international leasing company (ILC) and a lessee will be less than optimal, and their overall goals may be difficult to achieve. Before planning strategies and making decisions, one should be aware of the principles and requirements commanding the strategy and decision-making.

Principles

Maximisation of shareholders' wealth

Goals of a financial decision have traditionally attracted a large number of possible candidates including maximisation of profits, maximisation of sales, minimisation of costs, survival of a firm, achieving a target market share etc. However, modern finance theory explicitly states that the goal of a financial decision is to maximise the wealth of its shareholders, and the wealth should be determined on the capital market through the supply of and demand for the firm's stocks. Further, the maximisation of the NPV of an individual project generally leads to the maximisation of shareholders' wealth over a long run. The change in the shareholders' wealth due to the acquisition and the use of an asset is the market value of the asset incremental net cash flows to equity.

In reality, however, it is not enough just to say that the goal of financial decisions of a firm is to maximise the wealth of shareholders or to maximise an individual project NPV. In the leasing literature, it is well known that the maximisation of lessor/lessee shareholders' wealth can only be realised with the NPV maximisation of individual leasing projects or transactions. For example, if a leasing alternative among the options to obtain the use right of an asset has the largest NPV to the user (lessee), the user (lessee) will choose leasing alternative to be an optimal one to the shareholders' wealth maximisation. There is a question left. Should the lessee in decision making consider this alternative also to be the optimal option to the lessor? Similarly, if a lease proposal among others maximises the NPV, the lessor will regard this proposal as the best one. Will the lessor consider whether this will also be the best option to the user (lessee)? The question is whether a leasing transaction with the maximisation of NPV to the lessor or lessee shareholders, will simultaneously lead to the wealth maximisation to its counterpart's (lessee's or lessor's) shareholders.

It is argued that two parties (lessor and lessee) of any leasing transaction will both require to maximise their shareholders' wealth, and the optimal transaction is the one that can largely satisfy both (maximisation). Suppose a lease decision made by the lessor will result in the maximisation of its shareholders' wealth, but not of the lessee's shareholders. Of course, this decision will not be an optimal, since the lessee will not accept such a deal. In theory, the lessee and the lessor decision problems are exact mirror images of each other. In practice, game theory may be used to resolve the conflict of interests between parties concerned. Generally, if a leasing project or transaction maximises its goal (say NPVs), this project or transaction will maximise the goal (NPV) of individual parties who participate in the project or transaction under a competitive market.

Risk and return tradeoff

In theory, return differences between different leasing investments will provide an incentive for leasing capital flows. Investors can improve risk versus return performance by holding an internationally diversified portfolio of securities as compared with a domestically diversified portfolio. The tradeoff between the return on investment and risk is a very important consideration in analysing investment opportunities. Finance theories show that an investor can reduce the total risk by choosing several investment alternatives and holding a diversified portfolio.

The more variable the value of a portfolio is, the less certain an investor can be of the future value. According to the principles of finance, an investor should and can expect higher rates of return on risky investments than s/he can earn on less risky investments. That is because the required rate of return applicable to a particular investment consists of a risk free rate and a risk premium including premium for inflation. The relation is given by:

$$K_L = R_f + \text{Risk premium} \hspace{4cm} [8.1]$$

where K_L is the required rate of return on an investment L, and R_f is the nominal interest rate on a risk-free security.

It can reduce the variability of a portfolio by diversifying and selecting different investments contained in a portfolio. To see the effects of diversification, let us look at a simple example. Assume an ILC has two investment opportunities in two countries: Brazil and China. The ILC holds portfolio B (in Brazil) and portfolio C (in China) with the shares of the portfolio devoted to B denoted by b, and the share devoted to C by c. There are three options open to the ILC:

1) The ILC holds only B, then $b=1, c=0$;
2) The ILC holds only C, then $b=0, c=1$;

3) The ILC chooses some amount of diversification by holding both *B* and
   C.

The return on the portfolio (R_p) can be written as a weighted average of the
returns on the individual investments (R_b and R_c):

$$R_p = bR_b + cR_c \qquad [8.2]$$

The expected future return on the portfolio will then be:

$$R^*_p = bR^*_b + cR^*_c \qquad [8.3]$$

Where R^*_p, R^*_b, and R^*_c are the expected returns of the portfolio and
individual investments respectively. Since portfolio risk is associated with the
variability of the return on the portfolio, it is required to measure this
variability. The measure of the degree to which a variable varies about its
mean or average value is called the *Variance (Var)*. The variance of a
portfolio depends on the variances of individual investments, and their
Covariance (Cov). Specifically,

$$Var(R_p) = b^2 Var(R_b) + c^2 Var(R_c) + 2bcCov(R_b,R_c) \qquad [8.4]$$

If one return R_b or R_c is higher than the average, or, one return R_c or R_b is
lower than the average, the covariance is negative. In result, a negative
covariance contributes greatly to reducing the overall portfolio variance and
therefore risk.

Moreover, diversification does not eliminate all risks to an investor,
because there is a systematic risk that occurs in all investment opportunities.
A systematic risk stems from the fact that there are other economy-wide
perils which may threaten all businesses or investments. The risk that can
potentially be eliminated by diversification is known as a non-systematic risk.
The total risks of any investment may be written as:

$$\text{Total risk } r_t = \text{Systematic risk } r_s + \text{Non-systematic risk } r_n \qquad [8.5]$$

With international leasing, an investor or a lessor can gain with international
diversification. According to the principal theme of modern financial theory,

the risk of a well-diversified portfolio depends on the systematic risk (r_s) of the securities included in the portfolio. r_s is measured by Beta (β) defined by:

$$\beta = \frac{\text{Cov}(R_f, R_m)}{\text{Var}(R_m)} \qquad [8.6]$$

Where R_m is the market return of the portfolio; the numerator is the covariance between the return on a risk-free security f and the return from holding a portfolio containing every investment security in the market. The denominator is the variance of the return on the market portfolio. Beta (β) is a contribution of an individual investment to the variance of the market portfolio. A risk-free asset, where the return is certain and does not vary with the return on the market portfolio, has a $\beta = 0$. On the other hand, the market portfolio would have a $\beta = 1$, because the covariance of the market portfolio with itself is the same as the variance of the market portfolio. Accordingly, Eq.[8.1] can be written with a β as follows which is defined as capital asset pricing model (CAPM):

$$K_L = R_f + \beta(R_m - R_f) \qquad [8.7]$$

Four-step decision procedure
In the most embryonic form of an international leasing decision, like any other decision, the basic decision making procedure includes the following four steps:

- *Step I: Model-formulation.* Step I is to formulate and structure the decision problem, including to specify goals and criteria, to generate alternatives, and to enumerate possible scenarios and impacts. There are usually considerable complexities associated with model formulation due to the difficulties in recognising and specifying: a) goals and attributes of required achievement; b) alternative courses of actions and strategies; c) possible scenarios; and d) possible consequences or impacts associated with given alternative-scenario combinations.

- *Step II: Probability-assessment.* Step II is to assess probabilities of possible scenario realisations and/or impacts on the realisations. The assessment is concerned with the formulation of expectations about future developments in variables that are considered to be related to decision-making. To make the international lease vs. import decision, for example, it needs to assess cash flows associated with a particular scenario (lease or import), the risks involved in the cash flows, and so forth.

- *Step III: Function-determination.* Step III is to determine the preference (values, or risk attitudes) of a decision maker with respect to certain criteria (i.e., utility function, NPV maximisation). The function represents the fundamental relationships among the variables to the decision in question. Sometimes, it is extremely difficult to find out the precise relations between the variables concerned. In addition, non-quantitative factors involved in a decision are impossibly functioned in a quantitative way.[1] These non-quantitative factors, however, must be taken into consideration in decision-making.
- *Step IV: Alternative-optimisation.* Step IV is to optimise the alternatives, and to select a decision or strategy that maximises a decision maker's required goal (e.g., NPV, the maximisation of shareholders' wealth).

The essential relationships of these steps are profiled in Figure 8.1. Obviously, decision-making cannot be independent of the external factors representing decision-inputs or information-inputs. Without reliable inputs, no precise decision-outputs can be produced.

Value-additivity principle
One of the fundamentals of microeconomics and finance is the value additivity hypothesis. This hypothesis states that the market value of a cash flow series equals the sum of the market value of the individual elements constituting the series. That is:

$$CF = CF_1 + CF_2 + ... + CF_i + ... + CF_n;$$

or

$$CF = \sum_{i=1}^{n} CF_i \qquad [8.8]$$

Where CF_i is the cash flows in period i. However, this principle is easily questioned if risk of cash flows and size value of money are considered. Obviously, the risk of cash flows in total as a whole is expected to be higher

---

[1] For example, cultural, behavioural factors may influence both the decision and the decision making procedure.

than the accumulate risks of individual cash flows involved in a portfolio. However, this has been a puzzle for many years in the academics and an unsolved issue of the foundation of economics.

Figure 8.1 The four-step decision procedure

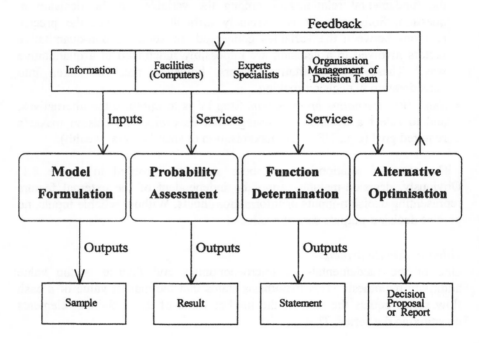

The application of this principle to some special cases may cause some difficulty. For example, the cash flows generated by an international leasing contract may express in terms of a multi-currency package. In this case, it is needed to concert these flows to a currency before adding them up. Also, if the cash flows cover inflation, the sum of these cash flows does not make sense, and thus it need transfer them in real terms before using the principle.

Considering quantitative and non-quantitative factors
In the decision-making literature, quantitative factors are usually paid more attention, leading to the formulation of mathematic equations or complex statistical models. However, it is well argued that non-quantitative factors should also be taken into account in decision-making, although they are not

easily measured. In making an international leasing decision, non-quantitative factors may be of relevance in some cases. For example, in the case of acquisition of the use of an asset a financial lease is preferable according to quantitative calculations. But management may favour importing the asset owing to the pride of ownership, or more disposition rights involved in the owned assets. The reverse is imaginable too: import may be preferable on account of a higher NPV, but management may choose to lease overseas in order to keep up the contracts it has previously made with the lessor. In some areas, leasing of some assets (e.g., agricultural tools) or real estate is prohibited due to the reason of religion.

Requirements

Herst (1984) points out the requirements in designing a model for solving the lease vs. buy/purchase problem, including: 1) taking into account the interactions of investment and financing decisions; 2) stating the grounds for the discount rates used; 3) indicating whether the model has been developed for evaluating financial leases, operating leases, or both types of leases; 4) quantifying the results of the lease evaluation model in NPV; and 5) paying attention to problems that may arise when applying the proposed model in practice (pp.8-14).

It is emphasised that taking into account the interaction of investment and financing decisions is a very important requirement. In the leasing literature there are broadly three schools of views regarding the function of leasing. The first school considers that leasing is only an alternative of financing the acquisition of the use of an asset (among others, Bierman 1988).

The second school argues that leasing is only related to the firm's capital investment and the decision of lease vs. purchase choice belongs to capital budgeting (among others, Sartoris and Paul 1973).

The third school regards that leasing is not only an alternative of financing the acquisition of the use of an asset, but also a way of capital investment (among others, Myers, *et al.* 1976). The first two schools prefer to separate financial decisions from investment decisions, and treat a leasing decision as a financial or an investment decision; whereas the third school prefers to combine both financing and investment decisions.

I argue that an international leasing decision is not a pure budgeting problem faced by a lessor or a pure financing selecting problem faced by a lessee, but a combined decision of budgeting, financing, currency exposure, and tax planning. It is a decision that has the value dependencies or interactions among capital budgeting, financing, exchange exposure and tax planning. For example, from a lessor's point of view, the leasing of assets to a foreign lessee seems just like an investment project which is subject to the capital budgeting decision. But in fact, this decision involves financing problems, and has an impact on the lessor's financial structure. From a lessee's point of view, a leasing decision seems just like a financial selecting decision among financing alternatives to acquisition of the use of an asset (e.g., borrowing, buying with equity). However, leasing may alter the initial capital asset acquisition decision, because it may add additional values to the project cash flows and change the project NPVs.[2]

On the other hand, there is no way that an investment decision can separate from its financing decision. This is because: 1) the market imperfections result in the impossibility of separating an investment decision from its financing decision; 2) international risk diversification mixes an investment decision with its financing decision;[3] 3) from the standpoint of managerial efficiency, it is more costly to separate an investment decision from its financing decision. Indeed, combining the investment and financing decision may very well be less time consuming than trying to make these decisions separate from one another (Herst 1984, p.122).

In addition to the Herst requirements, two additional requirements are proposed for international leasing financial decision-making: specifying certain circumstances to be the *status quo* for designing a model and making proper assumptions before designing a model. As considerable differences of economic systems and structures between countries exist, it requires to select a system to be the *status quo* for the model designing in the analysis. All the models in the leasing literature have been developed with some assumptions. The major assumptions made in the lease evaluation models or the lease vs. buy/borrow decision include 1) perfect market assumption (Miller and Upton 1976); 2) one-for-one debt displacement of leases (Myers, *et al.* 1976; Franks and Hodges 1987); 3) the same risk for all cash flow elements (Drury 1989); 4) the certainty of the future real interest rate (Brick, *et al.* 1987); 5) zero salvage value (Herst 1984); and 6) the lessee and lessor have the same tax bracket (Heaton 1986).

---

[2] A typical example is a double-dip leasing transaction which can offer more opportunities for a firm to accept a project that is rejected under the capital budgeting decision with a normal financing approach.

[3] In fact, to a large extent the profitability of a project may depend on the way it is financed.

Decision-making techniques

Present value (PV) and net present value (NPV)

The intention of the PV calculations is to determine the amount of money an investor or a firm would accept at present in place of a given amount at a certain future date. The NPV technique involves discounting all expected after-tax cash flows to their PV and then taking the difference between the PV of the inflow and the PV of the outflow. The difference is called the NPV. Both calculations require the use of a discount rate, which depends on the basis of its cost of capital and the degree of risk involved in a project (or proposal) being evaluated vis-a-vis the risk attached to the current composite portfolio.

In practice, the NPV technique is increasingly used by firms. Sykes (1976) shows that only 19% of his sample used the NPV (discounted cash flows method) to evaluated leases. The survey by Anderson and Martin (1977) displays that only 23% of firms of the survey uses the NPV technique, which is lower than traditional internal rate of return (IRR) method (50%). In the survey of Hull and Hubbard (1979), however, the number increased to 43% of the respondents. In the literature, the NPV method is popularly utilised as a basis for models building.

The risk-adjusted discount rate (RADR) technique

The RADR technique is a modification of the NPV method described above wherein the discount rate is adjusted either upward or downward, depending on whether the project under evaluation has greater or less risk than those normally undertaken by the investor. The reason to use the adjusted discount rate is that projects should achieve hurdle rates that reflect their degree of risk (i.e., more risky projects should offer greater expected returns). The rationale of the RADR technique states that cash inflows and outflows generated by a project should be discounted for both the time value of money (using a risk-free rate) and the degree of risk associated with the project (using a risk premium that is added to the risk-free rate). The way for financial managers or decision-makers to implement the RADR technique is to categorise projects according to their risk and then to utilise discount rates that are appropriate for the projects in that risk class.

Option theory

Options are a unique type of financial contract that have a throwaway feature. They give you the right, but not the obligation, to do something. Options are usually classified according to whether they are options to buy (calls) or options to sell (puts), and according to whether they can be used only on a specific date (European) or at any time prior to a specific date (American). A call option is a contract giving its owner the right to buy a fixed number of shares, for example, of a specified common stock (underlying asset) at a fixed price at any time on or before a given date. A put option is a contract giving its owner the right to sell a fixed number of shares of a specified common stock at a fixed price at any time on or before a given date. The act of making such transactions is referred to as exercising the options. The specified stock is known as the underlying security.

The most commonly used formula for pricing call options is the Black and Scholes Model. Black and Scholes (1973) use minor variations to determine the gap between the market price of a call option and its intrinsic value. The application of option theory in the analysis of leases is, for example, the valuation of any purchase options during, or at the end of the lease terms as the exercise price is the contracted price in the lease. In addition, the cancellation feature of operating leases is really an option. Especially it is an American put option held by a lessee (e.g., Copeland and Weston 1982).

Sensitivity Analysis Technique (SAT)

The SAT is probably the most common method of evaluating a project's risk in practice. Its major analytical framework is to determine the impact of changes in the data inputs on the preferred decision alternative. Using the SAT the firm can make its best estimate of the revenues and costs involved in a project by way of calculating the project's NPV, and then checking the sensitivity of the NPV to possible estimation errors of the gross revenue and the various cost items. It is well known that financial analysts or decision makers are interested in determining the extent to which error made in forecasting future financial and operating cash flows will affect the present value or NPV of the alternatives under evaluation. Certainly, various forecasting errors may make the preferred alternative more attractive, which other errors may alter the preferred alternative. In general, the SAT considers the following aspects:

1) Qualitative aspects of the decision setting;
2) Quantitative aspects that are too complex to incorporate directly into the evaluation model;
3) The extent to which conditions will have to change to result in a different preferred alternative.

Normally, every decision setting is surrounded by both quantifiable and non-quantifiable aspects that require consideration and evaluation in arriving at a final decision. In international leasing analysis, especially in measuring the impact of different tax rates affecting the tax savings, the SAT is a very useful method. The application of the SAT in the lease decision analysis is advocated by many authors (e.g., Bower 1973; Herst 1984).

Risk ranking technique

The main aim of the risk ranking technique is to provide the decision maker with a unified, consistent, comprehensive and defensible assessment of the acceptability of the various decision options (Chicken and Hayns 1989, p.18). To rank the acceptability of the various risk options the technique integrates the acceptability of the major factors (e.g., political stability, foreign exchange rate, technological development) associated with each option. Ideally the ranking technique requires a quantitative assessment of the related factors, but the technique may be used when only qualitative data is available. Generally, the ranking technique serves two vital purposes: it grades the acceptability of each factor in absolute terms and the width of each rank gives a measure of the uncertainty associated with each factor.

The general procedure of the risk ranking technique is shown in Figure 8.2 in the form of a flow diagram with six steps.

Step 1 is a definition of the risk to be ranked, this is important at the beginning of a risk assessment process.

Step 2 requires a definition of the criteria to be used for judging and scoring the acceptability of each factor in the assessment process.

Steps 3, 4, 5 are the evaluation of the data available and the determination of the ranking options.

In step 6 the risk decision is taken about the preferred option.

Figure 8.2 The risk ranking technique

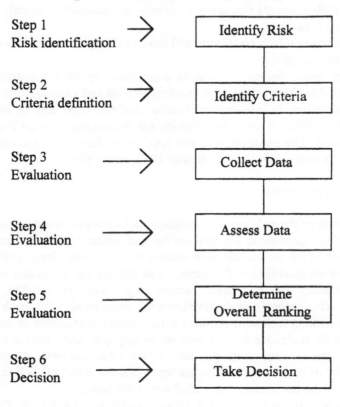

Step 1
Risk identification

Step 2
Criteria definition

Step 3
Evaluation

Step 4
Evaluation

Step 5
Evaluation

Step 6
Decision

Identify Risk

Identify Criteria

Collect Data

Assess Data

Determine
Overall Ranking

Take Decision

Factors in international leasing analysis

Cash flows

A fundamental of finance theory requires that a project need be evaluated by considering all of the cash inflows and outflows induced by the decision in question. These flows are the incremental cash flows, determined by the magnitude and timing of the cash flows. A decision to acquire an asset whether by either an import plan or an overseas leasing contract creates an incremental cash flow stream that need be estimated and calculated.

Forecasting a project cash flow stream plays a vital role in the international leasing analysis. For example, in evaluating the attractiveness of a lease or a purchase alternative, forecasting plays a role in determining all the direct and indirect cash flows. There may be differences between the net cash inflows with a lease and those with purchase, however. For example, the unit cost of a product manufactured using the asset may differ according to whether the asset is leased or owned. The fact is that in the former case the lease payments constitute a part of the unit cost of the product, whereas in the latter depreciation plus any interest are part of the unit cost. The lease payment does not need to equal interest, if any, plus depreciation (Herst 1984, p.127).

Moreover, the cash flows of international leasing differ between lessors and lessees. From a lessor point of view, a decision maker must forecast and qualify all the following cash flows and factors that are associated with a lease project:

a) The initial outlay required for a leasing project, including the purchase price of leased assets, service costs (e.g., installation, transportation, maintenance, and insurance costs), break-in and training costs etc.;

b) The lease return required by the project. This is a function of pricing, supply and demand relationships, reactions of competitors, fixed and variable costs of operation, the degree of risk aversion, and other variables;

c) The useful life of leased assets and the expected lease terms (especially in an operating lease) which is a function of technological change, wear and tear, obsolescence, customer's operating positions and competition, and the possibility of cancelling the leasing contract;

d) The market value of a leased asset at various points throughout its useful life and the lease term if the foreign lessee decides to cancel the leasing contract under its preference at any time, or ask for the replacement, as well as the market salvage value of the leased asset at the end of the leasing contract;

e) Tax impacts on the lessor's depreciation tax savings (DTS), investment tax credit (ITC), withholding tax, VAT, and other tax influences;

f) The value of disposition right and other variables such as delivery costs, customs duties, advertisement fees, registration costs and stamp duties etc.;

g) The value of a currency movement of the lease payments caused by the variability of foreign exchange rates, and so forth.

From a lessee point of view, all the following cash flows and factors must be projected:

a) The initial investment costs for the acquisition of the use right of a required asset, including the purchase price (or manufacture costs), service cost, transaction costs, and other costs (e.g., break-in and training, transportation, insurance costs);

b) The expected lease payments that the lessee will be able to negotiate if an international lease is under consideration. On the one hand, the payments will depend on the market conditions, the lessee's financial and operation positions, as well as the properties of assets. On the other hand, the expected leased payments will also depend on whether a lease is a financial lease, an operating lease, or other type of transactions (e.g., double-dip, leveraged leasing);

c) The foreseen useful life of an asset and the possible lease terms under different circumstances (e.g., economic recession, or war). Importantly, the lessee has to estimate the penalty costs if it cancels a (financial) lease;

d) The market reactions to the lessee in terms of market value change if an international leasing project is going to be undertaken, and the extent of the lessee's debt capacity affected by this leasing project;

e) The market salvage value of the leased asset at the end of the leasing contract and the value of option to purchase the leased asset if such an option is permitted;

f) Tax impacts on the lessee's DTS, ITC, withholding tax, VAT and other tax incentives;

g) The value of the currency movement of lease payments caused by the variability of foreign exchange rates, and the possible gains and losses stemming from the choices of import or lease overseas.

One important cash flow to both the lessee and the lessor is the lease payments over the term of the contract. In reality the lease payments can take on a wide variety of patterns: equal monthly payments at the beginning of each month; payments in arrears; ballooning payments at various times over the lease; payments with a multi-currency package and so on. Whatever the pattern is, cash flow must be discounted to present value using the appropriate discount rate. Further, in order to get a good position in bargaining, both the lessor and the lessee have to evaluate cash flows of their potential counterparts. For example, in evaluating tax benefits of an international lease, both the lessor and the lessee should evaluate not only its own available benefits from its jurisdiction, but its potential benefits from the partner's jurisdiction. This is particularly important in double-dip leasing as the lessor will be expected to pass on some of the tax savings to the lessee in the way of reduced lease payments.

Discount rates

The sensitivity of the lease decision to the choice of discount rates has been a matter of constant concern for financiers and decision-makers. In fact, the choice of discount rates is a highly controversial issue in the literature. I argue that the discount rate for valuing a cash flow is the rate that an investor or a firm in the market utilises to value a project's cash flows of like risk and taxability. The discount rates to be applied in the lease decision-making and lease analysis should depend on the following considerations:

a) The goal of decision-making. The goal of financial decision-making is the maximisation of wealth of the lessor's/lessee's shareholders. Thus, the present value of the cash flows should be calculated to the equity of a lessor/lessee and the equity market value is the discounted value of the expected aggregate future cash flows (wealth) allocated to equity-holders.

b) The nature of the cash flows being discounted. Different cash flows have different economic natures. For example, the economic nature of the lease payments from a lessee point of view is generally less risk, if given the future interest rate and the exchange rate. The only risk associated with the fixed lease payments obviously results from the uncertainty about the movement of the interest rate and/or the exchange rate. The discount rate used to discount the lease payments depends therefore on the degree of uncertainty about the future interest rate and exchange rate. However, the residual value of the lease asset is highly uncertain, since it depends on technological development and other factors such as wear and tear. According to this characteristic, the decision-maker should correlate the discount rate for the residual cash flow with the uncertainty about the future technological innovation, the time of replacement of the asset. If the firm as a whole reasonably expects to generate sufficient taxable income from its overall operations to use all tax deductions, tax shields should obviously be discounted at a low rate since they are virtually certain. From the above discussion, it can be concluded that the economic nature of a cash flow can be used to consider the establishment of discount rates in the leasing evaluation and decision-making.

c) Capturing degree of uncertainty or risk. A very appealing argument in the finance literature is that the discount rate of cash flows should capture degree of uncertainty or risk involved in the flows. The higher risk of cash flows, the higher the discount rate that should be used. As discussed previously, a discount rate appropriate to the tax savings resulting from the various tax deductible costs depends on a large extent on the tax system being in force, particularly on regulations relating to tax deductible losses issued by fiscal authorities. However, the choice of an appropriate rate to discount the tax shields from the non-interest portion of the lease payments (e.g., the ITSs of debts supported by the lease payments) is not so straight-forward, since these tax shields are closely related to many other factors like the lease payments. It is generally accepted that the use of market discount rates implies that leasing projects with different risks require different discount rates. For example, an asset imported or leased that has risk characteristics different from the rest of the firm will generally require a discount rate other than the firm's existing rate (usually cost of capital). Moreover, risk is not constant over time, therefore, to fix a constant discount rate to account for risk is at best an extremely crude device and may lead to an erroneous decision.

d) The extent of a firm's risk diversification. Apart from the general risk consideration, a key issue of international leasing transactions to an ILC is whether a higher rate of return should be required for foreign lease projects than domestic ones with comparable risks. Many ILCs believe that additional risks associated with international leasing (e.g., political instability, currency controls, exchange risk, expropriation, and other forms of government interventions) mean that the greater a firm's international involvement, the riskier its projects should be, hence the greater its cost of equity capital. In theory, leasing being international may actually reduce the risk. According to the capital asset pricing model (CAPM), by holding a portfolio of stocks whose returns are not all subject to the same risks, an investor can eliminate some of this return variability. The risk of a portfolio of stocks will be less than the average risk of its component's stocks. However, the application of the CAPM to international capital markets depends on whether the markets are integrated or segmented. Under the integrated markets, risky assets are priced according to their non-diversifiable world risk (i.e., international CAPM); under the segmented markets, risky assets are priced relative to domestic assets only (i.e., domestic systematic risk is the basis of asset pricing). Unfortunately, whether international leasing markets are integrated or segmented is still subject to further research.

Risk factors

Lease analysis needs to consider both business and financial risk and their impacts on the overall risk position of the lessor/lessee. Business risk is risk arising from the variability in earnings that is a function of the firm's normal operations. Business risk is affected by a variety of factors including the changing economic environment, market condition, management decisions on capital intensification etc.. The second primary element of the firm's overall risk is financial risk. Financial risk results from the variability in earnings that is a function of the firm's financial mix, in particular the use of debt financing (including lease financing). For a firm, the increasing use of leasing results in large fixed obligation (the lease payments) and, thereby increases the variability of earnings after taxes and earnings per share. For example, Laitinen (1991) finds that for firms under lease financing, their unadjusted operating margin and profit margin are always lower than for similar firms under normal financing (p.62).

There are three major types of financial risks in international leasing transactions: foreign exchange (currency) risk; interest rate risk and credit risk. The latter two also arise within purely domestic leasing. Foreign exchange risk results from the fact that the lease payments are priced or calculated in a currency other than the home currency. Interest rate risk arises primarily through offering a fixed rate lease that has been financed with variable rate borrowing from international capital markets or *vice versa*. Inflation is an important factor influencing interest rate risk. The measure of interest rate risk often appears very complicated, especially when different currencies are involved and alternative forms of financing are used. Credit risk is another important concern to a lessor in all leasing analysis. However, it would be more difficult to manage and measure it when a lease goes international simply because economic and political environments, cultural backgrounds, accounting and fiscal systems, and legal jurisdictions are complicated and different from a pure domestic lease. Those 'foreign factors' make the credit assessment of a potential lessee more difficult and expensive.

Besides, other risks may arise from the following sources: 1) the potential for equipment obsolescence due to changing technology and market demand or supply; 2) variability in the price of money (interest rate) associated with different types of leases; 3) difficulty in estimating salvage value of equipment at the termination of a lease or at the end of the asset's economic life. For a lessee, the difference in risk between leasing and other forms of financing may be negligible under fully competitive capital markets, although foreign lessors frequently overemphasise that leasing is less finance risk than other forms of finance. For example in the case of risk of obsolescence of a leased asset, any ILC would not accept the risks of obsolescence at the cost lower than that if incurred by a lessee. By contraries, in many circumstances it can be a real case that this cost is higher for the lessor than the lessee because the assets in question reflect a proportion of the lessor's capital employed which is much larger than the corresponding proportion of the lessee who only uses these assets for normal business purposes. Consequently, the lessor is likely to require a higher risk premium per asset for obsolescence.

Lessee's credit risk must be examined. The lessor (and, when nonrecourse debt financing is utilised, the lender) must look primarily to the lessee for the payments due under the lease. In the event of a default by the lessee, they will have to look at the resale value or revenue generating capacity of the leased asset to be repaid. If the leased asset is located within a larger project, repossession may be difficult, particularly in some emerging economies, and the lessor and lenders may be forced to look to project revenues for payment. These concerns can often be ameliorated through local government or central bank guarantees and, in appropriate cases, political risk insurance.

On the other hand, the creditworthiness of the lessor may be an issue of concern to the lessee. A bankruptcy or insolvency event relating to the lessor may make it unable to comply with its obligations to pass title to the lessee on exercise of a purchase option contained in the lease and may also interfere with the continuing use of the leased asset by the lessee.

It is obviously of great importance to lessors and lenders that the law applicable to the transaction is well-developed and clear as it relates to such matters as asset rights, enforcement of contractual rights and remedies (including perfection and enforcement of rights in collateral), the consequences of bankruptcy or insolvency of the lessee or a credit support provider and the like. Also of concern, particularly in emerging economies where local courts may be hostile, is the ability to obtain judicial relief in default and repossession scenarios. These concerns have usually been addressed by having the transaction documents governed by the law of a country having an internationally recognised body of commercial law precedents and by providing for the parties to submit to the jurisdiction of the courts in that country in the event of litigation. Also, where the lessee or a credit support provider is a governmental entity or is controlled by a governmental entity, the documents should provide for a waiver of sovereign immunity. Even with these contractual protections, however, the parties usually attempt to get comfortable (usually through legal opinions) that they are enforceable under local law.

Project risk is worthwhile considering in some cases. Most international leasing to date has been utilised to finance investment in transportation and other discrete assets (e.g., telecommunications equipment, printing presses etc.). In these cases, the principal risks are lessee defaults (which are covered by exercise of remedies under the lease) and loss or expropriation of the leased equipment (which are covered by insurance). In the case of equipment that is incorporated into a larger project, the financing parties may, as a practical matter, be unable to foreclose and be forced to look to project revenue for ultimate payment in the case of a lessee default. They thus may be exposed to additional project risks.

Foreign exchange rates and risks

Determining and measuring the foreign exchange rate is important to the international leasing analysis. Primarily, two types of exchange rates exist: a spot exchange rate and a forward exchange rate. As described in Chapter 5, a spot exchange rate is applied to the exchange of two currencies on the spot, that is, for immediate delivery, whereas a forward exchange rate is applied to the agreement for a future exchange of two currencies on an agreed date. The reason to select an exchange rate is the fact that international leasing transactions involve a foreign currency and payments over much longer period of time. The flexibility of foreign exchange rates causes foreign exchange risk (or called currency risk). Foreign exchange risk arises when the lease payment is priced in a currency other than the principal currency of the lessor/lessee. For instance, a Dutch lessor leasing assets paid for in Dutch guilders to a Swiss lessee who pays the lease payments in terms of Swiss france (SF) will generate considerable exposure to a falling SF. Also, in a multi-currency package transaction, different currencies involved in the lease payments require to transfer the currencies to a certain currency (mostly home currency) for the measurement in the analysis or the decision making. Specifically, the currency problem involved in the international lease payments can broadly be categorised as falling into three classes embracing the following situations:

1) Lease payments in terms of a currency in which cash inflows are expected;
2) Lease payments in terms of a currency other than in which cash inflows are expected, but with cover in the forward markets;

3) Lease payments in terms of a currency other than in which cash inflows are expected, but without forward cover;
4) Lease payments in terms of a multi-currency package covering the situation 3 and 2 or 1.

In general, leasing transactions in the first two situations avoid foreign exchange risk, but in the last two cases, foreign exchange risk is taken on. How to cope with and measure foreign exchange risk? As discussed in Chapter 5, various hedging strategies can be employed.

Eun and Resnick (1988) show that exchange risk is *nondiversifiable* to a large extent due to the high correlation among the changes in the exchange rates and, as a result, substantially contributes to the overall risk of the international portfolio. They therefore propose to simultaneously use two methods of exchange risk reduction, i.e., multicurrency diversification and the forward exchange contract on a currency-by-currency basis.

1) If under a hypothetical leasing transaction, the lease payments are in the form of a multicurrency package, whereby various currencies are fairly priced, firms can structure their liabilities so as to reduce their exposure to foreign exchange risk at no cost to the value of the firm. In this case, this simply involves matching net positive positions in each currency with borrowing of similar maturity;

2) If a firm leases an asset with lease payments in a foreign currency, its effect cost equals the after-tax cost of repaying the principal and interest in terms of its own currency. This includes the nominal cost of principal and interest in foreign currency terms, adjusted for any foreign exchange gains or losses. For example, when a Dutch lessee pays the lease rentals in terms of the US dollars for one year at 6% interest rate, and during the year the dollar appreciates by 8% relative to the guilders, the approximate before-tax cost of this debt is 14.48% (i.e., 6% x 1.08% + 8% = 14.48%). The calculation is derived as follows:

$$K_d = I_d \times \Delta I_d + \Delta P_d \qquad\qquad [8.9]$$

Where: K_d = the before-tax cost of the debt; I_d = interest in dollar; ΔI_d = additional interest due to exchange rate change; ΔP_d = additional principal due to exchange rate change. The added 8.48% cost of this debt in terms of Dutch guilders would be reported as a foreign exchange transaction loss, and would be deductible for tax purposes. Therefore the after-tax cost of this debt when the Dutch income tax rat (*t*) is 48% would be:

$$K_d(1-t) = 14.48\% \times .52 = 7.53\%$$

Inflation

Inflation is an important factor that causes difficulties for decision-makers in forecasting future real cash flows of a leasing project. It is known that future inflation is determined by a host of factors including past price increase, government fiscal and monetary policy, consumer behaviour in spending and saving, the market equilibrium position of supply of and demand for certain commodities, as well as firms' decisions on prices for their products and services. Inflation has a significant influence upon the international leasing analysis. For example, inflation has a direct impact on the DTS. In the absence of inflation the PV of the DTS is usually given by:

$$PV(TD) = \sum_{i=1}^{n} \frac{TD_i}{(1+R_f)^i} \qquad [8.10]$$

Where TD_i is the DTS in period i, and R_f is the discount rate (say a risk-free rate) for discounting the DTS. Since depreciation allowances are based on historical cost, the present value of the tax shield, *PV(TD)*, does not vary with inflation. As a result, *PV(TD)* in real terms falls in the presence of inflation. To be more specific, given an inflation rate *F%* per year, the *PV(TD)* reduces to:

$$PV(TD,F) = \sum_{i=1}^{n} \frac{TD_i/(1+F)^i}{(1+R_f)^i} = \sum_{i=1}^{n} \frac{TD_i}{(1+R_f)^i(1+F)^i} \qquad [8.11]$$

Where *PV(TD,F)* stands for the present value of the DTS under an inflation circumstance. Obviously *PV(TD) > PV(TD,F)*, which means that other things being equal, the DTS becomes less attractive under inflation. The higher the inflation rate, the greater the gap between *PV(TD)* and *PV(TD,F)*.

Dealing with inflation in the decision of leasing an asset, Pritchard and Hindelang (1980) recommend that firms, especially in times of high uncertainty about the future inflation, should consider the possibility of 'hedging' by signing a short-term lease, even at a higher annual cost.

According to the authors, this is because during the period of the lease a major portion of the uncertainty may be resolved so that probabilities of future outcomes can be more easily assessed, and the additional flexibility of being a lessee rather than an owner in such uncertainty times could be well rewarded during and at the end of the shorter term lease (p.67). I argue that inflation is a factor that contributes to a firm's overall risk. Dealing with inflation the firm should consider the overall position of risk and the preference of risk and return to the firm. Whether signing a short-term or long-term lease should depend on the firm's overall risk position and the required return. There is no reason to believe that a short-term lease is better than a long-term lease without comparing the costs involved. There are generally two ways to adjust a project NPV in an inflationary environment to real terms:

1) Adjust the nominal cash flows to real term and then discount them at the real required return of the project.

$$NPV_R = \sum_{i=1}^{n} \frac{CF_i/(1+F)^i}{(1 + K_R)^i} - A_0 \qquad [8.12]$$

Where: A_0 = the initial capital outlay; CF_i = the cash flows in period i; NPV_R= the net present value (NPV) in real term; K_R = the appropriate discount rate in real term; F = the inflation rate in percentage; n = the period of a project.

2) Adjust the appropriate discount rate to nominal term and then discount the nominal cash flows of the project.

$$NPV_N = \sum_{i=1}^{n} \frac{CF_i}{(1+K_R)^i(1+F)^i} - A_0 = \sum_{i=1}^{n} \frac{CF_i}{(1+K_N)^i} - A_0 \qquad [8.13]$$

Where: NPV_N = the NPV in nominal term; K_N = the appropriate discount rate in nominal term. Obviously, since both NPV_R and NPV_N are the correct net present value under an inflationary environment, the firm can separate its cash flows into two components. One part of the cash flows whose nominal value changes proportionally to the price level will not be affected by inflation. The other part whose nominal value changes randomly to the price level will be affected by inflation. For both parts it is true that one can apply either the real rate of discount to the constant cash flow or the nominal rate of discount to the nominal value of the cash flow.

Taxes

Leasing combines a number of attractions as a financing medium due to asymmetrical tax incentives. Most of the traditional literature on domestic leasing draws the conclusion that if markets are competitive, then there should be no advantage to a leasing contract for firms in the same tax bracket (Bower 1973; Lewellen, *et al.* 1979; and Miller and Upton 1976). The primary tax advantage from international leasing may be obtained when it is possible to structure 'double-dip leasing'. In a double-dip transaction, the disparate leasing rules of the lessor's and lessee's countries let both parties be treated as the owner of the leased asset for tax purposes. Thus, both the lessee and the lessor are entitled to the DTS and other possible tax credits. Generally, this kind of benefits to the lessor can be passed on to the lessee in the form of lower lease payments. However, different treatments of leases between countries may also lead to a situation where neither the lessee nor the lessor has the right to depreciate an asset for tax purposes.

Shapiro (1991) makes a very clear comparison. As an alternative to increasing the debt of foreign subsidiaries, US multinationals could expand their use of leasing in the US. Although leasing an asset is economically equivalent to using borrowed funds to purchase the asset, the international tax consequences differ. Prior to 1986, US multinationals counted virtually all their interest expenses as a fully deductible US expense. Under the new law, firms must allocate interest expense on general borrowing to match the location of their assets, even if all the interest is paid in the US. This allocation has the effect of reducing the amount of interest expense that can be written off against US income. Rental expense, on the other hand, can be allocated to the location of the leased property. The lease payments on equipment located in the United States, therefore, can be fully deducted. At the same time, leasing equipment to be used in the US, instead of borrowing to finance it, increases reported foreign income (since there is less interest expense to allocate against foreign income). The effect of leasing, therefore, is to increase the allowable foreign tax credit to offset US taxes owed on foreign source income, thereby providing another tax advantage of leasing for firms that owe US tax on their foreign source income (pp.537-8).

As far as corporate taxes are concerned, taxes are real outflows when measuring the cash flows of a leasing project. Note that when calculating tax effects of cash flows, depreciation is normally treated as tax-deductible factor that decreases the project's tax burden. Also, the tax benefit of deducting depreciation is normally certain under a single leasing project as this depends on a firm's overall tax position that is determined by the operations of the firm, not of a single project.

Further, there are different corporate tax treatments subject to different cases. If a financial lease is treated as a sale and the lessor has no permanent representation in the lessee's country, then the lessor is usually exempt from the corporate income tax in the lessee's country. If the lessor provides maintenance services in the local country, the lessor may be determined to be carrying on a domestic trade or business, then the lease payments will be subject to corporate income taxes. If the lessor provides maintenance services in the lessee country, the entire lease payments are rarely subject to the taxes. However, most countries allow some deductions, either on the basis of deemed rental payments to the lessor or be taking into account equipment depreciation and the relevant financing costs.

The taxation of the lease payments in the lessor's home country is mainly determined by whether the home country makes a distinction between operating and financial leases. In a country where the distinction is made, a financial lease transaction is usually considered an instalment sale and the gain is fully taxable. In a country where no distinction is made, the lease payments are normally treated as rental income, and the deduction of financing costs and the depreciation of the asset—usually based on its useful life, not on the term of the lease—are allowed. In addition, the lease payments can be sheltered from taxation by leasing from companies in a jurisdiction such as Saudi Arabia, Kuwait, the Emirates, Singapore or Switzerland, provided there are no withholding taxes in the lessee's country, the lease payments can be accumulated with only a light tax burden. For example, in Singapore only 10 per cent tax rate for any income from onshore leasing, which is substantially below the Singapore corporate tax rate of 31 per cent.

Taxes are an important consideration in structuring leasing, particularly international leasing. However, the tax problem involved in international leasing cannot be understood without knowing the development of national tax rules of leasing. In general, complicated tax treatments on leasing, even on a national level, are a recent phenomenon. Prior to the early 1980s, the tax rules on leasing seem to have been fairly simple everywhere in the world. For example, leasing was treated as renting, which meant that the lease payments were taxable income to the lessor and deductible costs to the lessee. Until recently, more detailed and complicated tax treatments on leasing have been introduced in some leading countries (e.g., the US, the UK, Germany and The Netherlands). In those countries a lease is required to strictly split between a financial and an operating lease. Different tax rules are imposed on different types of leases. In a financial lease, the lessee is treated as the owner of the leased asset for tax purposes. In many cases, a financial lease has been regarded as a conditional sales contract. In an operating lease, however, the lessor is the owner for tax purposes.

Some countries require the legal ownership to be the only basis for assets depreciation (e.g., Argentina, Brazil, Colombia, Italy, Sweden and Spain). In other countries like the US, the UK and The Netherlands, the economic ownership is the basis for assets depreciation. Because tax treatments of leases are different between countries, tax depreciation allowance in cross-border leasing may be given to both the lessee and the lessor or to neither of them. For example, double-dip leasing can be more easily achieved if the lessee is in a country (e.g., Australia, Germany, Mexico, New Zealand, The Netherlands, the UK or the US) which allows depreciation for tax purposes to be claimed by the lessee as the economic owner of the asset under the lease and the lessor is in a country (e.g., Argentina, Brazil, France, Italy or Sweden) which allows depreciation for tax purposes to be claimed by the lessor as the legal owner of the same asset. However, recently tax reforms in many countries have swept away many tax advantages that once could be claimed by the owner of an asset. Generally, it will be the fact for some time that the tax treatment of leases diverges from country to country. Even in the European Union, the difference of tax treatments of leases still remains. For details of taxes and law related to leasing in the European Union, see Rosen (1994).

International leasing obviously involves a number of tax-related concerns. All transactions involve an element of "structural" tax risk, which may or may not be covered by indemnities given by the lessee to the lessor against loss or disallowance of the tax benefits on which the transaction's economics are based. In most cross-border deals, however, each party takes the risk of tax problems in its jurisdiction. In some cases (e.g., Japanese leases), the lessor will nevertheless require special termination rights in the event the lessor is not allowed to claim the tax benefits. In such event, the lessee may be required to make a substantial payment to the lessor that may reduce the benefit it received in the transaction.

The location of the leased asset in the lessee's jurisdiction may also give rise to local income tax exposure, and the lessee may be expected to provide an indemnity against these taxes. For example, a number of tax treaties to which the US is a party (e.g., the treaty with Australia) treat ownership of leased assets located in the jurisdiction of one of the signatories as giving rise to a "permanent establishment", the profits from which may be taxed in that jurisdiction.

Import duties and stamp duties

Customs duties are also an area requiring consideration. In transactions involving the leasing of equipment/machinery that is to be imported into the lessee's country, the question of import duties can obviously be of great importance to the parties involved. However, the computation of export/import duties on leased assets is a too complex area. Duty is generally payable on the sale value of the assets on importation and the amount of duty payable depends on the type of assets. Sometimes, duty is computed by discounting the total rentals receivable under the lease agreement. Some countries like Hungary, have made imported leased equipment and machinery that is owned by lessors outside Hungary exempt from import duties. Stamp duties are another form of taxation that can have some importance in a transaction and which vary significantly between different countries. Many countries, if they have any at all, simply have a system of duties payable on the provision by the government authorities of notary services or, in the case of Hungary, on the grant of permission to a foreign company to conduct business in Hungary. Interestingly, Poland, though it has a rigorous system of stamp duties, has adopted the position that duties are not payable on leasing transactions with foreign lessors. However, rules on import and stamp duties are frequently changed to reflect the need of the fiscal policy of individual countries. International leasing analysis requires a full examination of these policies.

Conclusion

This chapter discusses the principles, theories, techniques, risk, taxes and other factors which influence international leasing decision-making. Maximisation of shareholders' wealth must be the objective of leasing decision-making. This can only be achieved by selecting leasing projects with positive NPV. Whether a project has a positive NPV is also subject to risk and return tradeoff which offers ground for choosing discount rates. A high discount rate leads to less present value of cash flows, consequently reduces the amount of a project's NPV given others being equal, and *vice versa*. However, leasing itself is financing and marketing tool which may have additional value that cannot be incorporated into normal cash flows based decision-making models. Risk, tax benefits, for example, are linked with other business activities of the firm, and are difficult to isolate from the overall business portfolio.

It is clear that these fundamentals are important in international leasing analysis. However, theories and techniques themselves are developing with the emerging of new ideas and models, and the evolution of disciplines and technology. Many of these factors will be discussed further in later chapters when they are selected to incorporate in the decision-making models.

Reference

Anderson, P.E. and J.D. Martin. 1977. Lease vs. purchase decisions: a survey of current practice. *Financial Management* Spring: 41-7.

Bierman, H. 1988. Buy versus lease with an alternative minimum tax. *Financial Management* Winter: 87-91.

Black, F. and M. Scholes. 1973. The pricing of options and corporate liabilities. *Journal of Political Economy* May-June: 637-54.

Bower, R.S. 1973. Issues in lease financing. *Financial Management* Winter: 25-34.

Brick, I.E., W. Fung and M. Subrahmanyam. 1987. Leasing and financial intermediation: comparative tax advantages. *Financial Management* Spring: 55-59.

Chicken, J.C. and M.R. Hayns. 1989. *The Risk Ranking Technique in Decision Making*. Oxford: Pergamon Press.

Copeland, T.E. and J.F. Weston. 1982. A note on the evaluation of cancellable operating leases. *Financial Management* Summer: 60-7.

Drury, C. 1989. Evaluating the lease or purchase decision. *Managerial Finance* 15, no. 1/2: 26-38.

Eun, C.S. and B.G. Resnick. 1988. Exchange rate uncertainty, forward contracts, and international portfolio selection. *Journal of Finance* March: 197-215.

Franks, J.R. and S.D. Hodges. 1987. Lease valuation when taxable earnings are a scarce resource. *Journal of Finance* September: 987-1005.

Gao, S.S. 1995. Leasing in Poland: privatisation, financing and current problems. *European Business Review*, no. 5: 31-40.

Heaton, H. 1986. Corporate taxation and leasing. *Journal of Financial and Quantitative Analysis* September: 351-359.

Herst, A.C.C. 1984. *Lease or Purchase: Theory and Practice.* Massachusetts: Kluwer-Nijhoff Publishing.

Hull, J.C. and G.L. Hubbard. 1979. Lease evaluation in the UK: current theory and practice. UK: Cranfield School of Management.

Laitinen, E.K. 1991. The effect of leasing on profitability ratios. *The International Journal of Management Science* 19, no. 1: 59-63.

Lewellen, W.G., M.S. Long and J.J. McConnell. 1979. Asset leasing in competitive capital markets. *Journal of Finance* June: 787-98.

Miller, M.H. and C.W. Upton. 1976. Leasing, buying, and the cost of capital services. *Journal of Finance* June: 761-786.

Myers, S.C., D.A. Dill and A.J. Bautista. 1976. Valuation of financial lease contracts. *Journal of Finance* June: 799-819.

Pritchard, R.E. and T.J. Hindelang. 1980. *The Lease/Buy Decision.* New York: Amacon, A Division of American Management Association.

Rosen, H. (ed.) 1994. *Leasing Law in the European Union.* London: Euromoney Books.

Sartoris, W.L. and R.S. Paul. 1973. Lease evaluation: another capital budgeting decision. *Financial Management* Summer: 46-52.

Shapiro, A.C. 1991. *Foundations of Multinational Finance Management.* Boston: Allyn and Bacon.

Sykes, A. 1976. The lease-buy decision: a survey of current practice in 202 companies. In *Management Survey Report.* London: British Institute of Management.

9 International leasing analysis: double-dip issue

Double-dip leasing

One of the main advantages of cross-border leasing is the tax savings through structuring double-dip deals in which both the lessor and lessee are qualified in their own tax system as the owner for tax purposes given to the leased asset. In principle, double-dip deals are based on 'dual ownership' thereby requiring that the lessor, according to the laws and practices in its jurisdiction, 'owns' the leased asset for tax purposes, and that the lessee, too, 'owns' the leased asset according to its (different) jurisdiction, both thereby being entitled to claim the tax benefits available to the owner of the asset according to the respective jurisdiction. This chapter will mainly examine the financial advantages of double-tip leasing with the application of the NPV method. It is not the intention of this chapter to study juridical systems for structuring the deals.

A major objective of international (especially cross-border tax) leases is to reduce the overall cost of financing through utilisation by the lessor of tax depreciation allowances to reduce its taxable income. The tax savings are passed through to the lessee as a lower cost of finance. Such tax advantages may be obtained when it is possible to structure 'double-dip leasing'. In a double-dip transaction, the disparate leasing rules in two countries let both the lessor and the lessee be treated as the owner of the leased asset for tax purposes. Thus, both the lessee and the lessor are entitled to the DTS and to other possible tax credits. Normally, this kind of benefits to the lessor can be passed on to the lessee in the form of lower lease payments. However, different treatments of leases between countries may also lead to a situation where neither the lessee nor the lessor has the right to depreciate an asset for tax purposes. As a result of the asymmetrical tax treatment, equality of before-tax costs of leasing will lead to inequality of after-tax costs to a lessee.

The basic prerequisites in a double-dip lease are relatively high tax rates in the lessor's jurisdiction, liberal depreciation rules and either very flexible or very formalistic rules governing tax ownership. Both the US and Japan meet these criteria. However, the Japanese Government is currently considering a number of tax law revisions, some of which, if enacted, may considerably curtail the availability and/or reduce the attractiveness of tax benefits to leasing. Other suitable jurisdictions include France, Germany, Hong Kong, Sweden and the UK. However, leasing from these jurisdictions has, for tax or political reasons, been largely confined to equipment which is manufactured or used locally.

Each country applies different rules for determining whether the party acting as lessor under an international lease is the 'owner' of the leased asset for tax purposes and is thereby entitled to claim tax allowances. In the US and some other jurisdictions, the principal focus is on whether the lessor possesses substantially all attributes of economic ownership of the leased asset. Other jurisdictions - such as Germany - apply more formalistic property law concepts and focus primarily on the location of legal title, although these jurisdictions usually also require that the lessor have some attributes of economic ownership or, at least, that the lessee have only a minimal economic interest in the equipment. For example, ownership of legal title is essential in Japan, but the lessor is only required under current law to obtain nominal incidents of economic ownership (all that is required is that the lease will provide a return of the equity investment plus a pre-tax profit of 1% of equipment cost). Japan has detailed tax guidelines for cross-border leases and the guidelines are designed primarily to circumscribe the tax benefits available to the lessor in a cross-border lease to prevent undue tax deferral; they do not require the lessor to have a significant economic interest in the leased asset.

From the point of view of tax authorities, there is one major difference between domestic leasing and international leasing. In a domestic case, it does not really matter who is the economic owner as the relevant taxes will be paid anyway, at least insofar as both the lessor and the lessee are taxpayers having more or less the same tax and depreciation situation. This is not the case in an international lease. The tax authorities tend to examine each case very carefully in terms of ownership and tax benefits. In addition, as cross-border leases very often run for a long period of time, the tax situation in the countries concerned may change prior to the expiration of the lease. Therefore the parties usually agree in advance on who shall bear the consequences of a change of tax law or of tax practices. To this end, tax risk involved in double-dip leasing will be higher than domestic leasing. Therefore, extra cover for such a risk should be available for the party that shall bear the costs of the change in tax.

Double-dip leasing evaluation models

Although there are many ways to create a double-dip leasing deal, the following two conditions need to be met at all times:

1. *The lease into the country of a lessee must be considered as a purchase under the tax rules applicable to the lessee;*
2. *The lease out of the country of a lessor must not be considered as a sale under the tax rules applicable to the lessor.*

Under the above conditions, the disparate tax rules of the lessor's and lessee's countries let both parties be treated as the owner of leased assets for tax purposes. Thus, both the lessee and the lessor are entitled to benefits such as DTS, ITC, and other possible tax credits. Generally speaking, the major concerns in structuring double-dip leasing are, among others, tax and financial considerations as well as accounting treatments. For example, a double-dip lease can be more easily achieved if the lessee is in a country which allows depreciation for tax purposes to be claimed by the lessee as the economic owner of an asset under the lease (e.g., Austria, Germany, Japan, Mexico, New Zealand, the Netherlands or the US) and the lessor is in a country which allows depreciation for tax purposes to be claimed by the lessor as the legal owner of the same asset (e.g., Argentina, Brazil, France, Italy or Switzerland). The best known examples of double-dip transactions are the aircraft leases from the UK to airlines in the US between 1980 and 1982, and from Australia to several Far East airlines in the same period. Sometimes, "a triple dip can be achieved by arranging a lease with a Swiss lessor (always entitled to allowances), a UK lessee with a purchase option (qualifying it for the 25% depreciation allowance in the first year), and a German sublessee who satisfies German economic ownership rules (qualifying it for a depreciation deduction as well)" (Shapiro 1989, p.717).

Similar to other financial decisions, a double-dip leasing decision from the lessee's point of view should also focus on the expected incremental cash flows associated with the leasing project.

Let us first briefly discuss some cash flows involved in a double-dip leasing transaction before presenting the evaluation models. Note that a prepayment on a double-dip lease is an up-front cash payment that is very similar to the down payment typically required when the import/purchase of an asset is financed with borrowed funds. In the models below, it is assumed that, for simplicity, there is no prepayment provision in the leasing contract. With respect to ITC, it is assumed that ITC has a near-zero effect on the firm's effective marginal tax rate. The basis of this assumption is that tax shields affect the tax rate by increasing the probability of tax exhaustion. As discussed previously, a major advantage of international leasing is that it enables the lessor and the lessee to construct a double-dip formula in which both the lessor and the lessee are able to claim to be the owners of the leased asset for tax purposes. From this context, the lessee is also assumed to obtain DTS and ITC.[1] However, the amount of the lessee's DTS is different from that of the lessor, because the base of both depreciation shields (e.g., amounts of depreciation, and tax rates) is different. In developing the following model, the foreign exchange problem is also ignored for simplicity at this stage. In addition, it is also assumed that in the first model a lease displaces debt on an one-for-one basis for simplicity. This assumption will be dropped in the second model which is more complicated.

First, the value of a leasing contract under a double-dip case is defined as the advantage of leasing over normal financing. This value is presented as:[2]

$$V = 1 - PV[L_i(1-T)] + PV(D_iT) + PV(K_dTW_i) \qquad [9.1]$$

Where: V = the value of a lease under a double-dip case; L_i = the lease payments in period i per dollar of an asset leased; D_i = the depreciation per dollar of the leased asset's value; T = the lessee's marginal corporate income tax rate; W_i = debt displaced in period i per dollar of the asset leased, by definition: $W_i \equiv \partial Y_i/\partial A_0$ (Y_i is the total debt obligation of the lessee in period i and A_0 is the initial value of the leased asset); K_d = the firm's borrowing rate; PV = the present value of cash flows. As a first approximation, the present values may be estimated by discounting at different rates, K_1, K_2, K_3.

---

[1] In some countries, there is no ITC available. For simplicity, in our model we omit the ITC.

[2] The detail of this definition is shown at Appendix 9-A to this chapter. The difference of this formula from a non double-dip lease is the sign of $PV(D_iT)$.

$$V = 1 - \sum_{i=1}^{n} \frac{L_i(1-T)}{(1+K_1)^i} + \sum_{i=1}^{n} \frac{D_iT}{(1+K_2)^i} + \sum_{i=1}^{n} \frac{K_dTW_i}{(1+K_3)^i} \qquad [9.2]$$

As Schall (1974), Herst (1984) and others have emphasised, each distinct cash flow stream should be discounted at a different rate. In this section, however, for simplicity, it is assumed that the streams of the lease payments and tax shields have the same risk characteristics as the stream of interest and principal payments on the lessee's debt. Therefore, $K_1 = K_2 = K_3 = K_d$. Then Eq.[9.2] is changed as:

$$V = 1 - \sum_{i=1}^{n} \frac{L_i(1-T)}{(1+K_d)^i} + \sum_{i=1}^{n} \frac{D_iT}{(1+K_d)^i} + \sum_{i=1}^{n} \frac{K_dTW_i}{(1+K_d)^i} \qquad [9.3]$$

Let's turn to the debt constraint of the lessee. As already presented by Myers, *et al.* (1976), the debt constraint of the lessee is given by:

$$Y_i + \sum_{\tau=i+1}^{n} \frac{L_iA_0}{(1+K_d)^{\tau-i}} = \Psi_i + \sum_{\tau=i+1}^{\infty} \frac{S_i + K_dTY_\tau}{(1+K_d)^{\tau-i}} + \sum_{\tau=i+1}^{n} \frac{TL_iA_0}{(1+K_d)^{\tau-i}} \qquad [9.4]$$

Where: A_0 = the initial value of the leased asset; K_d = the lessee's borrowing rate; L_i = the lease payments in period i per dollar of an asset leased; n = the lease term; S_i = the lessee's total tax shield due to book depreciation on all assets owned in period i; T = the lessee's marginal corporate income tax; Y_i = the aggregate debt outstanding in period i, $i = 0.1,...n$; Ψ_I = optimal borrowing for the firm in period i excluding any contribution to debt capacity made by depreciation and interest tax shields.

Now, calculate V, the value of the leasing contract. In period n, the lease expires, $W_n = 0$ and $V_n = 0$. In period $n-1$, from Eq.[9.4] we know:

$$Y_{n-1} + \frac{L_nA_0}{(1+K_d)} = \Psi_{n-1} + \frac{S_n}{(1+K_d)} + \frac{K_dTY_{n-1}}{(1+K_d)} + \frac{TL_nA_0}{(1+K_d)} \qquad [9.5]$$

For simplicity, let us drop variables depending on Y_i and S_i for $i > n$. Also, it determines that the marginal amount of debt displaced by the lease by way of differentiating with respect to A_0. Note $\partial \Psi_{n-1}/\partial A_0 = 0$, and $\partial S_n/\partial A_0 = D_n T$ since by definition $S_n = D_n T A_0$.

$$W_{n-1} \equiv \partial Y_{n-1}/\partial A_0 = \frac{TD_n}{1 + K_d} - \frac{L_n(1-T)}{1 + K_d} + \frac{K_d T W_{n-1}}{1 + K_d} \qquad [9.6]$$

Solving from Eq.[9.6] for W_{n-1},

$$W_{n-1} = \frac{TD_n - L_n(1-T)}{1 + K_d - K_d T} \qquad [9.7]$$

Now, turn to V_{n-1}, the value of the lease liability in period $n-1$. From Eq.[9.3],

$$V_{n-1} = \frac{TD_n - L_n(1-T)}{1 + K_d} + \frac{K_d T W_{n-1}}{1 + K_d} \qquad [9.8]$$

Note that $V_{n-1} = W_{n-1}$. Substituting for W_{n-1} and simplifying

$$V_{n-1} = \frac{TD_n - L_n(1-T)}{1 + K_d - K_d T} \qquad [9.9]$$

The analysis for the period $i = n-2$ is somewhat different, since W_{n-2} and V_{n2} are the explicit functions of W_{n-1} and V_{n-1}. The debt constraint is:

$$Y_{n-2} + \frac{L_{n-1}A_0}{(1+K_d)} = \Psi_{n-2} + \frac{S_{n-1}}{(1+K_d)} + \frac{K_d T Y_{n-2}}{(1+K_d)} + \frac{TL_{n-1}A_0}{(1+K_d)} + \frac{V_{n-1}A_0}{(1+K_d)}$$

$$[9.10]$$

Again differentiating and simplifying

$$W_{n-2} = \frac{TD_{n-1} - L_{n-1}(1-T) + V_{n-1}}{1 + K_d + K_d T} \qquad [9.11]$$

V_{n-2} is given by:

$$V_{n-2} = \frac{TD_{n-1} - L_{n-1}(1-T) + V_{n-1}}{1 + K_d} + \frac{K_d T W_{n-2}}{1 + K_d} \qquad [9.12]$$

Substituting for W_{n-2} and simplifying

$$V_{n-2} = \frac{TD_{n-1} - L_{n-1}(1-T) + V_{n-1}}{1 + K_d - K_d T} \qquad [9.13]$$

Obviously, this reasoning repeats for the periods, *n-3, n-4*, etc. In general, the following formula is held:

$$V_i = W_i = \frac{TD_{i+1} - L_{i+1}(1-T) + V_{i+1}}{1 + K_d - K_d T} \qquad [9.14]$$

For the period *i = 0*, it should recognise the funds provide by the lease (+1). In this case, $W_0 = V_0 - 1$,

$$V_0 = 1 + \frac{TD_1 - L_1(1-T) + V_1}{1 + K_d - K_d T} \qquad [9.15]$$

Now substituting for V_1:

$$V_0 = 1 + \frac{TD_1 - L_1(1-T)}{1 + K_d - K_d T} + \frac{TD_2 - L_2(1-T) + V_2}{(1 + K_d - K_d T)^2} \qquad [9.16]$$

By successive substitution, the V_i's drop out and finally obtain

$$V = 1 + \sum_{i=1}^{n} \frac{TD_i - L_i(1-T)}{1 + K_d - K_dT} = 1 - \sum_{i=1}^{n} \frac{L_i(1-T) - D_iT}{(1+K^*)^i} \qquad [9.17]$$

Where $K^* = K_d(1-T)$. This is a basic double-dip lease valuation formula. To employ it, a lessee needs only to know the schedule of the lease payments, the asset tax depreciation schedule, the corporation borrowing rate and the firm marginal tax rate. Clearly, this formula is different from the model developed by Myers, *et al.* (1976). The difference appears in the signs of D_iT. A double-dip lease enables the lessee to claim the DTS. As a result, the DTS is added to the value of the lease.

In the above model, it is assumed that the lessee borrows 100 per cent of the tax shields created by interest payments, the lease payments and depreciation. Also, it is assumed that a debt is perfectly (i.e., 100 per cent) replaced by a lease. Now, these assumptions are released in order to include a more practical situation. Let λ stand for the proportion of debt replaced by the lease,[3] and γ stand for the proportion of the tax shields that the lessee borrows against. In this new case, the value of a double-dip lease is formed in Eq.[9.18]:[4]

$$V = 1 - \sum_{i=1}^{n} \frac{L_i(1-T) - TD_i}{(1 + K_d - \gamma K_dT)^i} + \sum_{i=0}^{n-1} \sum_{\tau=i+1}^{n} \frac{K_dTL_\tau(\gamma - \lambda)}{(1+K_d-\gamma K_dT)^{i+1}(1+K_d)^{\tau-i}}$$

$$[9.18]$$

Conclusion

This chapter specially discusses double-dip leasing and its financial evaluation. Double-dip deals are based on 'dual ownership' thereby requiring that the lessor 'owns' the leased asset for tax purposes, and that the lessee, too, 'owns' the leased asset according to its jurisdiction, both thereby being entitled to claim the tax benefits available to the owner of the asset. This chapter examines the financial advantages of double-dip leasing with the

---

[3] It is not necessary that $0 \le \lambda \le 1$.
[4] The derivation process is similar to the above case. The detail of the derivation is shown in Appendix 9-B.

application of the NPV method. A model measuring the value of a double-dip lease has been developed.

It should be aware of that there is an increasing difficulty to design a double-dip deal as most tax authorities recently take extraordinary measures to prevent the double-tax advantages in international leasing. Accordingly, risk involved in the deal may be quite high if the tax rules are changed during the lease term. Both the difficulty and risk should be considered for an ILC to plan its strategies. In addition, there is an increasing call for the harmonisation of tax and accounting rules, as a result the opportunity for structuring double-dip will be difficult to find. However, some opportunity may be available between western developed countries and east European countries as countries in eastern Europe are encouraged to engage in the leasing of capital assets by providing tax incentives including the tax available to double-dip leasing.

Reference

Herst, A.C.C. 1984. *Lease or Purchase: Theory and Practice.* Massachusetts: Kluwer-Nijhoff Publishing.

Myers, S.C., D.A. Dill and A.J. Bautista. 1976. Valuation of financial lease contracts. *Journal of Finance* June: 799-819.

Schall, L.D. 1974. The lease-or-buy and asset acquisition decisions. *Journal of Finance* September: 1203-14.

Shapiro, A.C. 1989. *Multinational Financial Management.* Boston: Allyn and Bacon.

Appendix 9-A Definition of the value of a double-dip lease

Let X_j be the value invested in investment project j ($j = 1,2,....,J$), Y_i be the aggregate debt outstanding in period i, and Z_j be the amount of lease financing obtained for project j. Also assume that other factors such as foreign exchange and dividend policy are irrelevant in the analysis at this stage. Obviously, the current market value of a firm (M) is the function of X_j, Y_i and Z_j. That is $M = M(X_j, Y_i, Z_j)$. If the value additivity principle holds, there appears the following linear function.

$$M = \sum_{j=1}^{J} X_j \theta_j + \sum_{i=0}^{n-1} Y_i \varphi_i + \sum_{j=1}^{J} Z_j \omega_j \qquad \text{[9.1A]}$$

The ultimate objective of financing decisions is to maximise M.

$$\text{Max } M = \sum_{j=1}^{J} X_j \theta_j + \sum_{i=0}^{n-1} Y_i \varphi_i + \sum_{j=1}^{J} Z_j \omega_j$$

Subject to:

$$\Lambda^1{}_i = Y_i - g_i(X_j, Z_j) \leq 0$$

$$\Lambda^2{}_j = X_j - X_j(\text{Max}) \leq 0$$

$$\Lambda^3{}_j = Z_j - X_j \leq 0 \qquad \text{[9.2A]}$$

Where: θ_j = the present values of the after-tax cash flows associated with X_j; φ_I = the present values of the after-tax cash flows associated with Y_i; ω_j = the present values of the after-tax cash flows associated with Z_j; g_i = the firm debt capacity in period i, and is a function of the X_j's and Z_j's; $\Lambda^1{}_I$ = a constraint that debt in any period must be less than the debt capacity; $\Lambda^2{}_j$ = a constraint that the firm is limited to a certain maximum investment in each project; $\Lambda^3{}_j$ = a constraint that an asset which is not a part of the firm's investment plan cannot be leased.

Let's consider the Kuhn-Tucker conditions for the lease variables.

$$\theta_j + \sum_{i=0}^{n} \rho^1{}_i (\partial g_i / \partial Z_j) - \rho^3{}_j \leq 0 \qquad \text{[9.3A]}$$

Where $\rho^1{}_i$ and $\rho^3{}_j$ are the shadow prices for $\Lambda^1{}_i$ and $\Lambda^3{}_j$ respectively. If the lease of asset j is worthwhile it will be in the optimal solution. $\rho^3{}_j$ will be positive and equal to sum of the first two terms on the left hand side of Eq.[9.3A]. If it is not included, these two terms will have a negative sum. Therefore, the lease is worthwhile only if

$$\theta_j + \sum_{i=0}^{n} \rho^1{}_i (\partial g_i/\partial Z_j) > 0 \qquad\qquad [9.4A]$$

V_{0j}, the marginal contribution to M of leasing asset j, must equal this quantity.

$$V_{0j} = \theta_j + \sum_{i=0}^{n} \rho^1{}_i (\partial g_i/\partial Z_j) \qquad\qquad [9.5A]$$

The Kuhn-Tucker condition for debt is:

$$\varphi_i - \rho^1{}_i = 0 \qquad\qquad [9.6A]$$

Note that by definition, $\partial g_i/\partial Z_j = W_{ji}$. Substituting $\partial g_i/\partial Z_j = W_{ji}$ and $\varphi_i = \rho^1{}_i$ of Eq.[9.6A] into Eq.[9.5A], obtain:

$$V_{0j} = \theta_j + \sum_{i=0}^{n} \varphi_i W_{ji} \qquad\qquad [9.7A]$$

According to the Modigliani and Miller theory, φ_i is simply the present value of the tax shields generated by debt interest in i. Therefore, Eq.[9.7A] can further be expressed as:

$$V_{0j} = \theta_j + \sum_{i=1}^{n} \frac{K_d T W_{ji-1}}{(1 + K_3)^i} \qquad\qquad [9.8A]$$

Now θ_j is defined as the present value of the after-tax cash flows directly associated with a double-dip lease. Again substituting,

$$V_{0j} = 1 - \sum_{i=1}^{n} \frac{L_{ji}(1-T)}{(1+K_1)^i} + \sum_{i=1}^{n} \frac{D_{ji}T}{(1+K_2)^i} + \sum_{i=1}^{n} \frac{K_d T W_i}{(1+K_3)^i} \qquad\qquad [9.9A]$$

Eq.[9.9A] can be simply expressed as:

$$V = 1 - PV[L_i(1-T)] + PV(D_iT) + PV(K_dTW_i) \qquad [9.10A]$$

Appendix 9-B   Model of the value of a complicated double-dip lease

Incorporating λ and γ into the debt constraint of the lessee, Eq.[9.5] can be rewritten:

$$Y_i + \lambda \sum_{\tau=i+1}^{n} \frac{L_iA_0}{(1+K_d)^{\tau-i}} = \Psi_i + \gamma[\sum_{\tau=i+1}^{\infty} \frac{S_i + K_dTY_\tau}{(1+K_d)^{t-i}} + \sum_{\tau=i+1}^{n} \frac{TL_iA_0}{(1+K_d)^{\tau-i}} \qquad [9.1B]$$

Let us differentiate Y_{n-1} with respect to A_0 and solve for W_{n-1}:

$$W_{n-1} \equiv \partial Y_{n-1}/\partial A_0 = \frac{\gamma TD_n - L_n(\lambda-\gamma T)}{1 + K_d - \gamma K_dT} \qquad [9.2B]$$

Now, turn to V_{n-1}. From Eq.[9.8] and get:

$$V_{n-1} = \frac{TD_n - L_n(1-T)}{1 + K_d} + \frac{K_dTW_{n-1}}{1 + K_d} \qquad [9.3B]$$

Substituting for W_{n-1} and simplifying

$$V_{n-1} = \frac{TD_n - L_n(1-T)}{1 + K_d - \gamma K_dT} + \frac{L_nK_dT(\gamma-\lambda)}{(1+K_d)(1+K_d-\gamma K_dT)} \qquad [9.4B]$$

Let's turn to the analysis for $i = n-2$. Similarly,

$$Y_{n-2} + \lambda \frac{L_{n-1}A_0}{(1+K_d)} = \Psi_{n-2} + \gamma[\frac{S_{n-1}+K_dTY_{n-2}}{(1+K_d)} + \frac{TL_{n-1}A_0}{(1+K_d)}] + \frac{V_{n-1}A_0}{(1+K_d)}$$

$$[9.5B]$$

Differentiating Y_{n-2} with respect to A_0 and solving for W_{n-2}.

$$W_{n-2} \equiv \partial Y_{n-2}/\partial A_0 = \frac{\gamma TD_{n-1} - L_{n-1}(\lambda-\gamma T) + W_{n-1}}{1 + K_d - \gamma K_d T} \qquad [9.6B]$$

Substituting Eq.[9.2B] into Eq.[9.6B] and then substituting Eq.[9.6B] into the expression for V_{n-2} and simplifying:

$$V_{n-2} = \frac{TD_{n-1} - L_{n-1}(1-T) + V_{n-1}}{1 + K_d - \gamma K_d T} + \sum_{\tau=n-1}^{n} \frac{L_\tau K_d T(\gamma-\lambda)}{(1+K_d-\gamma K_d T)(1+K_d)^{\tau-n-2}} \qquad [9.7B]$$

Clearly, this reasoning repeats and in general (except for $i = 0$):

$$V_i = \frac{TD_{i+1} - L_{i+1}(1-T) + V_{i+1}}{1 + K_d - \gamma K_d T} + \sum_{\tau=i+1}^{n} \frac{L_\tau K_d T(\gamma-\lambda)}{(1+K_d-\gamma K_d T)(1+K_d)^{\tau-i}} \qquad [9.8B]$$

For $i = 0$,

$$V_0 = 1 + \frac{TD_1 - L_1(1-T) + V_1}{1 + K_d - \gamma K_d T} + \sum_{\tau=1}^{n} \frac{L_\tau K_d T(\gamma-\lambda)}{(1+K_d-\gamma K_d T)(1+K_d)^{\tau}} \qquad [9.9B]$$

By successive substitution, $V_1, V_2, ..., V_{n-1}$ are eliminated to obtain:

$$V_0 = 1 - \sum_{i=1}^{n} \frac{L_i(1-T) - TD_i}{1 + K_d - \gamma K_d T} + \sum_{i=0}^{n-1} \sum_{\tau=i+1}^{n} \frac{L_\tau K_d T(\gamma-\lambda)}{(1+K_d-\gamma K_d T)(1+K_d)^{\tau-i}} \qquad [9.10B]$$

10 Lessees: strategy and decision of international leasing

Why do firms lease overseas?

As previously discussed, international leasing is an important financing source which attracts many firms in many countries. Why does a firm take a lease rather than use other alternatives (e.g., buy or borrow) to obtain the use of an asset? Why do firms lease overseas rather than domestically? The first question has been discussed by among others Clark (1978), Pritchard and Hindelang (1980), Erickson (1987), Glass in Clark (1991), and Riahi-Belkaoui (1998). Riahi-Belkaoui (1998) identifies the advantages of leasing as "shifting the risks of ownership, avoidance of restrictions associated with debt, effect on cash borrowing capacity, and tax advantages".

Generally, the reasons why leasing is chosen differs considerably from lessee to lessee. Leasing may occur whenever there are differences between firms in their tax position, so that different tax rules applied to different firms may also provide an incentive for tax transfer via leasing (Edwards and Mayer 1991, p.192). Under conditions where firms (insiders) have more information than investors (outsiders), leasing may offer investors an opportunity to monitor inexpensively the actions of the better informed insiders (Torre 1990). Leasing may also have lower associated bankruptcy costs relative to secured debt, and is a preferred financial options for firms with a higher potential for financial distress or bankruptcy (Krishnan and Moyer 1994). Other factors (e.g., size of firm, type of industry, growth rate of firm and type of asset) may have different influences on the extent of the use of leasing (Adams and Hardwick 1998). For example, some empirical findings show that the use of leasing increases as a firm's turnover increases.

However, "this does not imply that these positive aspects of leasing will be of importance in every conceivable situation. The advantages and the disadvantages of leasing are mainly determined by the conditions of a lease contract and by the financing alternatives open to a firm's management" (Herst 1984, p.209).

From an international perspective, leasing may offer some additional advantages. For example, leasing finance may be more readily obtainable overseas. A lessee may be exempt from taxation upon its income in its own jurisdiction and may therefore allow a lessor in another jurisdiction to obtain benefits associated with the asset ownership. These benefits may be shared with the lessee. International leasing may be arranged so as to provide for double-dip or triple-dip of taxation deductions or other investment incentives as discussed in Chapter 9.

The advantages of international leasing as a form of international financing stem from two sources: reduction in taxes and lower financing costs. Many large international leasing transactions provide both elements. The main advantages of international leasing are summarised as follows:

1. It may be the cheapest (or only) option of obtaining the use of assets due to import (or export) controls or the existence of patent rights or another form of monopolistic constraint on the flow of the asset. Leasing of the asset may provide the possibility of avoiding import duties which can be as high as twenty percent of the asset's cost (Isom and Amembal 1982).

2. It may offer an additional foreign source of finance and extend the range of methods of financing the acquisition of assets. By international leasing, the use of an asset is obtained without domestic capital outlay. Many companies, in particular MNCs adopt a mixed financing strategy with the leasing of some of the facilities which they employ simultaneously to finance their capital investments. Especially, in order to reduce the balance of payments deficits, the governments of debt-crisis countries may restrict the amount of local or foreign borrowing by firms and consequently encourage them to take international leasing.

3. It may provide lessees worldwide with a steady supply of long- or medium-term financing during periods of credit scarcity and interest-rate volatility. The service has proved to be invaluable to many borrowers in recent years, at a time when government deficits and tight monetary policies have crowded out many firms from the more traditional term credit markets. In some countries, leasing from overseas is very often the only form of medium-term financing as there may be no other capital market instruments available.

4. It may offer tax advantages. International leasing opens up many tax planning opportunities and can substantially reduce the cost of financing. For example, double-dip leasing provides an opportunity for both the lessee and the lessor to be treated as the "owner" of leased assets for tax purposes and thereby gaining tax benefits (Shapiro 1989).
5. It may provide investors the diversification benefits. Modern portfolio theory implies that an investor can improve risk vs. return performance by holding an internationally diversified portfolio of securities as compared with a domestically diversified portfolio. International leasing provides investors and lessees more opportunities to diversify their portfolios.
6. It may reduce political risk of a lessee. International leasing may be preferable where a lessee is located in an area of political instability since ownership of the assets may be kept outside that area.
7. It may be used to take advantage of accounting or legal differences. There are countries which treat a lease transaction strictly in accordance with its legal form (e.g., in Sweden, Italy). If legal ownership of the asset remains with the lessor, the lessor will show the asset in its accounts and will depreciate it for tax purposes, and accept the legal obligations and privileges associated with ownership of the asset. There are also countries which adopt the approach of "substance over form" and, in the case of a finance lease, where the lessee has economic ownership of the asset, the lessee will show the asset in its accounts and depreciate it for tax purposes, notwithstanding the fact that legal ownership remains with the lessor (e.g., US, the Netherlands, Germany). In this case, international leasing may be used to take advantage of the differences of accounting or legal treatments between the countries to satisfy the firm's objectives (e.g., depreciation tax savings, or off-balance sheet).
8. It may lower other costs of acquiring the use of assets (e.g., research and search costs). Particularly, international leasing may enable the user of an asset to avoid overseas search and contracting costs associated with buying and selling the asset under the buying option.

Following the growing expansion of leasing since the 1997s, there are considerable studies focusing on 1) lease or buy/borrow choice of a firm (among others, Levy and Sarnat 1979; Herst 1984; Steele 1984; Schall 1987; Bierman 1988; Drury 1989; Holmes 1991; Lewis and Schallheim 1992; and Krishnan and Moyer 1994); 2) the impact of leasing financing decisions on firm's value and taxes (among others, Miller and Upton 1976; Heaton 1986; Franks and Hodges 1987; Brick, *et al.* 1987; Loewenstein and McClure

1988; Bayless and Diltz 1990; Edwards and Mayer 1991; and Gutman and Yagil 1994), and the determinants of the leasing policy/decision (e.g., Smith and Wakeman 1985; Adams and Hardwick 1998; Waring 1995). However, as criticised by Cason (1987), many recurring actual business situations are not really covered in these studies. For example, none of them seems to cover filling a projected long-term need with a series of back-to-back short-term leases. Uncertainty of the lessee's revenue stream is also ignored, and operating leases are not addressed as a possible part of a larger economic (financial) evaluation (Cason 1987, p.14). Especially, international leasing has generally been ignored (exceptions include, Parrish 1983; Meidan 1984; Thompson 1990; and Gao 1994).

Strategies and decisions of a lessee

It is well recognised that leasing is one of several options of acquiring the use of an asset. Options include: 1) producing the assets/equipment; 2) leasing the asset either domestically or internationally; 3) borrowing to purchase the asset; 4) purchasing the asset using a firm's available funds; or 5) purchasing the "used" asset. Each alternative has its own advantages, and accordingly there are different strategies and decisions, and impacts on a firm's value.[1] Moreover, other options are also available to the lessee or the user of assets in both an international and a domestic setting: among others financial leasing, operating leasing, sale-and-leaseback, leasing versus producing, leasing versus purchase/borrowing, and overseas leasing versus import. In the literature there are a lot of discussions on domestic leasing decision-making. However, very few studies are specifically addressed to the leasing decisions and strategies in an international setting.

For a firm to consider the use of a lease, it is necessary to first examine the firm's capital structure as a lease will alter the existing level of financial leverage. Probably no topic in the finance literature has received more attention than that of capital structure.[2] The main result of the well-known papers by Modigliani and Miller (1958) and Miller and Modigliani (1961) is that, for a given investment policy in the absence of taxation and bankruptcy, corporate financial policy is irrelevant: the owners of a firm are indifferent to

---

[1] At least, decision makers have to measure the costs of every alternative, to compare the costs between these alternatives and to choose the alternative with the lowest cost.

[2] See the surveys by Masulis (1988), and Harris and Raviv (1991).

the debt-to-equity ratio. This is equivalent to that a firm cannot change the total value of its shares just by splitting the cash flows into different streams. A firm's value is determined by its underlying real assets and not by the shares it issues. As a consequence investment decisions and financing decisions are independent of each other.[3] However, corporate tax provides a strong incentive to debt-finance because interest payments are generally deductible from earnings before taxes. Also, different taxes imposed on interest income, dividends, and capital gains, as well as different individual (shareholders and bondholders) tax positions provide some other incentives to debt/equity-finance. Empirical studies show that the capital structure of a firm is related to the firm's value and the firm's choice of leasing or other forms of financing in the acquisition of the use of assets has financial impact on the firm's value (Bayless and Diltz, 1986; Lewis and Schallheim, 1992). Moreover, market imperfections arising from government intervention, transaction costs etc. usually lead to an optimal financial policy, as well as an optimal capital structure. Also, a firm may have a set of debt-equity or debt-asset ratios, not just a single one, which is consistent with value maximisation (Lewis 1990).[4] The case study by Rutterford (1988) shows that Japanese firms appear to rely most heavily on debt finance, where the US and UK firms show the greatest use of equity financing. French and German firms have leverage ratios somewhere between the US/UK and Japanese extremes. As a consequence, Japanese firms are more likely to lease than firms from other countries, other things being equal. This is because lease finance is a very important part of debt finance. We know from Chapter 1 that the Japanese leasing industry currently is the most active one in the world, and the Japanese leasing market is one of the world largest leasing markets.

In general, the evaluation of international leasing by a lessee is a complex decision process that involves an assessment of a multitude of often conflicting factors, both economic and non-economic. On the one hand, the fundamental theoretical notion underlying the economic rationale is that of maximising the discounted cash flows of a leasing project. This requires that all potential impacts of a project are quantified in cash flow terms. On the

---

[3] This could be a theoretical reason why many firms separate their asset acquisition decision from the financing (e.g., leasing) policy.

[4] Particularly, from a long-run perspective the capital structure of a firm is dynamic. On the one hand, the debt ratio of a firm is changing associated with the firm's financial strategies and operations. On the other hand, within the same debt-equity ratio the proportion of the debt elements (e.g., long-term loan, short-term borrowing and financial leasing) is also changing over time.

other hand, the impact of many factors such as political risk, market growth, foreign attitudes towards leasing and cultural variables etc. that cannot be fully quantified in cash flow terms have to be taken into account in decision-making.[5]

Noticeably, some studies on leasing put much emphasis on sophisticated computing techniques to deal with evaluation of a financial lease (e.g., Steele 1984; Bayless and Diltz 1990). This narrow focus has increasingly been criticised (e.g., Cason 1987). For example, the existing models on analytical techniques, with its over simplified assumptions or too complicated assumptions,[6] is inapplicable in practice.

The lease vs. make decision

Most studies in the literature analyse the lease vs. purchase decision, and the lease vs. borrowing decision. No one has so far paid attention to the lease vs. make decision. It is unclear why leasing an asset should directly compare with purchase, rather than producing or making it. It is argued that the lease vs. make, lease vs. purchase, lease vs. borrowing decision should have the same place in decision-making related to the acquisition of the **use** of an asset. In terms of the use of an asset, there should be no difference whether the asset is leased, made, or purchased, although those alternatives may have different costs and economic impacts on the firm's value. If a firm has the capacity, ability and economical advantages to produce an asset, the firm will of course produce the asset itself, rather than lease or buy it. In other words, if the firm wants to obtain the use of an asset and the firm has capacity and economically advantages to produce the asset, why should the firm consider the benefits of leasing or borrowing to buy the asset, rather than to produce it?

Almost every firm at one time or another is confronted by the problem of choosing between the make or lease and buy either domestically or overseas of the required asset. The decision to make, buy, or lease an asset depends on many factors such as technological feasibility, costs and financial advantages. For instance, technology, quality or secrecy may preclude a firm utilising the services of an outside supplier even when the profitability calculation

---

[5] Partially in recognition of this phenomenon, a separate body of literature has emerged, stressing the importance of non-economic and strategic factors in evaluating a leasing contract (for example, Flath 1980; Barnard 1985; and Loewenstein and McClure 1986).

[6] Many models derived from econometrics, mathematics, and statistics have recently been developed grounding on very complicated assumptions.

indicates that leasing or purchase is the preferred alternative. Usually, the attention is focused on the quantitative analysis of the very large and important subset of decisions in which both the make and lease/buy alternative are technically feasible. Under these circumstances, the make or lease/buy decision, like any other decisions, should base on a comparison of present values of the cash flows generated by the three alternatives with the criteria of maximisation of net present value (NPV) of the project.

The lease payments decision

As discussed previously, the currency for lease payments is also a very important factor in leasing decision-making. Normally, exchange risk is nondiversifiable and substantially contributes to the overall risk of a firm's portfolio. With respect to lease payments, a lessee is subject to a variety of choices under the principle of maximising the shareholders' value: 1) the lessee may make all payments as promised; 2) the lessee may make a number of the lease payments as promised, make a few late payments, and then continue payments as promised; 3) the lessee may make several lease payments as promised, miss a few, and then pay off the lease; 4) the lessee may make a few payments as promised and then default on the contract (of course it has to pay penalty for the default, or go to bankruptcy), and so on. These choice may not be free and may involve legal problems. Every alternative has its own impact on the firm's market price.

The operating leasing decision

There are not so many discussions on the operating leasing in the finance literature (Gao 1998). Imhoff, *et al.* (1997) examine the impact of constructive capitalisation of operating leases on both operating income and net income from an accounting point of view. Unlike straight financial leases, operating leases may be cancelled at the option of the lessee. From the lessee's point of view, expenses under an operating lease transaction are usually variable cost (rather than fixed) because the lease contract may be terminated (sometimes requiring a penalty) and the leased asset can be returned if economic conditions become unfavourable. The advantages to the lessee therefore include risk reduction, the benefits of the lessor's specialist skill and economies of scale in purchasing, servicing arrangements and advantageous rental structures as a result of the lessor taking account of the residual value of the asset.

According to Imhoff, *et al.* (1997), operating leasing has gained increased popularity in recent years because it provides a source of off-balance sheet financing, in the US, for example, and usually does not transfer ownership of the asset to the lessee at the end of the lease term. The advantages of non-ownership to the lessee include the elimination of residual risk. That is particularly useful in high-tech assets where obsolescence is rapid. The asset is also off-balance sheet, which appeals to companies with high debt ratios. Under a standard international operating lease, the lessee makes periodic rental payments in a contracted currency, but may terminate the lease by suspending to make the payments and returning the asset to the foreign lessor. In some cases (e.g., aircraft leasing, high-tech equipment leasing), the right to sublease contracted in a lease may grant the lessee an opportunity to obtain highest-and best-use returns from the asset (by subleasing in the market) and using these returns to service the underlying primary lease. Sometimes, a purchase option involved in an operating lease also implicitly provides the lessee with the right to terminate the lease whenever the purchase option can be exercised. In addition, international operating leasing may offer chances for the lessee to diminish foreign exchange risks.

Strategically, if the user of an asset is highly uncertain about how long a lease will provide the asset's highest-and-best-use, it may be desirable to include in the lease a cancellation, sublease or purchase option. Although the foreign lessor will charge for these options, benefits provided to the user may exceed the charge for the options imposed by the lessor. Normally, the foreign lessor and lessee can negotiate a cancellation option or its equivalent if there are likely future situations in which the value of the asset to parties other than the lessee significantly exceeds the value to the lessee. Moreover, if the asset is held for only a short period of time, there is a greater likelihood of some salvage value. If the asset has become technologically obsolete, the salvage value is likely to be relatively small. The uncertainty of the salvage value may lead the lessee to select operating leasing in practice.

International financial leasing decision and strategy

Decision procedure

International financial leasing is considered as a source of finance. Financial leasing is for a long term, provides for full payout and is not cancellable without penalty. Financial leasing is usually perceived in the theoretical literature as a standardised type of financial instrument that is economically equivalent to other methods of acquiring assets, except for its tax treatment. In other words, financial leases are just loans by another name, and are often perceived as a substitute for debt.

As mentioned previously, financial leasing asks for a simultaneous investment and financing decision and a leased asset generates both operating and financial cash flows. Under an international financial lease, the lessee is obligated to make all rental payments agreed upon under the terms of the lease. At the maturity date of the lease, the lessee may buy the leased asset at the fair market price under the purchase option provision,[7] or return the leased asset back to the foreign lessor who can release or sell the asset to a third party, or perhaps, use the asset internally.

Generally, the decision to lease assets overseas initially involves the same considerations as those in a domestic case. However, there are some unique factors that should be considered in international leasing cases including: 1) the risk of overseas capital transfers, 2) the availability of tax credits, 3) the impact of foreign tax rates, 4) the effect of foreign borrowing rates, 5) difficulties in foreign leasing arrangement, 6) differences in the domestic and foreign accounting practices, 7) the types of foreign institutions that are entitled to grant leases, and 8) differences in local banking customs and practices.

Similarly, from the lessee's point of view an international financial leasing decision focuses upon the expected incremental cash flows associated with the leasing project. The decision to lease depends upon its financial effects on the firm. The difference of the lessee's decision from a lessor's decision is that the former primarily concentrates on the financing costs of leasing with other forms of financing options in order to obtain the use of assets required, whereas the latter is mainly concerned with the return of leasing with other forms of financing the lessor could offer.

Using capital budgeting techniques within a perfect market framework, Miller and Upton (1976) analyse the financial leasing decision and find no financial advantages accrued from financial leasing. Leasing is just a window-dressing activity that generates no positive net present value. Lewellen, *et al.* (1979) and Myers, *et al.* (1976) explore whether there are risk-adjusted advantages to leasing in a world of taxation. They demonstrate that there can be a nontrivial tax advantage from leasing, where the direction of the tax

---

[7] Some countries (e.g., UK) do not allow such a purchase option in a financial lease. Otherwise, this kind of lease will be treated as a hire-purchase contract.

effect depends on the specific asset life and relevant depreciation and capitalisation rates. MacKie (1990) argues that tax shields do affect financing when they are likely to change the marginal tax rate on interest deductions.

There are also cases where non-financial considerations may tip the scales of a decision where the financial factors are finely balanced, but a satisfactory financial prospect must be in view before non-financial factors become relevant (Taylor 1982, p.7). In financial decision-making, a lessee usually concentrates on a comparison between leases and debt obligations since financial leases are equivalent to secured debt to a certain extent. However, it is also argued that lease and debt obligations can imply significantly different burdens on a firm, and consequently the total present value of the firm's debt and lease obligations may be different. This is because a lease is not a one-for-one substitute of debt.[8] In addition, a lease and debt have different risks, so that a lessee needs to neutralise financial risk in the evaluation of the lease and other financial alternatives in order to have a comparable comparison.

Following the Lessard and Shapiro (1988) decision theory, the following decision model/procedure with respect to the leasing of assets overseas is presented in Exhibition 10.1. According to Lessard and Shapiro, passive decisions logically precede active decisions. Thus, the lessee should first make a passive decision assuming that a leasing contract is a normal financial leasing transaction (i.e., in the absence of a double-dip lease) in which the lessee is unable to obtain depreciation tax savings (DTS) according to legal or taxation regulations. In this case, if the NPV of the project is positive, this project should be undertaken; if the NPV is negative, the lessee should continue the decision-making process and make an active decision considering a double-dip leasing case. If the NPV of the project under a double-dip case is still negative, then the project should definitely be rejected.[9] Whereas if the NPV in this case is positive, then the project should be undertaken.

The models that are developed in this Chapter are related to the second stage of the above procedure. They are derived from active decisions. However, practical decision-making is much more complicated. In many real cases, it is not easy to separate a passive decision from an active decision.

---

[8] Many empirical results support this point (for example, Ang and Peterson 1984, Bayless and Diltz 1986).

[9] In an extreme, the lessee may consider the possibility of structuring a triple-dip leasing deal and further make a choice decision. However, it is extremely difficult to structure a triple-dip leasing deal. But, the process of decision making is the same as a double-dip case. For simplicity, we do not include the triple-dip decision process in the exhibition.

Sometimes there may be more than one positive NPV basing on active decision making as a number of double-dip deals are available. In this case, the lessees should try to select one with the largest positive NPV.

Exhibition 10.1 International leasing decision-making procedure by a lessee

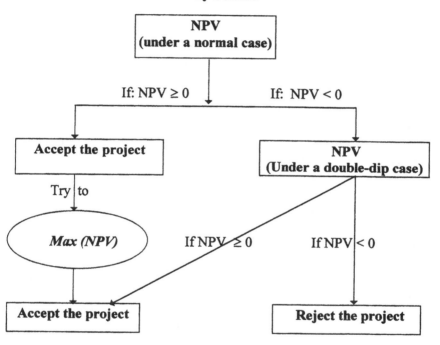

It is often questioned whether the lessor in a double-dip leasing transaction has to charge more lease payments or require a higher rate of return due to the lessee's ability of claiming DTS. Is the lessor going to share the lessee's DTS? The answers to these questions will depend on the bargaining power, competition, risk and many other factors. In theory, there should be no such a problem for the cases, because the market discounted cash flows have already considered the factors as discount rates used to calculate the present value of cash flows reflects the market condition consisting of the bargaining power, competition, risk and so on.

Evaluation models

A firm that wishes to make use of an asset may either lease it or finance the purchase price by borrowing. If the firm leases the asset either domestically or internationally, it saves the purchase price but it usually loses the DTS under a normal financial lease in some countries and incurs the net of tax lease payments. Generally accepted models for selecting a lease or purchase require estimation and valuation of incremental cash flows for each option.

The starting point in the decision-making process is whether the firm should first make an investment decision (i.e., asset acquisition decision basing on purchase), and then a separated financing decision. The models proposed in the literature differ with regard to the separation of these decisions. However, the survey conducted by O'Brien and Nunnally (1983) regarding the question "the firm analyses a leasing alternative only if the asset would have been profitable on a purchase basis", shows that the majority of the answers (75 per cent) support this. The similar evidence is also found in McInnes and Carleton (1982), and Drury and Braund (1989).

The models proposed in the literature differ also with regard to discount rates. The models are primarily based on the following two arguments: firstly, the discount rate for valuing a cash flow is the rate that investors in the market use to value cash flows of like risks and taxability. This is associated with the perfect market assumptions underlying discounted cash flow (present value) analysis. Such markets are characterised by competition, and the absence of transaction costs, information costs and governmental constraints on trading etc. In such markets, shareholders prefer firm's policies that maximise current equity market value, where equity market value is the discounted (using the appropriate risk-adjusted market discount rate) value of the expected future cash flows to equity holders. The use of market discount rates implies that lease arrangements with different risks require different discount rates. An asset purchase or a lease that has risk characteristics different from the rest of the firm will generally require a different discount rate than the firm's existing cost of capital. And even if all the firm's assets have identical business risk, DTS and lease rentals usually have different risk and require different discount rates than do revenues and operating expenses.[10] Second, changes in a firm's borrowing associated with leasing should be explicitly recognised in the cash flows computations. This is based

---

[10] See, for example, Bower (1973); Schall (1974); Lewellen, *et al.* (1976); Miller and Upton (1976); and Myers, *et al.* (1976).

on the assumption by the lessee of a financial obligation similar to debt, hence leasing may cause a firm to change its level of borrowing and the proportion of the firm's capitalisation derived from borrowing. Such changes affect the incremental cash flows of leasing and should therefore be taken into account.[11]

In addition, the traditional models usually assume that a lessee will pay the lease payments with the cash flows generated by the asset/equipment leased. These models isolate a leasing project from the rest of the firm's operation. I argue that a firm that makes a leasing decision should explicitly take the firm's entire operation into account. For example, it is not unusual that the lessee may borrow money to pay the lease payments in order to maintain the firm's capital structure.

Let's look at a well-known model of a lease evaluation.[12] Myers, *et al.* (1976) illustrate the costs and benefits of leasing by an analysis of the following cash flows:

1) Cash savings amounting to the dollar amount of the investment outlay, A_0, which the firm does not have to incur if it leases;

2) A cash outflow amounting to the present value of the after-tax lease payments, $PV[L_i(1-T)]$;

3) The present value of the opportunity cost of the lost depreciation tax shield, $PV[TD_i]$;

4) The present value of the change in the interest tax shield on debt that is displaced by the lease financing, $PV[T(K_dB_i)]$, where B_i is the remaining book value of debt outstanding in period i.

Putting these four terms together, Myers, *et al.* (1976) obtain an equation of evaluating a financial lease in a domestic setting (Eq.[10.1]).

$$V(\text{to lessee}) = A - PV[(1-T)L_i] - PV[TD_i] - PV[T(K_dB_i) \qquad [10.1]$$

Where V is defined as the value of the leasing contract as the advantage of leasing vs. normal financing. Further, Myers *et al.* develop a basic lease evaluation formula as follows:

---

[11] See, among others, Myers *et al.* (1976); Schall (1974); Brealey and Young (1980); Smith and Wakeman (1985) and Franks and Hodges (1987).

[12] I use different symbols in introducing the Myers *et al.* model and the Herbst model that follows, for the purpose of convenience and consistence.

$$V = 1 - \sum_{i=1}^{n} \frac{L_i(1-T) + D_iT}{(1+K^*)^i} \qquad\qquad [10.2]$$

Where: $K^* = K_d(1-T)$. In this model, the salvage value and foregone ITC are assumed to be zero to simplify the model, and operating maintenance expenses absorbed by the lessor are also assumed to be zero. Particularly, the authors assume that the lessee borrows 100 per cent of the tax shields created by interest payments, the lease payments and depreciation. Also they assume that a dollar of debt is displaced by a dollar of lease. Using the Myers *et al.* model as the starting point and assuming the lessee borrows a portion of the tax shields and a dollar of debt is not perfectly displaced by a dollar of lease, Herbst (1982) generates a model shown in Eq.[10.3].

$$V = 1 - \sum_{i=1}^{n} \frac{L_i(1-T) + TD_i}{(1 + K_d - \gamma K_dT)^i} + \sum_{i=0}^{n-1} \sum_{\tau=i+1}^{n} \frac{K_dTL_\tau(\gamma - \lambda)}{(1+K_d-\gamma K_dT)^{i+1}(1+K_d)^{\tau-i}} \ [10.3]$$

Where: L_i = The lease payments in period i (normalised by dividing by the purchase price of the asset); D_i = the normalised depreciation foregone in period i, if the asset is leased instead of purchased; K_d = the lessee's borrowing rate; T = the lessee's marginal tax rate on income; n = the life of the lease; λ = proportion of debt displaced by a dollar of the lease; γ = proportion of the tax shields the lessee borrows against.

Note that above two models are based on a domestic case in which the lessee will loss the DTS by definition. Obviously they cannot be used in an international double-dip leasing case because in double-dip leasing cases both the lessee and the foreign lessor can claim the DTS as discussed in Chapter 9.

International lease vs. import decision

Lease vs. borrow/buy decision and lease vs. import decision

A firm that wants to make use of an asset that is not available in the national market may either lease it overseas or import it directly. If the firm leases the asset, it will save the purchase price in a normal financial leasing case but lose the DTS and incur the lease payments. Generally, the international lease vs. import decision is quite similar to the lease vs. borrow or the lease vs. buy decision. Ben-Yosef (1988) already argues that the lease/buy decision should be viewed as part of the broader topic of internalisation. In the literature, the suggested solution to the lease-buy problem is to determine whether a lease provides a better financing alternative to that which would be employed if the asset were purchased. This procedure is referred to as a "net advantage to leasing (NAL)" analysis. Similarly, the lease or import choice can be approached by computing and comparing the NPV of the import purchase and lease, and then adopting the option—import or lease—with the higher NPV (the asset is rejected entirely if the NPV is negative). Proceeding in this way (or using most other approaches), it needs to compare choices with uncertainty and potentially different time spans (Schall 1987, p.19).

The lease vs. buy decision is very simple if the lessee has extended its line of credit to the limit, as borrowing costs then become excessive and may involve a shareholder's giving a personal guarantee. Leasing in this situation is much more attractive regardless of tax implications. Alternatively, if a company can arrange the required borrowing with an acceptable financing cost, the buy/lease decision becomes more difficult (Bowman 1990, p.22). Furthermore, an implication for lease-buy analysis is that the evaluation must often contend with uncertainty about the lease term as well as about the holding period under purchase (Schall 1987, p.20).

There is a variety of models in the literature regarding the lease vs. buy/borrow decision. However, Bowman (1990) criticises that many of these models determining the required rate of return on the lease and buy are usually somewhat arbitrary and most of the required income tax assumptions are over-simplified. Wolfson (1985) criticises that the risk sharing motive for shared ownership has largely escaped the attention of contributors to the lease vs. buy/purchase decision (p.160). The marginal rate of income tax is generally another area of over-simplification used in the various lease vs. buy/purchase decision models. This is because the tax rate is not a static amount, but changes depending on governmental budgets (Bowman 1990). In addition, some papers do not clearly distinct the lease vs. buy and the lease vs. borrow decision.

A leasing decision is not just a financing decision faced by the lessee, but a compound of financing, investment and tax planning decision. Precisely, the lease vs. buy/borrow decision should be regarded as a decision consisting of capital budgeting, financing, tax planning and marketing. Therefore, either the lease vs. buy decision or the lease vs. borrow decision involves the interactions among budgeting, financing, tax planning and marketing decisions. In the literature, "lease vs. buy/purchase" is used more commonly than "lease vs. borrow".

The literature in leasing reveals persistent disagreement regarding the appropriate method for the evaluation of the lease vs. buy/purchase alternatives.[13] Most of the controversy centres around the appropriate method of incorporating into the evaluation of the effects of the implicit debt financing embodied in a lease. The difficulty is caused by the fact that a lease represents a simultaneous investment and financing decision, and a leased asset generates both operating and financial cash flows. Further, the impact of a lease on the firm's financial structure as well as financial risks which are different from those generated by a regular asset acquisition should be quantified and incorporated into the evaluation.

An international lease vs. import decision model

The following model is derived from the objective of maximising the equilibrium market value of the firm with consideration of the interactions between capital budgeting decision, financing decision and other variables. In deciding whether to import (purchase) or overseas lease, it is essential that relevant data must be made comparable. A valid comparison requires recognition of the interest charge implicit in the lease payments, the exchange gains or losses due to the timing span of the cash flows between the two alternatives as well as their income tax aspects. For a cancellable lease, it is also necessary to determine the total cost of leasing for different periods of time and to estimate the probability distribution of various possible holding periods in order to determine an expected cost of leasing which can be compared validly to an import alternative. Note that the real term under a lease may also be unknown at the beginning of the transaction. Although a financial (non-cancellable) lease requires the lessee to pay rentals until the lease expires, it may be possible to negotiate cancellation before the lease expiration date.[14] The cost of such cancellation by the lessee includes the payments to the lessor for allowing early termination as well as legal expenses, negotiating costs, and any other expenses required.

---

[13] Herst (1984) presents a detailed analysis and comparison of the lease vs. purchase models.

[14] In reality, if the productivity or profitability of the asset has fallen for the lessee by significantly more than it has declined in alternative uses, a mutually satisfactory termination might be possible and be negotiated.

Also, risks involved in the two alternatives are usually not identical. The lease option, for example, commits the firm to a stream of rental payments, normally fixed in advance. Therefore, in order to neutralise the risk differential, the analysis of the import option must be made on the explicit assumption that the import is partially financed by a loan which commits the firm to a stream of fixed payments (principal and interest), thereby equating the cash flows terms of the import and lease alternatives. Otherwise, comparing the NPV of import and lease alternatives just involves us in a comparison of apples and oranges, because the two cash flows differ in a fundamental sense. The lease arrangement is like borrowing in that it commits the firm to a series of fixed rental payments. Thus, even if the lease alternative has a greater NPV, it may also expose the firm's shareholders to greater risk (Levy and Sarnat 1979, p.48).

Moreover, it should note that if the corporate tax rate is uncertain or systematically varies with the economy, or if income cannot always be found to exploit the tax shelter, risk is not neutralised.

The models relating to the international lease vs. import decision is developed as follows. First, the NPV of an import alternative *NPV(I)* is written as:

$$NPV(I) = -A^f_0 F^s + A^f_0 F^s \pi + \sum_{i=1}^{n} \frac{(1-T)R_i}{(1+K_a)^i} - \sum_{i=1}^{n} \frac{(1-T)B^i_i}{(1+K_b)^i}$$

$$+ \sum_{i=1}^{n} \frac{TD^i_i}{(1+K_c)^i} + \frac{S^i_n}{(1+K_d)^n} - G(I) \qquad [10.4]$$

Where: A^f_0 = cost of the asset in terms of a foreign currency at $i = 0$; F^s = the spot foreign exchange rate; π = the home country's investment credit rate, assuming ITC exists; T = the firm's corporate tax rate; R_i = cash flow before taxes and depreciation at period i as a consequence of the investment; B^i_i = cash outlays (e.g., insurance and property tax) at period i; D^i_i = tax allowed depreciation at period i; S^i_i = expected residual value of the imported asset in period n; $G(I)$ = other cash flows relating to the import like custom duties, stamp duties, registration taxes etc., expressed in the home currency; n = the economic useful life of the asset imported; all K= discount rates used to arrive at NPV of the cash flows.

Normally, the lease alternative is used to finance an import because of the tax advantage in writing off the lease payments instead of the depreciation. The tax advantage of the debt financing involved in the lease is not a *true* advantage since the debt financing may be obtained without the lease. In order to offset the tax advantage in the lease option due to the implicit debt financing, I define that:[15]

$$Af_0F^s = (1-T)L_0^h + \sum_{i=1}^{j} \frac{(1-T)(M_i-N_i) + N_i}{(1+K_e)^i} \qquad [10.5]$$

Where: L_0^h = the lease payment in the home currency at period $i = 0$; M_i = payment of interest and principal on the loan at period i; N_i = amortisation of loan's principle for tax purposes at the period i; j = the period of loan repayments;[16] K_e = a discount rate (or the firm's borrowing rate under the certainty of T). Incorporating Eq.[10.5] into Eq.[10.4], a formula of calculating the present value of an import alternative is obtained as follows:

$$NPV(I) = -(1-T)L_0^h + Af_0F^s\pi + \sum_{i=1}^{n} \frac{(1-T)R_i}{(1+K_a)^i} - \sum_{i=1}^{n} \frac{(1-T)B^i_i}{(1+K_b)^i}$$

$$+ \sum_{i=1}^{n} \frac{TD^i_i}{(1+K_c)^i} + \frac{S^i_n}{(1+K_d)^n} - \sum_{i=1}^{j} \frac{(1-T)(M_i-N_i) + N_i}{(1+K_e)^i} - G(I)$$

$$[10.6]$$

Secondly, the proposed lease evaluation is written as follows:

$$NPV(L) = -(1-T)L_0^h - \sum_{i=1}^{m-1} \frac{(1-T)L_i^h}{(1+K_f)^i} + \sum_{i=1}^{m} \frac{(1-T)R_i}{(1+K_g)^i} + \sum_{i=1}^{m} \frac{(1-T)B^l_i}{(1+K_h)^i}$$

---

[15] It is assumed the amount of the loan is $Af_0F^s - (1-T)L_0^h$ and it will be paid in j periods by means of equal annual payments that cover interest and principal at the interest rate at which the firm borrows.

[16] The period of loan repayment is not necessarily equal to the economic life of the asset. The lease term in the lease option will be discussed later.

$$-\sum_{i=1}^{m} \frac{TD^l_i}{(1+K_i)^i} - \frac{S^l_m}{(1+K_j)^m} - G(L) \qquad [10.7]$$

Where: $L_i{}^h$ = the lease payments at period i; F^i_i = cash outlays (e.g. insurance and property taxes) at period i that are assumed by the foreign lessor; S^l_i = expected residual value of the leased asset at the end of the lease;[17] $G(L)$ = other cash flows relating to the lease like contract fees, stamp duties, registration taxes etc., expressed in the home currency; m = the lease terms; all K = discount rates used to arrive at NPV of the cash flows.

In order to compare the two alternatives, it is further assumed: 1) the useful life of the asset imported equals the lease terms (i.e., $n = m$); 2) cash outlays (e.g., insurance cost, maintenance fee, and property taxes) are the same for two alternatives (i.e., $B^i_i = B^l_i = B_i$); 3) the expected residual value of the asset is the same regardless of whether the asset is leased or imported (i.e., $S^i_i = S^l_i = S_i$); 4) there is no difference between tax allowed deprecations (i.e., $D^i_i = D^l_i = D_i$). Now, combining Eq.[10.6] and Eq.[10.7] and re-naming discount rates in terms of numbers, the advantage of an international lease over an import option is:

$$NPV(L)-NPV(I) = -Af_0F^s\pi - \sum_{i=1}^{m-1} \frac{(1-T)L_i{}^h}{(1+K_1)^i} + \sum_{i=1}^{j} \frac{(1-T)(M_i-N_i) + N_i}{(1+K_2)^i}$$

$$+ 2\sum_{i=1}^{m} \frac{(1-T)B_i}{(1+K_3)^i} - 2\sum_{i=1}^{m} \frac{TD_i}{(1+K_4)^i} - 2\frac{S_n}{(1+K_5)^n} + [G(L)-G(I)]$$

$$[10.8]$$

Again, it is suggested to use the risk ranking method to determine the discount rates in Eq.[10.8]. However, a detailed discussion of the relations of these discount rates is beyond the scope of this book. Instead, I further consider the advantage of an international lease over an import option. In doing so, I presume that there is no investment credit available, and the total

---

[17] Note that S^i_n is not the same as S^l_m, even in the case of $n = m$. This is because the owner of the imported asset may have a different attitude/way from the lessee in using and maintaining the asset.

PV of the after-tax lease payments is equal to the total PV of the loan and interest for the alternative of import. Also, let $G(L) = G(I)$. Thus, the advantage of an international lease over an import option, Adv(L), will be simply expressed in terms of function as follows:

$$Adv(L) = f(B, TD, S)$$

It is clear that the criterion of selecting an international lease or import alternative depends mainly on variables B, TD, and S. B has a positive effect on the advantage of an international lease over import, whereas both TD and S have a negative effect on the advantage. In theory, a lessee or an importer in decision making of an international lease vs. import should concentrate on the evaluation and measurements of the costs of insurance, maintenance, property tax, the DTS, and the expected residual value of the asset.

There are a few practical issues that need to be considered as well. Customs duties are in most countries levied on goods imported in accordance with the normal customs regulations of the countries. Duty is normally payable at the point of entry before an asset is cleared for transmission to the importer. However, in the case of hire-purchase agreement the customs duties may be delayed until the date ownership of the asset is actually transferred to the lessee. In this case, the expected present value of the duties should be calculated. In some countries like Mexico assets imported under operating leases are not subject to import taxes or VAT but a bond to guarantee the return of the assets to its country of origin. In Singapore there are no customs duties or VAT levied on equipment into the country. Moreover, the tax shelter involved in either an international lease or import contract is almost completely certain in practice since it can be obtained against the income of other projects should the project in question fail to generate any taxable income. However, even in the case in which the firm suffers an overall loss, the tax claim can still be carried forward (or backward) in some countries and applied against the firm's future (or past) year taxable income. Thus the discount rate which is used to calculate the present value of the tax shield is only slightly higher than the risk-free interest rate (Levy and Sarnat 1979, p.49). In addition, the legal, tax and accounting aspects may affect the decision making relating to international leasing vs. import-purchase.

Conclusion

This chapter discusses international leasing strategies and decisions from the lessee's perspective. Apparently, the lessee must first find out the advantages of international leasing before entering any international leasing deal. The advantages of international leasing include among other: 1) it may be the cheapest (or only) procedure of obtaining the use of assets; 2) it may offer an additional foreign source of finance; 3) it may, in its various forms, provide lessees world-wide with a steady supply of long- or medium-term financing during periods of credit scarcity and interest-rate volatility; 4) it may take advantage of the tax difference between countries of a lessee and a lessor; 5) it may provide investors the diversification benefits; 6) it may reduce political risk of the lessee; 7) it may be used to take advantage of the accounting treatment; 8) it may lower other costs of acquiring the use of capital assets (e.g., custom duties, research and search costs).

International leasing decisions from a lessee's perspective consist of passive and active decisions. The major objective of decision-makers should try to minimise the expected after-tax cost of leasing and keeping risk within acceptable levels. However it should be noted that asymmetrical tax system is a most important concern in international leasing decision making. Leasing may alter a firm's optimal capital structure and affect the market value of the firm. This chapter concentrates on the strategies and decisions of a lessee, and provides decision-making models. There are many variables to consider in determining whether a particular lessor may be right for the lessee, so care must be taken in the selection of a lessor. Also, this chapter particularly look at the international lease vs. import decision, providing an evaluation model for decision-making.

Reference

Adams, M. and P. Hardwick. 1998. Determinants of the leasing decision in United Kingdom listed companies. *Applied Financial Economics* 8: 487-94.

Ang, J. and P.P. Peterson. 1984. The leasing puzzle. *Journal of Finance* September: 1055-65.

Barnard, J. 1985. Technical skills: lease or buy? *SAM Advanced Management Journal* Winter: 36-9.

Bayless, M. E. and J.D. Diltz. 1986. An empirical study of the debt displacement effects of leasing. *Financial Management* Winter: 53-60.

Bayless, M.E. and J.D. Diltz. 1990. Corporate debt, corporate taxes and leasing. *Managerial and Decision Economics* 11: 13-19.

Ben-Yosef, E. 1988. *Contractual Arrangements for the Acquisition of Capital Equipment and Machinery: Another Look At the "Lease or Buy" Decision.* PhD Dissertation, New York University.

Bierman, H. 1988. Buy versus lease with an alternative minimum tax. *Financial Management* Winter: 87-91.

Bower, R.S. 1973. Issues in lease financing. *Financial Management* Winter: 25-34.

Bowman, S. 1990. Lease or buy? *CMA Magazine* February: 22-25.

Brealey, R.A. and C.M. Young. 1980. Debt, taxes and leasing: a note. *Journal of Finance* December: 1245-50.

Brick, I.E., W. Fung and M. Subrahmanyam. 1987. Leasing and financial intermediation: comparative tax advantages. *Financial Management* Spring: 55-59.

Cason, R.L. 1987. Leasing, asset lives and uncertainty: a practitioner's comments. *Financial Management* Summer: 13-16.

Clark, T.M. 1978. *Leasing.* UK: McGraw-Hill Book Company Limited.

Clark, T.M. 1991. *Leasing Finance.* London: Euromoney Publications.

Drury, C. 1989. Evaluating the lease or purchase decision. *Managerial Finance* 15, no. 1/2: 26-38.

Drury, C. and S. Braund. 1989. A survey of UK leasing practice. *Management Accounting* April: 40-43.

Edwards, J.S.S. and C.P. Mayer. 1991. Leasing, taxes, and the cost of capital. *Journal of Public Economics* 44: 171-79.

Erickson, S.M. 1987. *The Cross Sectional Determinants of Lease Use: a Theoretical and Empirical Study.* PhD dissertation, University of Washington.

Flath, D. 1980. The economics of short-term leasing. *Economic Inquiry* April: 247-59.

Franks, J.R. and S.D. Hodges. 1987. Lease valuation when taxable earnings are a scarce resource. *Journal of Finance* September: 987-1005.

Gao, S.S. 1994. *International Leasing: Its Financial and Accounting Application.* Preston: UCL Publications.

Gao, S.S. 1998. An alternative solution to the operating lease evaluation. *Working Paper No.8,* Faculty of Business, Glasgow Caledonian University.

Gutman, E. and J. Yagil. 1994. Leasing and the US 1986 tax reform act. *Journal of Business Finance & Accounting* July: 749-761.

Harris, M. and A. Raviv. 1991. The theory of capital structure. *The Journal of Finance* 56, no. 1: 297-355.

Heaton, H. 1986. Corporate taxation and leasing. *Journal of Financial and Quantitative Analysis* September: 351-359.

Herbst, A.F. 1982. *Capital Budgeting: Theory, Quantitative Methods and Applications*. New York: Harper & Row Publisher.

Herst, A.C.C. 1984. *Lease or Purchase: Theory and Practice*. Massachusetts: Kluwer-Nijhoff Publishing.

Holmes, B.J. 1991. Lease-buy decision analysis. *International Journal of Purchasing and Materials Management* Fall: 35-40.

Imhoff, E.A., R.C. Lipe and D.W. Wright. 1997. Operating leases: income effects of constructive capitalisation. *Accounting Horizons* 11, no. 2: 12-32.

Isom, T.A. and S.P. Amembal. 1982. *The Handbook of Leasing: Techniques & Analysis*. New York: Petrocelli Books, Inc.

Krishnan, V.S. and R.C. Moyer. 1994. Bankruptcy costs and the financial leasing decision. *Financial Management* Summer: 31-42.

Lessard, D.R. and A. Shapiro. 1988. Guidelines for global financing choices. In *new Developments in International Finance*, ed. J.M. Stern and D.H. Chew. New York: Basil Blackwell Inc.: 181-93.

Levy, H. and M. Sarnat. 1979. Leasing, borrowing, and financial risk. *Financial Management* Winter: 47-54.

Lewellen, W.G., M.S. Long and J.J. McConnell. 1976. Asset leasing in competitive capital markets. *Journal of Finance* June: 787-98.

Lewis, C.M. 1990. A multiperiod theory of corporate financial policy and taxation. *Journal of Financial and Quantitative Analysis* March: 25-43.

Lewis, C.M. and J.S. Schallheim. 1992. Are debt and lease substitutes? *Journal of Financial and Quantitative Analysis* 27, no. 4: 497-511.

Loewenstein, M.A. and J.E. McClure. 1986. Managing the lease-sell decision. *Sloan Management Review* Spring: 77-82.

Loewenstein, M.A. and J.E. McClure. 1988. Taxes and financial leasing. *Quarterly Review of Economics and Business* Spring: 21-38.

MacKie, M.J. 1990. Do taxes affect corporate financing decisions? *Journal of Finance* December: 1471-93.

Masulis, R.W. 1988. *The Debt/Equity Choice*. New York: Ballinger Publishing Company.

McInnes, J.M. and W.J. Carleton. 1982. Theory, models and implementation on financial management. *Management Science* September: 957-78.

Meidan, A. 1984. Strategic problems in international leasing. *Management International Review* 24, no. 4: 36-47.

Miller, M.C. and F. Modigliani. 1961. Dividend policy, growth and the valuation of shares. *Journal of Business* October: 411-33.

Miller, M.H. and C.W. Upton. 1976. Leasing, buying, and the cost of capital services. *Journal of Finance* June: 761-786.

Modigliani, F. and M.H. Miller. 1958. The cost of capital, corporate finance and the theory of investment. *American Economic Review* June: 261-97.

Myers, S.C., D.A. Dill and A.J. Bautista. 1976. Valuation of financial lease contracts. *Journal of Finance* June: 799-819.

O'Brien, T.J. and B.H. Nunnally. 1983. A 1982 survey of corporate leasing analysis. *Financial Management* Summer: 30-6.

Parrish, K.M. 1983. International leasing. In *The International Banking Handbook*, ed. W.H. Baughn and D.R. Mandich. Homewood Illinois: Dow Jones-Irwin:173-82.

Pritchard, R.E. and T.J. Hindelang. 1980. *The Lease/Buy Decision*. New York: Amacon, A Division of American Management Association.

Riahi-Belkaoui, Ahmed. 1998. *Long-Term Leasing - Accounting, Evaluation, Consequences*. Westport, CT: Quorum Books.

Rutterford, J. 1988. An international perspective on the capital structure puzzle. In *New Developments in International Finance*, ed. J.M. Stern and D.H. Chew. New York: Basil Blackwell Inc.

Schall, L.D. 1974. The lease-or-buy and asset acquisition decisions. *Journal of Finance* September: 1203-14.

Schall, L.D. 1987. Analytic issues in lease vs. purchase decision. *Financial Management* Summer: 17-20.

Shapiro, A.C. 1989. *Multinational Financial Management*. Boston: Allyn and Bacon.

Smith, C.W. and L.M. Wakeman. 1985. Determinants of corporate leasing policy. *Journal of Finance* 40: 895-908.

Steele, A. 1984. Different equation solutions to the valuation of lease contracts. *Journal of Financial and Quantitative Analysis* September: 311-328.

Taylor, P.J. 1982. Leasing in theory and practice. *Managerial Finance* 8, no. 2: 6-14.

Thompson, A. 1990. International leasing. In *Handbook of International Financial Management*, ed. M.Z. Brooke. London: Macmillan Publishers: 284-92.

Torre, C.De.La. 1990. *Leasing, Information Asymmetries and Transaction Cost Economies: A Theoretical and Empirical Investigation*: PhD Dissertation, The University of Texas at Austin.

Waring, A. 1995. Determinants of corporate leasing policy: some UK evidence. *Journal of Industrial Affairs* 4: 19-31.

Wolfson, M.A. 1985. Tax, incentive, and risk-sharing issues in the allocation of property rights: the generalised lease-or-buy problem. *Journal of Business* 58, no. 2: 159-211.

11 Lessors: strategy and decision of international leasing

General considerations

Traditional analysis of leasing has focused almost exclusively on the problem of the lessee, the user of equipment (e.g., Levy and Sarnat 1979; Steele 1984; Loewenstein and McClure 1988; Bowman 1990; Lewis and Schallheim 1992; Grenadier 1995). Very little has been written on the lease analysis from the lessor's point of view.[1] As mentioned previously, the practice of both domestic and international leasing retains its existence primarily to numerous and significant asymmetries between lessors and lessees. For instance, a lessor and a foreign lessee may have different beliefs about the economic life of the leased asset, and different degrees of confidence with which those beliefs are held. They may also have different criteria for judging risks involved. A lessor may have different decision-making procedures and methods with respect to an international leasing project compared with a lessee.

International leasing and domestic leasing have much in common, but there are also many ways in which they differ. As a lessor's portfolios of assets and liabilities have become internationally diversified, the differences stemming from the cross border nature of leasing have become more apparent. The most obvious difficulties are those associated with differing cultural and financial traditions, and accounting practices, complicated by legal barriers, transaction costs and taxation. However, the principles of domestic and international leasing strategies and decisions are generally identical, except that

---

[1] Exceptions are Flavell and Salkin (1982), and Smith (1982).

international leasing strategy-planning and decision-making is a more complicated exercise. International leasing usually involves manipulation with more than one currency, more than one legal jurisdiction, more than one taxation system, and more than one accounting practice.

When moving leasing to an international arena, a number of factors relating to international cases may extremely inhibit and constrain the managers from the normal procedure of making domestic leasing decisions. For instance, one of the most significant considerations is the qualification of a real lease in a foreign country. A real lease in one country may not be a real lease in another country since their legal definitions may be different.

Evaluation of an international lease by the lessor is regarded in itself as an international capital budgeting problem. The decision has to depend on the factors such as the terms of the lease contract,[2] the financial credit of the foreign lessee, the assessments of political and currency risks, and so on. Smith (1982) argues that the capital budgeting problem of an international leasing project is uniquely sensitive to the simultaneous effects of tax and funding considerations as global constraints (p.346). The two basic tasks in leasing decision making from the lessor's perspective are: to develop a decision model or rule to value the risky cash flows emanating from a leasing project; and to foresee the size and risk of the incremental after tax cash flows of the project. The first task has long been the focus of the leasing finance literature (See, among others, Lewellen, *et al.* 1979; Myers, *et al.* 1976; Flavell and Salkin 1982; Loewenstein and McClure 1988; Bayless and Diltz 1990; and Edwards and Mayer 1991). This task involves answering two questions. Firstly, what is the appropriate opportunity cost of capital for the project cash flows to the lessor? Secondly, how can the interactions among investment, financing, exchange exposure, tax planning decisions be analysed? The second task is concerned with how to create high quality information on the project's expected cash flow streams and the foreign lessee's credit worthiness. Unfortunately, very few discussion on this task can be found in the literature.

More specifically, a lessor has to clarify what is meant by incremental cash flows of an international leasing project. In particular, whether the project cash flows should be incremental to the parent, subsidiary (in the case if the

---

[2] However, this is not to say that an international leasing decision to the lessor is a pure capital budgeting problem. There are many arguments on this point. It may be appropriate to say that a decision of international leasing consists of capital budgeting, financing, foreign exchange exposure, and tax planning decisions.

lessor is a subsidiary of a bank, an insurance company or other financial institutions), or both. Like domestic leasing decisions, international leasing decisions from the lessor's point of view also focus primarily upon the expected incremental cash flows. The lessor's analysis of a leasing project involves: 1) determining the net cash outlay, which is usually the invoice price of the leased asset less any investment tax credit; 2) determining the annual cash inflows in terms of a desirable currency, which consist of the lease payments minus the income taxes, the lessor's maintenance expense and insurance costs etc.; 3) estimating the residual value of the asset when the lease expires; 4) determining whether the present value of the inflows exceeds the net cost of acquiring the asset; and 5) determining the lease rate to charge the lessee in order to maximise the shareholders' wealth.

International leasing is more complicated because of certain factors peculiar to international circumstances. For example, an international leasing project may be estimated in a foreign currency to produce very considerable cash flows in a foreign territory but, because of exchange control restrictions, the bulk of these foreign cash flows may not be distributable to the lessor's shareholders. In such a case, looking at the project purely in terms of cash flows accruing in the foreign territory may not be enough to an international leasing decision. Also, trust between a lessor and a foreign lessee tends to complicate international leasing more than domestic leasing since in many cases parties to an international transaction have limited knowledge about the financial or business reputation each other. Difficulties in international leasing may also result from longer transportation and communication lines, and the possibility of misunderstanding because of language and cultural barriers.[3] In sum, the factors presented in Figure 11.1 must be taken into account in the lessor's international leasing decision-making. Decision makers must fully consider these factors and the economic consequences resulting from these factors must be reflected in the aggregate cash flows generated by a leasing project.

Strategies and models

The leasing industry is currently undergoing **internationalisation**: the expansion of leasing firms into countries outside their headquarters. The

---

[3] For example, because no proper words in Thai mean leasing and a lease, foreign leasing companies find it difficult to sign a lease contract with a Thai company directly.

strategies to undergo internationalisation vary with different countries and different lessors. For independent lessors, the major strategies are to set up subsidiaries, joint-ventures, and licenses in foreign countries, or conduct direct cross-border leasing.

> ### Figure 11.1 Factors needed to be considered by a lessor
>
> 1. Cash flows differences associated with a foreign project;[4]
> 2. Foreign exchange risks;
> 3. Different tax rates;
> 4. Withholding taxes, and interests and profits remittances;
> 5. Different accounting treatments and information assessment;
> 6. Reinvestment and remittance problems;[5]
> 7. Home/foreign duties on exported/imported assets;
> 8. Different inflation and interest rates;
> 9. Possibilities of financial gains or losses derived from internationally segmented leasing and/or capital markets;
> 10. The increased complexity of determining the terminal value of leased assets on a foreign country basis and the lack of foreign second markets;
> 11. Political risk and expropriation;[6]
> 12. Royalties of subsidiaries, management fee and other costs such as custom duties, transportation and insurance costs, consultation charges.

---

[4] The cash flows of a lease project in a foreign country may differ from parent cash flows if the leasing project is conducted by the subsidiary of an international leasing firm. For example, royalties and management fees are cash outflows from the subsidiary point of view, but cash inflows from the parent point of view. Therefore, there is a need to distinguish between project cash flows and cash flows contributed to the parent company. Also the treatment of deductions for lease payments and depreciation may differ.

[5] Full remittance of cash flows arising from a lease project may be sometimes restricted in terms of payment to the home country. Therefore there is a need for an explicit consideration of financing and remittance problems. Also, some foreign countries may require a certain proportion of profits to be reinvested locally.

[6] Phillips (1985) describes the relationship between political risks and the asset types defined by Myers (1977) which consist of two parts: "assets in place" derived from its real assets and "real options" derived from intangible assets, and concludes that firms whose values depend more on "real options" are subject to low political risk. Accordingly, for a leasing firm it may be subject to high political risk because of "assets in place".

In fact, the most prominent lessors have already established extensive networks of affiliates and subsidiaries to strengthen their position in the growing world market and more firms are entering into the game at a rapid rate.

One common strategy of a lessor involved in international leasing is to establish leasing ventures within the domestic markets of foreign countries, which could be a vehicle for international transactions if the need arose. This is generally a common feature amongst many international leasing corporations (ILCs). The main criteria and considerations used for setting up an international leasing branch network are: 1) the political stability of the country concerned; 2) the existence or otherwise of controls on foreign investment; 3) the strength of demand in the country; 4) the relative availability of other forms of finance; 5) impositions on leasing via tax, legal or accounting systems; 6) regulations on debt and equity ratios; 7) the likelihood of change of any of the above (Meidan 1984, p.42).

If a lessor is a manufacturer-lessor, it may face the decision of choosing selling or leasing products to other buyers or lessees in other countries.[7] In most instances, the lease vs. sale decision confronted by the seller/lessor and the lease vs. purchase or import decision faced by the buyer/lessee are not in parity. That is, the indifference point between sale or lease that the seller/lessor calculates will not be the same as the buy or lease indifference point that the buyer/lessee calculates, even though their expectations regarding asset life and salvage value are the same, and even though two firms have identical after tax costs of capital. Thus, it is possible for an international manufacturer to work the lease vs. export decision to his advantage. For the most time, the lessee or buyer considers the choice, according to the price difference between the lease and buy of products. As mentioned previously, marketing managers usually take a strategy of increasing the price of sales or leases so as to obtain more marketing penetration. For bank-lessors,[8] establishing a subsidiary to hold international leasing is a common strategy. Most US banks have chosen to form separate subsidiaries for their leasing operations. Such operations usually consist of a

---

[7] However, in some cases, the international leasing option is less attractive or not available at all. Some kinds of equipment (e.g., military equipment) can be sold, but not leased.

[8] According to Harris (1990), the various ways that a bank may engage in leasing include: 1) financing equipment leasing companies; 2) engaging in full-payout, non-tax-motivated leasing; 3) engaging in full-payout, tax-motivated leasing; 4) automobile leasing; and 5) purchasing an existing equipment leasing company (p.24).

domestic subsidiary and one or more international subsidiaries to hold investment in foreign leasing operations (Parrish 1983, p.175).

Financial, operating, leveraged leasing and others (export leasing etc.) are among the categories which can be chosen to serve foreign customers' needs. Within a category there may also be some different sub-categories to select. For example, major financial leasing contracts in the USA and the UK are commonly written on a variable interest rate basis. The purpose of the variable rate leases to the lessor is to protect from the risk of changes in the interest rate during the period of the lease (Hodges 1985). Any selection has its own impacts on the firm's return versus risk consequences which may considerably differ from those of other selection. In turn, different financial decision models subject to those categories should be designed to meet different requirements involved. In this chapter, I shall concentrate on those financial decision models.

I start with a general discussion of the basic model in terms of formulated cash flows (CF_i^f). There are numerous ways to reach a final selection decision. Here I present two basic approaches shown in Figure 6.2.[9] Let CF_i^f be local cash flows receivable in period i; R_i be end-year exchange rates in terms of number of units of the home currency to one of the foreign currency; f_i^f be local anticipated inflation rate in period i; K_R be the appropriate return required for a project in real terms; Q_i be the percentage of distributable cash flows to the parent company in period i. Obviously, whichever of the models we use, the final result in home currency terms comes out as identical, so long as purchasing parity holds throughout the period of analysis.

The adjusted present value (APV) approach involves discounting cash flows at a rate that, by removing the effects of financing, reflects only the business risks of the project. This rate, called the all-equity rate, represents the required rate of return on a project financed entirely with equity. The all-equity rate, K_e, can be used in capital budgeting by reviewing the value of a project as the sum of the following components: 1) the present value of project cash flows after taxes but before financing costs, discounted at K_e; 2) the present value of the tax savings on debt financing, discounted at the company's normal domestic borrowing rate, K_d, and 3) the present value of any savings on (or penalties from) interest costs associated with project-specific financing, discounted also at K_d. This latter differential would

---

[9] There is no difference between the two approaches.

generally be due to governmental regulations and/or subsidies that caused interest rates on restricted funds to diverge from domestic interest payable on unsubsidised, arm's-length borrowing.

Figure 11.2 Decision models for an international project

Steps	Approach I	Approach II	Explanations
1	$\sum_{i=1}^{n} CF_i^f$	$\sum_{i=1}^{n} CF_i^f$	Estimate the project's future cash flows in a local currency.
2	$\dfrac{\sum_{i=1}^{n} CF_i^f}{(1 + f_i^f)^I}$	$\dfrac{\sum_{i=1}^{n} CF_i^f}{(1 + f_i^f)^I}$	Calculate real term flows in a local currency by discounting for local inflation.
3	$\dfrac{\sum_{i=1}^{n} CF_i^f Q_i}{(1 + f_i^f)^I}$	$\dfrac{\sum_{i=1}^{n} Cf_i^f}{(1 + f_i^f)^i (1 + K_R)^i}$	I: Determine the distributable portion of cash flows to the parent company; II: Calculate real terms PV in local cash flows by a real discount rate.
4	$\dfrac{\sum_{i=1}^{n} CF_i^f Q_i R_i}{(1 + f_i^f)^i}$	$\dfrac{\sum_{i=1}^{n} CF_i^f Q_i}{(1 + f_i^f)^i (1 + K_R)^i}$	I: Convert to the home currency using a spot exchange rate; II: Determine the distributable portion of cash flows to the home in a local currency.
5	$\dfrac{\sum_{i=1}^{n} CF_i^f Q_i R_i}{(1 + f_i^f)^i (1 + K_R)^i}$	$\dfrac{\sum_{i=1}^{n} CF_i^f Q_i R_i}{(1 + f_i^f)^i (1 + K_R)^i}$	I: Calculate present values using home country real terms discount rate; II: Convert to the home currency present value using a spot rate.
6	NPV or APV?	NPV or APV?	Compare the result and select the alternative.

In an equation form, the APV of a project can be expressed as follows:

$$APV = -A_0 + \sum_{i=1}^{n} \frac{CF_i}{(1+K_e)^i} + \sum_{i=1}^{n} \frac{T_i(K_d DF_i)}{(1+K_d)^i} + \sum_{i=1}^{n} \frac{T_i(K_d - K_d')DF_i'}{(1+K_d)^i} \quad [11.1]$$

Where A_0: the initial investment, assuming a one-time initial outlay; CF_i: the expected annual operating after-tax cash flow, assuming the project is all equity financed; K_e: the risk-adjusted required rate of return on the specific project, assuming the project is financed solely with equity; K_d: the firm's normal domestic borrowing rate; K_d': the rate of interest (translated into its domestic equivalent) on foreign source financing; DF_i: the amount of domestic debt financing supported by the project in period i; DF_i': the amount of foreign source debt financing supported by the project in period i; T_i: the company's tax rate in period i.

It should be emphasised that the all-equity cost of capital equals the required rate of return on a specific project; this in turn can be broken down into the risk-free rate of interest plus an appropriate risk premium based on the project's particular risk.

Financial decisions of international financial leasing

Financial leasing is for a long term, provides for full payout, and is not cancellable without penalty by the lessee. A financial lease is primarily a source of financing.[10] Similarly, an international financial lease is a source of international financing. The Unidroit Convention describes an international financial leasing as "one party (the lessor) on the specifications of another party (the lessee) enters into an agreement with a third party (supplier) under which the lessor acquires plant, capital goods or other equipment on terms approved by the lessee so far as they concern its interest, and enters into an agreement with the lessee, granting to the lessee the right to use the equipment in return for the payment of rentals". According to the Convention, a financial leasing transaction includes three characteristics: a) the lessee specifies the equipment and selects the supplier without relying primarily on the skill and judgement of the lessor; b) the equipment is acquired by the lessor in connection with a leasing arrangement which, to the knowledge of

---

[10] This view is the same as Brealey and Myers (1988). Strictly speaking, both a financial lease and an operating lease are sources of financing. However, a financial lease is more likely to be "a loan in kind" financing, the term defined by (Herst 1984). This is because a financial lease is usually a "full pay-out" and long-term lease, and particularly it provides complete financing for an object, except for a first payment, if any, made at the beginning of the lease term (Herst 1984, p.5).

the supplier, either has been made or is to be made between the lessor and the lessee; and c) the rentals payable under the leasing agreement are calculated so as to take into account in particular the amortisation of the whole or a substantial part of the cost of the equipment. Like other financial decisions, financial decisions of international financial leasing from the lessor's point of view will also focus upon the expected incremental cash flows associated with a leasing project.

Model-designing

The adjusted present value (APV) approach is used in the following model.[11] Lessard (1981) expanded the traditional APV into a specific formulation in which each of the terms would be discounted at an appropriate rate to reflect its unique systematic risk.

$$APV = PV(A) + PV(CF) + PV(TD) + PV(FS) + PV(DC) + PV(TS) + PV(AR) + PV(RV) \qquad [11.2]$$

Where:
- PV(A): the present value of capital outlays;
- PV(CF): the present value of the after-tax operating cash flows that are remitted;
- PV(TD): the present value of tax savings due to depreciation;
- PV(FS): the present value of financial subsidies;
- PV(DC): the present value of project contribution to corporate debt capacity;[12]
- PV(TS): the present value of other tax savings;
- PV(AR): the present value of additional remittance;
- PV(RV): the present value of the residual asset.

The Lessard formulation is applied to design a decision model for international financial leasing from the lessor's perspective. First, it is concerned with the present value of capital outlays of the project. Assuming

---

[11] Many scholars (among others, Herst 1984) advocate this approach.

[12] In my view, PV(DC) should be the present value of the interest tax savings of project contribution to corporate debt capacity, since the only value of using debt financing instead of equity is the tax savings generated by the deductibility of interest from taxable income according to the Modigliani-Miller view.

that the capital outlays of this project are measured in terms of the lessor's home currency, then the present value of capital outlays of this project is:

$$PV(A) = A^h \qquad\qquad [11.3]$$

where: A^h is the capital outlays in terms of the home currency of the leasing project. The present value of the remitted after-tax operating cash flows of an international leasing project is related to the lease payments from the foreign lessee. The lease payments can be made in terms of foreign currencies or the lessor's home currency, depending on the negotiation.[13] If the lease payments are paid in a foreign currency, the lessor has to take foreign exchange risks into consideration. Also, the tax treatment of rental income should be considered. Note that most countries in the world have no specific legislation relating to lease rentals paid to non-residents. If both the lessor and the lessee countries have a tax treaty, the lease payments are usually taxed by one tax system, otherwise, double taxation may exist.[14] Without specifying the discounted rate at the moment, we formulate the present value of the fully remitted after-tax lease payments in Eq.[11.4].

$$PV(CF) = \sum_{i=1}^{n} \frac{(1-T^*)L_i^h}{(1+K_a)^i} \qquad\qquad [11.4]$$

---

[13] In some countries, such as South Korea, the government requires that all local costs, such as inland transportation of leased asset, insurance, and installation costs, must be financed via the local currency. In such countries a leasing transaction may involve two separate lease payment agreements.

[14] The way in which the lease payments are taxed in different countries depends on different circumstances. Sometimes, the taxation of the lease payments in the lessor's home country is largely determined by whether the home country makes a distinction between an operating and a finance lease. If this distinction is made, the transaction of a finance lease is normally treated as an instalment sale and the gain is fully taxable. However, in many countries it is possible to defer the recognition of the gain until a certain amount of the payments has been received. The interest income included in the payments is taxable upon receipt. In countries where no distinction is made, the lease payments are usually treated as rental income, and deduction of financing costs and depreciation of the asset is allowed. Generally speaking, few countries have introduced specific legislation relating to the lease payments made to non-residents. But most the developing countries have charged tax on lease rentals by way of withholding tax.

Where: $L_i{}^h$ is the expected lease payments received in the home currency in period i; T^* is the combined tax rate on the lease payments including the lessor's home income tax rate and the lessee's tax charges (if applicable). Specifically, if let T^h be the home country corporate tax rate and T^f the foreign country tax rate, then T^* may equal to $T^h + T^f - T^hT^f$, since $(1 - T^h)(1 - T^f) = 1 - T^h - T^f + T^hT^f$; K_a is the appropriate discount rate for discounting the after-tax lease payments. In some cases the lease payments paid by the lessee are not fully remitted because of restrictions (e.g., reinvestment provision) imposed by the authorities, therefore, the percentage of remitted lease payments must be determined by the lessor. Writing Eq.[11.4] in more detail to include the case of not fully remitted to the home country of the lease payments as well as the lease payments in other than the lessor's home currency, then we have Eq.[11.5] and Eq.[11.6] respectively:

$$PV(CF) = \sum_{i=1}^{n} \frac{(1-T_i^f)(1-T_i^h)L_i^hQ_i}{(1+K_b)^i} \qquad [11.5]$$

$$PV(CF) = \sum_{i=1}^{n} \frac{(1-T_i^f)(1-T_i^h)L_i^fR_iQ_i}{(1+K_c)^i} \qquad [11.6]$$

Where: $L_i{}^f$ is the contracted lease payments received in a foreign currency in period i; Q_i is the percentage of the remitted lease payments; R_i is a forward exchange rate to the period i, assuming the existence of such a forward market;[15] K_b and K_c are the appropriate discount rates for discounting two stream cash flows respectively. Obviously, the following relationship usually holds:

$$K_a \leq K_b \leq K_c \qquad [11.7]$$

---

[15] In reality, however, the forward exchange beyond 12 months is only limited to a few hard currencies. But the non-availability of the forward market for most currencies for periods beyond 12 months does not mean that financiers cannot obtain the forward cover for long-term borrowing in foreign currencies. In fact, financiers can manufacture long-term cover by conducting a spot and forward swap. In our theoretical models, we assume that there exists a long-term forward market of the currencies concerned.

Tax savings due to depreciation depend to a large extent on the tax system being in force, including the availability of a bilateral double-tax treaty and depreciation methods adopted. In a double-dip lease transaction, measures of tax savings due to depreciation are much more complicated. In this stage, for simplicity we assume that there is no double depreciation available. Also it is assumed that the tax system being in force does not provide compensation for the losses of the lessor, thus the tax savings have to be attained as the tax deductible costs have been earned. The present value of tax savings due to depreciation for the lessor is:

$$PV(TD) = \sum_{i=1}^{n} \frac{T_i^h D_i^h}{(1+K_d)^i}$$ [11.8]

Where: D_i^h is depreciation expense in terms of the lessor's home currency in period i; K_d is the appropriate discount rate for discounting tax savings. If the lessee depreciates the asset, then the tax savings due to depreciation for the lessee will be:

$$PV(TD) = \sum_{i=1}^{n} \frac{T_i^f D_i^f}{(1+K_e)^i}$$ [11.9]

Where: D_i^f is depreciation expense in terms of a foreign currency in period i; K_e is the appropriate discount rate for discounting tax savings by the lessee. Note that the tax savings due to depreciation received by the lessor is not identical to those received by the lessee, even though they have the same depreciation schedule, tax rate, as well as discount rate. This is due to the fact that the basis of depreciation between the lessor and the lessee is different.

PV(FS) is the present value of financial subsidies. There are various subsidies involved in international leasing associated with different industries and countries. One of the most common financial subsidies around the world is the investment tax credit (ITC) received by investors. Usually, the lessor claims the ITC in either the home country or a foreign (lessee) country, or both.[16] Assuming the ITC is received at the end of a fiscal year, then, we have:

$$PV(FS) = A^h \pi^h / (1 + K_f) \qquad \text{(in the home country)} \qquad [11.10]$$

$$PV(FS) = A^f \pi^f / (1 + K_g) \qquad \text{(in a foreign country)} \qquad [11.11]$$

$$PV(FS) = [A^h \pi^h + A^f \pi^f] / (1 + K_h) \quad \text{(in both countries)} \qquad [11.12]$$

Where: A^f is the amount of leasing investment in a foreign country; π^h or π^f is the percent of investment credit obtainable in the lessor home country or in a foreign country respectively; K_f is the risk-free rate; K_g and K_h are discount rates for discounting the cash flows ($A^f \pi^f$; $A^h \pi^h + A^f \pi^f$) respectively. Obviously, the relations, $K_f \leq K_g \leq K_h$, usually hold.

In our case, PV(DC) is the present value of project's contribution to corporate debt capacity. We are specially concerned with the issue of debts supported.[17] Obviously, a lessor is always in the position of a "creditor" before the lease payments have fully been paid by the lessee. In other words, leasing supports the debt capacity of the lessor until the lease payments are fully received. However, the only advantage of using debt financing is the tax savings generated by the deductibility of interest from taxable income, and debts themselves have no real value to the firm (Modigliani and Miller, 1973). The attention here is to formulate the present value of ITS on these debts supported, rather than to find out exactly the amount of the debts supported. Whether one dollar of lease receipts supports one dollar of lessor's debt capacity is a further study area.[18] At present, it only deals with

---

[16] This is not true for all cases. Sometimes only the lessee can claim the ITC, according to his country's tax regulation.

[17] Because an international leasing project is an investment to the lessor, and the project has an impact on the lessor's debt capacity to some extent. We term such an impact as "debts supported". Myers, *et al.* (1976) are the first authors defining this concept. Let *DS* be the debt supported by a lease; *DO* the total debt obligation of the lessor; *IV* the initial value of the leased asset. The authors define the debt supported in period *t* as: $DS_t \equiv \partial DO_t / \partial IV$ (i.e., the debt supported by a lease is obtained by differentiating the total debt obligation with respect to the initial value of the lease asset).

[18] Financial theories usually suggest that a lease and debt substitute each other. There are three views on the magnitude of the substitution coefficient: 1) one-to-one substitution (i.e., trade-off between debt and lease as one-to-one); 2) less-than-one substitution; and 3) more-than-one substitution. However, Ang and Peterson (1984) studying the sample of approximately 600 firms from 1976 to 1981, find that none of the three views is supported

the present value of the ITS of the debts supported by the prospective DTS, and the foreign lessee's commitment to make future rental payments. I present it in Eq.[11.13]:[19]

$$PV(DC) = \Phi \sum_{i=1}^{n} \left[\frac{\mu^d D_i^h T^h}{(1+K_s)^i} + \frac{\mu^L Q_i L_i (1-T^h)}{(1+K_p)^i} \right] \qquad [11.13]$$

For simplicity, PV(TS) and PV(AR) are not discussed in the model because they are insignificant. The present value of the residual asset is:

$$PV(RV) = \frac{S_n^f R_n}{(1+K_i)^n} \qquad [11.14]$$

Where: S_n^f is the cash flow of the residual asset in a foreign currency in period n; R_n is the forward exchange rate to the period n, assuming the existence of such a forward market; K_i is the appropriate rate for discounting the value of the residual asset.

Taking the signs of the elemental cash flows into account, it can formulate one of the lessor's decision models for an international financial leasing project by adding Eq.[11.3], Eq.[11.4], Eq.[11.8], Eq.[11.10], Eq.[11.13] and Eq.[11.14]. That is:

$$APV(L) = -A^h + \frac{A^h \pi^h}{(1+K_f)} + \sum_{i=1}^{n} \frac{(1-T_i^*)L_i^h}{(1+K_a)^i} + \sum_{i=1}^{n} \frac{T_i^h D_i^h}{(1+K_d)^i}$$

$$+ \Phi \sum_{i=1}^{n} \left[\frac{\mu^d D_i^h T^h}{(1+K_s)^i} + \frac{\mu^L Q_i L_i (1-T^h)}{(1+K_p)^i} \right] + \frac{S_n^f R_n}{(1+K_i)^n} \qquad [11.15]$$

---

by their empirical results. Their results indicate that lease and debt are complements: greater use of debt is associated with a great use of leasing. No empirical research on the lease supporting debt from the lessor's point of view, however, has been seen in the literature. Myers, *et al.* (1976) argue that the degree to which the present value of lease payments displaces debt capacity is less than one, reasoning that no firm can operate at 100% debt. Therefore, a lease supports less than an equivalent amount of debt.

[19] The detailed derivation of Eq.[11.13] is presented in Appendix 11.A.

Eq.[11.15] is a basic model for a lessor to make a decision for international financial leasing.[20] In principle, if APV(L) is positive, the project should be undertaken, whereas if APV(L) is negative, the project should not be undertaken. Apparently, in applying the model it is essential to select appropriate discount rates for the cash inflows in Eq.[11.15].

Ranking discount rates

First, it is emphasised that the discount rates used depend on the nature of the cash flows of which the present value is calculated. Also, it is advocated that each of the project cash flows should be discounted at an appropriate rate to reflect its risk.

Then, some relationships are determined amongst discount rates with the ranking technique in order to find out which rates are suitable to the model. Presume that a lessor decides to own an asset and operate it rather than to lease the asset to a foreign user. What rate of return would be required by the lessor due to owing and operating the asset? Clearly, owning the asset is riskier than a lending position of an equivalent amount because owning the asset consists of the total risk of its cash flows, not purely the risk of a debt position. Also, a lessor usually argues that leasing is less risky than financing a loan because it retains the legal ownership of the asset. The asset legal ownership retained can provide better security for the lessor than a mortgage or charge arising from a loan. Therefore, the required rate of return for financial leasing ought to be less than the return required of a loan because of the lower risk, or equal to the return of a loan if both have the same risk in the extreme. Thus, the following relations hold:

$$K_o \text{ (own assets)} > K_l \text{ (lending)} \geq K_L \text{ (lease)} \qquad [11.16]$$

If the lessor borrows to undertake leasing investment, the Modigliani-Miller definition of the cost of capital can be applied. Let the capital structure of a lessor be $B/(B+C)$ (B and C are the market values of debt and equity respectively), the appropriate weighted averaged cost of capital (K_w) then is:

---

[20] It is possible to formulate a number of particular models associated with different circumstances. However, the difference among these models is insignificant.

$$K_w = K_L \left(1 - T \frac{B}{B + C}\right)$$
[11.17]

Where: T is the lessor's marginal tax rate. Clearly, $K_w \leq K_L$, since $T[B/(B+C)] < 1$, or $= 0$ (in a 100% equity financing case). Hence the relations hold:

$$K_o > K_l \geq K_L \geq K_w$$
[11.18]

Further, such a ranking method is used to determine the discount rates in the model. Firstly, it is common for a lessor to compare the leasing of an asset with the lending of a certain amount of money to the user to buy the asset, because the majority of leasing firms are financial institutions or their subsidiaries. In this sense, it is reasonable to compare the discount rate for lease receipts with the firm's lending rate. However, a lessor usually regards that leasing is less risky than financing a loan (i.e., the user's debt) because it retains legal ownership of the asset. As a result the required rate of return on leasing ought to be less than the required return of a loan because of the lower risk. From the marketing point of view, the objective of a lessor is to negotiate a lending or lease financing agreement on the most favourable terms it can agree with a customer to obtain larger marketing penetration. Thus, it is suggested that the discount rate for discounting the after-tax lease payments should be a rate that is lower than K_l, or equal to K_l (in an extreme case that both have the same risk). This suggestion accords to a certain extent with the FASB No.13.[21] However, according to Lease, *et al.* (1990), few lease contracts pay out exactly as specified in the original leasing agreement (p.12). To incorporate such a risk this rate should be larger or at least equal to the lessor's weighted averaged cost of capital, K_w. That is:

$$K_w \leq K_a \leq K_l$$
[11.19]

Secondly, it is assumed that the tax system being in force does not provide compensation for leasing losses of the lessor, and tax is imposed on the entire

---

[21] FASB No.13 states that a lessee of a capital lease shall compute the present value of the minimum lease payments using the implicit rate when the implicit rate computed by the lessor is less than the lessee's incremental borrowing rate (p.11).

income of the lessor. That is the tax shields whether or not generated by a leasing project depend not only on a single project, but eventually depend on the lessor's entire operation, or the taxable income the lessor earned as a whole. Essentially, the tax shields take on some of the business risk of the firm's operations, since the shields have little value if the firm's operating income evaporates. Tax shields are worthless unless there are taxes to shield. The higher the debt ratio, the more difficult it will be for the firm to use all of its tax shields on schedule (Myers, *et al.* 1976). Thus, it is argued that the discount rate to calculate the present value of tax savings due to depreciation will be the firm's required return from the whole operation. That is the weighted average costs of capital.

$$K_d = K_w \qquad [11.20]$$

Thirdly, K_s is the discount rate for discounting the interest tax savings due to the debt supported by the depreciation. The above discussion of K_d is helpful in determining both K_s and K_p below. From Eq.[11.13] and Eq.[11A.12] in Appendix 11.A, it is known that if $\Phi = \{[T^h r(1+r)]/(1+r-r\mu^i T^h)\}$ and μ^d are given (or certain), then K_s must be equal to K_d, and Eq.[11.20] holds. However, both Φ and μ^d are uncertain by definition. Therefore K_s should be larger than K_d. K_p is the rate for discounting the interest tax savings due to the debt supported by the lessee's commitment of paying lease rentals. Similarly, K_p should be larger then K_a. On the other hand, comparing K_p with K_s, it is quite clear that $K_p \geq K_s$, since the actual lease payments paid by the foreign lessee are uncertain. In sum, the following relations hold:

$$K_p \geq K_s \geq K_d$$
$$K_p \geq K_a \qquad [11.21]$$

Finally, the discount rate for discounting the residual asset should be equivalent to the firm's cost of owning the asset, because the lessor usually has the right of the disposal of a leased asset at the end of a lease, which is the same as the lessor owning the asset at the same period. Normally, the salvage value of the asset leased is extremely difficult to be foreseen accurately, thus the highest premium should be required. Therefore:

$$K_i = K_o \qquad\qquad\qquad [11.22]$$

To summarise, the discount rates used in our model associated with the assumptions will generally follow the following relationships presented in Eq.[11.23]. Also, it is recommended to use the sensitivity analysis technique or the risk ranking technique to determine individual rates in particular cases.[22]

$$K_i > K_p \geq K_a \geq K_d > K_f$$

$$\qquad\qquad\qquad\qquad\qquad [11.23]$$

$$K_p \geq K_s \geq K_d$$

To understand the model a hypothetical example is presented as follows: West Leasing Company (lessor) in the US wants to lease construction equipment to a firm (lessee) in the Far East. The equipment costs $1,000,000, funded with 60% of equity of the lessor and 40% of the loan at the before-tax borrowing rate 14%. The lessor will claim the depreciation of the equipment valued 980,000 with the sum of the year-digits method, and obtain the investment credit of 10% of the investment, according to the regulations. The lessee proposes to pay a series of lease payments of $110,000 per annum which are fully remitted with the first payment in advance, and the lessee is responsible for the transportation, insurance costs and maintenance of the equipment. The lessor's income tax rate of the first five year is 40%, and it is expected to be 45% in the remaining five years. Also, it is known that the debt capacity supported is followed on the basis of "less than one substitution" with $\mu^l = 80\%$, $\mu^d = 90\%$, and $\mu^i = 80\%$,). At the termination of the lease, the lessor will sell the leased asset at the forecaster price of ¥5,000,000. The exchange rate in year 10 is expected to be ¥240 per dollar. The risk free rate is 5%. Using the ranking method, the firm selects: 8% as the discount rate for the tax savings due to depreciation; 9% and 11% for discounting the interest tax savings of debts supported by depreciation tax savings and by the lessee's commitment of the lease payments respectively; 10% for discounting the lease payments; and 13% for discounting the residual value of the leased equipment. Based on the above information, West Leasing Company has to decide whether this project should be undertaken or not.

---

[22] Many authors advocate the use of the sensitivity analysis in determining discount rates for discounting cash flow streams (e.g., Bower 1973; Herst 1984; and Weingartner 1987).

Table 11.1 is the calculation of the present values of tax savings due to depreciation of the leased equipment. Table 11.2 is the calculation of the present values of the after-tax lease payments. Table 11.3 is the calculation of the present values of the interest tax savings of the debt supported by the depreciation tax shelters. Table 11.4 is the calculation of the present values of the interest tax savings of the debt supported by the lessee's commitment of the lease payments. Applying Eq.[11.15], we can measure APV of the project.

$$
\begin{aligned}
APV(L) &= -1,000,000 + 10\%(1,000,000)/(1+5\%) + 431,790 + \\
&\quad 300,589 + 15,693 + 20,341 + \\
&\quad (5,000,000/240)(1+13\%)^{10} \\
&= -1,000,000 + 95,238 + 431,790 + 300,589 + 15,693 + \\
&\quad 20,341 + 6,146 \\
&= -\$130,203.
\end{aligned}
$$

Table 11.1 The present values of tax savings due to depreciation

Year	Initial capital outlay $	Depreciation (the sum of year-digits)	Depreciation tax savings (T=40%,45%)	Discount factor (8%)	The present value
0	1,000,000				
1		178,182	71,273	0.924	65,856
2		160,364	64,146	0.857	54,973
3		142,546	57,018	0.794	45,272
4		124,727	49,891	0.735	36,670
5		106,909	42,764	0.681	29,122
6		89,091	40,091	0.630	25,277
7		71,273	32,073	0.583	18,699
8		53,455	24,055	0.540	12,990
9		35,636	16,036	0.500	8,018
10		17,818	8,018	0.463	3,712
Total					300,589

Table 11.2 The present values of the after-tax lease payments

Year	Lease payments ($)	After-tax lease payments	Discount factor (10%)	The present value
0				
1	110,000	66,000	1.000	66,000
2	110,000	66,000	0.909	59,994
3	110,000	66,000	0.826	54,516
4	110,000	66,000	0.751	49,566
5	110,000	66,000	0.683	45,078
6	110,000	66,000	0.621	37,571
7	110,000	66,000	0.564	34,122
8	110,000	66,000	0.513	31,037
9	110,000	66,000	0.467	28,254
10	110,000	66,000	0.424	25,652
Total				431,790

Table 11.3 The present values of the ITS of the debt supported by the DTS

Year	depreciation tax savings x μ (90%)	x $(\Phi)^{23}$ ($\Phi_1 = .058$ $\Phi_2 = .066$)	Discount factor (9%)	The present value
0				
1	64,145	3,721	0.917	3,412
2	57,731	3,348	0.842	2,819
3	51,316	2,976	0.772	2,298
4	44,902	2,604	0.708	1,844
5	48,488	2,232	0.650	1,451
6	36,082	2,831	0.596	1,419
7	28,866	1,905	0.547	1,094
8	21,650	1,429	0.502	717
9	14,432	953	0.460	438
10	7,216	476	0.422	201
Total				15,693

---

[23] When the income tax rate in the first five years is 40%, Φ_1= .058; the income tax rate is expected to be 45% in the remaining five years, then Φ_2= .066 (also apply to Table 11.4).

Obviously, this project should not be undertaken, according to the rule: if APV(L) is positive, the project should be undertaken, whereas if APV(L) is negative, the project should not be undertaken.

Table 11.4 The present values of the ITS of the debt supported by the lessee's commitment of the lease payments

Year	After-tax lease payments x μ (80%)	x (Φ) (Φ_1 = .058 Φ_2 = .066)	Discount factor (11%)	The present value
0	52,800	3,062	1.000	3,062
1	52,800	3,062	0.901	2,759
2	52,000	3,062	0.812	2,486
3	52,000	3,062	0.731	2,238
4	52,000	3,062	0.659	2,018
5	48,400	3,194	0.593	1,894
6	48,400	3,194	0.535	1,709
7	48,400	3,194	0.482	1,540
8	48,400	3,194	0.434	1,386
9	48,400	3,194	0.391	1,249
10				
Total				20,341

Financial decisions of international leveraged leasing

International leveraged leasing

Leveraged leasing is one of the most complex and sophisticated vehicles for financing capital equipment in today's financial marketplace. Worldwide, leveraged leasing has played a predominant role as a vehicle for financing expenditure assets (e.g., aircraft, ships, construction equipment, etc.). The high costs of such assets preclude most users from purchasing these assets. In leveraged leasing, however, the lessor may offer a financing rate significantly lower than that available through other forms of financing. This is because in leveraged leasing the equity is highly leveraged by means of a non-recourse loan, and the lessor may receive all the tax benefits of ownership even when it contributes only a small portion of the investment so that the lessor can pass some of the benefits to the lessee in a reduction of the cost of financing. Since the 1970s, the academic research on leveraged leasing has received much attention (e.g., Packham 1975; Dyl and Martin 1977; Perg 1978; Athanasopoulos and Bacon 1980; Capettini and Toole 1981; and Marks 1983). However, none of them has been concerned with international leveraged leasing.

An international leveraged lease is a multinational financial leasing agreement in which the lessor borrows, from a third party lender, a substantial portion (usually 50% to 80%) of the purchase price of the asset. The debt instrument provides for a non-recourse loan by the lender to the lessor who, in turn, leases the asset to the foreign lessee. The lessor receives tax savings through the asset depreciation expense deductions, loan interest deductions, ITC, interest tax savings on the debts supported by the lease as well.[24] Usually, an equity participant is domiciled in a different country than the lessee.[25] One attraction of leveraged leasing is that the lessor obtains the title of the leased asset by providing only a relatively small proportion of its overall costs. With the title the lessor receives any relative taxation incentives and government subsidies. Some of these benefits are passed on to the foreign lessee by a reduction in the lease payments and, hence the implicit lease rate is often well below the current asset loan interest rate. In essence, leveraged leasing is a device to optimally allocate tax subsidies (e.g., ITC, DTS) with the private sectors (Miller and Upton 1976; Dyl and Martin 1977).

In international leveraged leasing, more than two parties, coming from at least two different nations, are involved. Usually, the lessor (or equity participant) is domiciled in a different country than the lessee. In normal financial leasing, there are only two parties (the lessor and the lessee) involved, whereas in leveraged leasing there are more than two parties involved. The difference in the number of parties involved results from the fact that in leveraged leasing the lessor puts up only a portion of the investment cost and borrows the rest from other sources. The reason for borrowing by the lessor is the fact that leveraged leasing involves significant capital outlays. The structure of most leveraged leasing transactions is

---

[24] The interest tax savings on the debts supported by a leveraged lease were not recognised in the literature (for example, Capettini and Toole 1981; Marks 1983).

[25] A lessor, or a group of financial institutions acting together as a lessor, is known as an equity participant.

basically the same, and involves five parties: a lessor (owner); a lessee (user); a financing source; a leasing company; and a manufacturer (or a supplier). The owner (lessor) is a bank, an individual, or an equity participant that purchases the equipment for all of the benefits associated with ownership. The financing source is typically a bank or an insurance company that is willing to provide funds based on the user-lessee's credit worthiness on a non-recourse basis that will typically correlate to an assignment of the lessee's rental stream. The leasing company is responsible for getting all of the parties together, documenting the entire transaction, arranging the purchase, and installing equipment. The leasing company is typically paid a fee which represents a percentage of the purchase price of equipment for arranging the transaction, and may also take an equity position.

Generally speaking, international leveraged leasing is a relatively complex financial instrument in many ways. First, it is legally complex in that it depends on different tax laws and accounting treatments involved, specific tax rulings of parties involved, and complicated trust and security agreements; Secondly, it is high risk business since the bankruptcy of any party participating in the transaction may result in a considerable risk to the other parties; and Thirdly, leveraged leasing is computationally complex because of its multiple signs of cash flows streams. In particular, as a result of the special tax provisions associated with leveraged leasing, in many instances there are multiple sign changes in the after-tax cash flow patterns. The two predominant patterns are: i) after the initial outlay, a series of positive cash flows is followed by a series of negative cash flows (i.e., negative-positive-negative cash flows); ii) after the initial outlay, a series of positive cash flows is followed by a series of negative cash flows, and then followed by another series of positive cash flows (i.e., negative-positive-negative-positive cash flows). These mixed cash flows patterns make extremely difficult for the lessor to calculate the return to equity.

There is no financial model on international leveraged leasing in the literature. A number of models have been proposed to design a leveraged lease in a domestic setting, or to calculate the return to equity. The methods or models include the sinking fund method (SFM), the separate phases (or called two-stage) method (SPM), the averaged growth rate method (AGR), the internal rate of return method (IRR), the net present value method (NPV), the net terminal value method (NTV), and the Mixed Integer Linear Programming Model (MILPM).

Perhaps the most widely used method for determining the return on a leveraged lease is the SFM (see Smith 1973). The SFM suggests that the positive cash flows in the early years have two components: one represents returns to the lessor, and the other represents funds that must be reinvested to offset the negative flows in later years. Under the SFM, early positive cash flows are presumed to be set aside in an amount that, when compounded at a pre-specified interest rate,[26] is enough to cover negative cash flows in the later years of the lease. The remaining cash flows are then used to settle an implicit rate of return. We take the cash flows foregoing pattern II to illustrate the SFM. The return to the equity can be determined from the relation:

$$A_0(1+K_e)^n = CF_1(1+K_e)^{n-1} + CF_2(1+K_e)^{n-2} + ... + CF_{m-1}(1+K_e)^{n-(m-1)}$$
$$+ [CF_m(1+K_s)^{n-m} + CF_{m+1}(1+K_s)^{n-(m+1)} + ...$$
$$+ CF_{s-1}(1+K_s)^{n-(s-1)}] + CF_s(1+K_e)^{n-s} + CF_{s+1}(1+K_e)^{n-(s+1)}$$
$$+ CF_n$$
$$or = \sum_{i=1}^{m-1} CF_i(1+K_e)^{n-i} + \sum_{j=m}^{s-1} CF_j(1+K_s)^{n-j} + \sum_{k=s}^{n} CF_k(1+K_e)^{n-k}$$

$$[11.24]$$

Where A_0: the initial investment outlay of the lessor; CF: the cash flows; K_s: the interest rate assumed for the sinking fund; K_e: the implicit rate of return on the lease for the lessor; n: the number of periods of the lease ($n = m + s + k$); m: the period in which the sinking fund is started; s: the period in which the sinking fund is ended; k: the remaining periods, $k = n - m - s$.

However, the SFM has been the subject of some controversy (Dyl and Martin 1977). Also, the financial policy of the SFM is contradictory to the traditional assumption in corporate finance theory that a company maintains constant financial leveraged throughout the life of an investment (Marks 1983). Noticeably, the SFM fails to ensure maximisation of present value whenever K_s is set at less than the cost of capital and/or whenever the lessor faces conditions of capital rationing (Hughes and Weide 1982).

Under the SPM, when the accumulated compounded cash flows less income recognised to date are positive, then the compounding rate for that period is assumed to be the cost of capital, or zero; when they are negative, then the compounding rate for the period is assumed to be the implicit rate (Shanno and Weil 1976; and Brief and Owen 1978). Generally speaking, the SPM has the same problems as the SFM. The mathematical relations, according to Hughes and Weide (1982), are:

---

[26] In fact, such a rate is difficult to pre-specify.

$$F_1 = \begin{cases} F_0(1 + K_e) + CF_1, & \text{if } F_0 < 0 \\ \\ F_0(1 + K_s) + CF_1, & \text{if } F_0 \geq 0 \end{cases}$$

$$F_2 = \begin{cases} F_1(1 + K_e) + CF_2, & \text{if } F_1 < 0 \\ \\ F_1(1 + K_s) + CF_2, & \text{if } F_1 \geq 0 \end{cases}$$

$$\begin{matrix} \vdots & \vdots & \vdots \\ \vdots & \vdots & \vdots \end{matrix}$$

$$F_n = \begin{cases} F_{n-1}(1 + K_e) + CF_n, & \text{if } F_{n-1} < 0 \\ \\ F_{n-1}(1 + K_s) + CF_n, & \text{if } F_{n-1} \geq 0 \end{cases} \qquad [11.25]$$

Where, to initialise the process, $F_0 \equiv A_0$. By successive substitution, we have:

$$\begin{aligned} F_n = {} & -A_0(1 + K_e)^{\alpha 0}(1 + K_s)^{\beta 0} + CF_1(1 + K_e)^{\alpha 1}(1 + K_s)^{\beta 1} \\ & + CF_2(1 + K_e)^{\alpha 2}(1 + K_s)^{\beta 2} + ... \\ & + CF_t(1 + K_e)^{\alpha t}(1+K_s)^{\beta t} + ... + CF_n \qquad [11.26] \end{aligned}$$

Where $\alpha_t + \beta_t = n - t$, for $t = 0, 1, ..., n-1$. Thus, F_n is a polynomial in K_e and K_s. If we now fix $K_s = 0$, we can set F_n equal to zero and solve for K_e. Then moving the first term on the right-hand side of Eq.[11.26] to the left, we have:

$$\begin{aligned} A_0(1 + K_e)^{\alpha 0} = {} & CF_1(1 + K_e)^{\alpha 1} + CF_2(1 + K_e)^{\alpha 2} + ... \\ & + CF_t(1 + K_e)^{\alpha t} + ... + CF_n \qquad [11.27] \end{aligned}$$

Under the AGR proposed by Hughes and Weide (1982), all future cash flows are compounded at the cost of capital, and an implicit rate of return (i.e., average growth rate), K_e, is determined from the following relation:

$$A_0(1+K_e)^n = CF_1(1+K_s)^{n-1} + CF_2(1+K_s)^{n-2} + ... + CF_n$$

$$\text{or} \ = \ \sum_{i=1}^{n} CF_i(1+K_s)^{n-i} \qquad\qquad [11.28]$$

This is, the internal rate K_e is simply the rate at which the initial investment would have to be compounded in order to achieve an amount equal to the sum of the future cash flows compounded at the cost of capital. This method provides a means of ranking investments from most to least preferred in the sense of maximising present value under capital rationing (Hughes and Weide 1982, p.39). However, it does not represent the characteristic of cash flows of a leveraged lease. On the other hand, this method is purposely used for the accounting purpose, not for financial decision purpose.

With respect to the IRR, the NPV and the NTV, Athanasopoulos and Bacon (1980) demonstrate that all the methods for evaluating leveraged leases lead to the same accept or reject decision, given the same assumptions regarding the reinvestment rate and provided the reinvestment rate is equal to the required rate of return.[27] However, such assumptions do not always hold, in particular in uncertainty circumstances. An important weakness of all the methods and models is the disregard of dependencies between investment and financing, instead they only treat a leveraged leasing project as a pure investment problem. Also, most of the models fail to maximise the NPV of a leveraged leasing project. Further, all the discussions of the above methods and models are based on a certainty world. Risks involved in leveraged leasing, and premiums on these risks have not been addressed, and in many cases a risk-free rate is selected in calculating the present value without giving reasons of the selection. Moreover, external constraint factors (such as the tax authorities' qualification of a true leveraged lease, firm's limited borrowing capacity) have not been examined in the above methods and models, except the MILPM.

The mixed integer linear programming model (MILPM) proposed by Capettini and Toole (1981) takes a number of external constraint factors into account and aims to maximise the NPV of a leveraged leasing project, despite some weaknesses. For example, Capettini and Toole do not consider the financial impact on the lessor's debt capacity.[28] Instead, they assume that

---

[27] For simplicity, we shall not discuss them in detail. The readers are recommended to Athanasopoulos and Bacon (1980) and Herbst (1982) (pp.174-86).

[28] In the literature, it is well recognised that the impact of lease financing on a corporate debt capacity must be included in the cash flows. Myers, *et al.* (1976) develop a procedure that may solve for the debt capacity effect.

leases are independent (i.e., investing in one leveraged lease does not affect the lessor's cost of capital, or the lessor's ability to invest or not invest in other leveraged leases). This assumption is obviously unrealistic and may lead to undermine the NPV of a project. Also, their model only uses a single discount rate (i.e., the after-tax cost of capital) to discount all cash flow streams. As these streams have different risk characteristics, they should be discounted with different rates.

Financial decisions of international operating leasing

International operating leasing

International operating leasing is a lease transaction for a short term and is cancellable during the lease at the option of the foreign lessee. In such a transaction, the lessor purchases an asset, and leases it out to a foreign lessee, but at a rate or term which does not cover the cost, interest and profit of the lessor. Operating leasing is a further potential area of expansion in an international market where there is little tax advantage. From the lessor's point of view, international operating leasing is riskier than its financial counterpart. The risk that the lessor must bear includes the economic depreciation of the asset, and business risks stemmed from the uncertainty of the foreign lessee's financial position, as well as exchange rate fluctuation, and political risk.

Operating leasing owns its existence primarily to numerous and significant asymmetries between lessors and foreign lessees. These often include the lessor's specialisation in a limited set of assets in the home country, which permits the lessor to know more about the market for the asset than most foreign lessees/users. Economies of scale exist in gathering and assessing information about obsolescence risk and in projecting future asset values. Constant contact with the market enhances the lessor's ability to re-market an off-lease asset and lowers the cost of bearing these risks. Operating leases are accounted for in different ways, in the main not being capitalised on the books of the lessee. In addition the lessor may have some good reasons (e.g., marketing) to lease the asset to more than one lessee.

One characteristic of operating leasing is that the cost of a leased asset is not wholly recovered by the lessor out of the rentals receivable during the non-cancellable period which is normally significantly shorter than the estimated useful life of the asset. Operating lessor's profits may arise in a number of ways: from re-leasing the asset to other lessees; from selling the asset; and from the provision of ancillary service. In these circumstances, residual value is of utmost importance and the lessor has to rely on the residual value of the asset to recover the balance of the net investment and to earn profits. Therefore operating leasing is normally confined to the transactions of those types of assets with an established used or second-hand market opened in the lessee's country particularly. Moreover, operating lessors typically specialise in a range of specific assets and pass some of the benefits of specialist knowledge and large-scale purchase of assets on to lessees. It is very difficult for lessors that have no asset marketing experience to enter the market.[29] Aircraft, computers are frequently leased under international operating leases.

An operating lease is a flexible financing instrument, and has tended to be far less sensitive to tax considerations than a finance lease. By definition, an operating lease does not involve any significant commitment by the lessee to continue to rent the asset. Because of this, all operating leases provide for at least a significant function to be performed by the lessor: the absorption of a major part of the risk of early obsolescence of the asset due to the economic life of the asset is less than anticipated.

Financial models of international operating leasing

Operating leases are virtually equivalent to having the lessor own the asset and operate it (Weston and Copeland 1986, p.636). Therefore the required rate of return should be something higher than the rate on a portfolio of assets of loaned funds, since owning assets has more risk than lending position as discussed before. The following three uncertain factors are of great importance to decision-making: 1) the cash flows received from the lease; 2) the expected market or salvage value of the leased asset at the end of the lease; and 3) the value of an American put option, defined by Copeland and Weston (1982). The put option captures the present value of the lessee's right to cancel the lease and return the asset whenever the value of the economic rent on the asset falls below the lease fees. The evaluation of an operating lease is traditionally based on the following steps (e.g., Copeland and Weston 1982). First to assume the lease is non-cancellable and calculate the competitive adjusted present value of the lease by way of applying Eq.

---

[29] This is the reason why a bank leasing company has currently been reluctant to undertake international operating leasing.

[11.15]; next to determine the competitive lease payments assuming the above contract is a cancellable operating lease. Eq.[11.15] can be modified with valuing out the present value of the American put option. The new evaluation equation is as follows:

$$APV(L) = -A^h + \frac{A^h \pi^h}{(1+K_f)} + \sum_{i=1}^{n} \frac{(1-T_i^*)L_i^h}{(1+K_a)^i} + \sum_{i=1}^{n} \frac{T_i^h D_i^h}{(1+K_d)^i}$$

$$+ \Phi \sum_{i=1}^{n} [\frac{\mu^d D_i^h T^h}{(1+K_s)^i} + \frac{\mu^L Q_i L_i (1-T^h)}{(1+K_p)^i}] + \frac{S_n^f R_n}{(1+K_i)^n} - PO$$

[11.29]

Where *PO* is the value of the American put implied by the cancellation feature.[30] As the risk of obsolescence increases so does the value of the put option held by the lessee. Now, we present an alternative analysis of operating leasing. If we split the value of an operating lease into two elements: Element A (*EA*) and Element B (*EB*). *EA* is merely used to summarise those terms (in terms of the present value) relating to the DTS, the ITC, and the interest tax savings of debt supported by the DTS. *EB* is merely used to refer those terms (in terms of the present value) which are dependent of the lessee's cancellation of the lease contract, such as the lease payments, the residual value, and the interest tax savings of debt supported by the lessee's commitment of future lease payments. Let $-A_0$ be the initial cost of the asset leased, the net present value of an operating leasing *NPV(OL)* will be:

$$NPV(OL) = -A_0 + EA + EB$$

[11.30]

Where:

$$EA = \frac{A^h \pi^h}{(1+K_f)} + \sum_{i=1}^{n} \frac{T_i^h D_i^h}{(1+K_a)^i} + \Phi \sum_{i=1}^{n} \frac{\mu^d D_i^h T^h}{(1+K_d)^i}$$

[11.30a]

---

[30] See Copeland and Weston (1982) for an analysis of an American put option involved in an operating lease.

$$EB = \sum_{i=1}^{n} \frac{(1-T_i^*)L_i^h}{(1+K_d)^i} + \Phi \sum_{i=1}^{n} \frac{\mu^L Q_i L_i(1-T^h)}{(1+K_p)^i} + \frac{S_n^f R_n}{(1+K_i)^n} \qquad [11.30b]$$

Obviously, the initial cost of the asset leased and *EA* are not affected whether and whenever the lessee cancels the lease. For simplicity we assume that $Q_i = 100\%$, $K_d = K_p$, and only one tax system T^h is in force. Also, we assume that the lessor will be able to get the leased asset back when the lessee cancels the lease. Then, the above *EB* (Eq.[11.30b]) can be rewritten as:

$$EB = (1 + \Phi\mu^L) \sum_{i=1}^{n} \frac{L_i(1-T^h)}{(1+K_d)^i} + \frac{S_n^h}{(1+K_i)^n} \qquad [11.31]$$

Note that *EB* is a function of the term (say *m*) when the lessee cancels the lease, that is $EB = f(m)$. Thus Eq.[11.31] can be expressed as follows:

$$EB = f(m) = (1 + \Phi\mu^L) \sum_{i=1}^{m} \frac{L_i(m)(1-T^h)}{(1+K_d)^i} + \frac{S_m^h}{(1+K_i)^m} \qquad [11.32]$$

Where: $L_i(m)$ refers to the future lease payments which are a function of *m*. However, *EB* is difficult to assert as it could be various possibilities in response to the lessee's cancellation of a lease. In this circumstance, we assign a probability *P* to each possible cancellation, denoted by *m*. The expected *EB*, *E(EB)* is:

$$E(EB) = \sum_{i} P_i EB$$

$$= (1 + \Phi\mu^L) \sum_{i} P_i \sum_{i=1}^{m} \frac{L_i(m)(1-T^h)}{(1+K_d)^i} + \frac{S_m^h}{(1+K_i)^m} \qquad [11.33]$$

In sum, the criterion of accepting an operating leasing project is:

$$E(EB) \geq A_0 - EA \qquad [11.34]$$

or:

$$(1 + \Phi\mu^L) \sum_i P_i \sum_{i=1}^{m} \frac{L_i(m)(1-T^h)}{(1+K_d)^i} + \frac{S_m^h}{(1+K_i)^m}$$

$$\geq A_0 - \frac{A^h\pi^h}{(1+K_f)} + \sum_{i=1}^{n} \frac{T^hD_i^h}{(1+K_a)^i} + \Phi \sum_{i=1}^{n} \frac{\mu^dD_i^hT^h}{(1+K_d)^i} \qquad [11.35]$$

Conclusion

International leasing is a very popular but complex method of international financing. It offers advantages of marketing, investment, financing and provides opportunities of reducing the cost of financing. International leasing diverges from domestic leasing in many aspects. International leasing usually involves manipulation with more than one currency, more than one legal jurisdiction, more than one taxation system, and more than one accounting practice. Therefore, an international leasing decision differs from the decision of domestic leasing that is based on the environment of a single accounting, currency, taxation and legal system. This chapter focuses on international leasing strategies and decisions from the lessor's point of view.

The focuses are mainly on international financial leasing, international leveraged leasing and international operating leasing. A number of decision models have been designed. Our models differ from the traditional models relating to domestic cases in some aspects. For example, the currency problem has been taken into consideration in the models. In addition, a multi-discount-rate system is used in the models so as to reflect different cash flows with different risks. Particularly, all the models consider the ITS of debts supported by an international leasing project, and these savings are formally formulated in the models.

Reference

Ang, J. and P.P. Peterson. 1984. The leasing puzzle. *Journal of Finance* September: 1055-65.

Athanasopoulos, P.J. and P.W. Bacon. 1980. The evaluation of leveraged leases. *Financial Management* Spring: 76-80.

Bayless, M.E. and J.D. Diltz. 1990. Corporate debt, corporate taxes and leasing. *Managerial and Decision Economics* 11: 13-19.

Bower, R.S. 1973. Issues in lease financing. *Financial Management* Winter: 25-34.

Bowman, S. 1990. Lease or buy? *CMA Magazine* February: 22-25.

Brealey, R. and S. Myers. 1988. *Principles of Corporate Finance.* New York: McGraw Hill.

Brief, R.P. and J. Owen. 1978. Accounting for leveraged leases: a comment. *Journal of Accounting Research* Autumn: 411-13.

Capettini, R. and H. Toole. 1981. Designing leveraged leases: a mixed integer linear programming approach. *Financial Management* Autumn: 15-23.

Copeland, T.E. and J.F. Weston. 1982. A note on the evaluation of cancellable operating leases. *Financial Management* Summer: 60-67.

Dyl, E.A. and S.A. Martin. 1977. Setting terms for leveraged leases. *Financial Management* Winter: 20-27.

Edwards, J.S.S. and C.P. Mayer. 1991. Leasing, taxes, and the cost of capital. *Journal of Public Economics* 44: 171-179.

Flavell, R. and G.R. Salkin. 1982. A model of a lessor. *The International Journal of Management Science* 10, no. 4: 413-431.

Grenadier, S.R. 1995. Valuing lease contracts: a real-options approach. *Journal of Financial Economics* 38: 297-331.

Harris, M.M. 1990. Equipment leasing in the 1990s. *The Journal of Commercial Bank Lending* January: 24-27.

Herbst, A.F. 1982. *Capital Budgeting: Theory, Quantitative Methods, and Applications.* New York: Harper & Row Publisher.

Herst, A.C.C. 1984. *Lease or Purchase: Theory and Practice.* Massachusetts: Kluwer-Nijhoff Publishing.

Hodges, S.D. 1985. The valuation of variable rate leases. *Financial Management* Spring: 68-74.

Hughes, J.S. and J.V. Weide. 1982. Incentive considerations in the reporting of leveraged leases. *Journal of Bank Research* Spring: 36-41.

Lease, R.C., J.J. McConnell and J.S. Schallheim. 1990. Realised returns and the default and prepayment experience of financial leasing contracts. *Financial Management* Summer: 11-20.

Lessard, D.R. 1981. Evaluating international projects: an adjusted present value approach. In *Capital Budgeting Under Conditions of*

Uncertainty, ed. R.L. Crum and F.G. Derkinderen: Chapter 6: Martinus Nijhof Publishing.

Levy, H. and M. Sarnat. 1979. Leasing, borrowing and financial risk. *Financial Management* Winter: 47-54.

Lewis, C.M. and J.S. Schallheim. 1992. Are debt and lease substitutes? *Journal of Financial and Quantitative Analysis* 27, no. 4: 497-511.

Loewenstein, M.A. and J.E. McClure. 1988. Taxes and financial leasing. *Quarterly Review of Economics and Business* Spring: 21-38.

Marks, B.R. 1983. Calculating the rate of return on a leveraged lease: a constant leverage approach. *Journal of Bank Research* Winter: 297-99.

Meidan, A. 1984. Strategic problems in international leasing. *Management International Review* 24, no. 4: 36-47.

Miller, M.H. and C.W. Upton. 1976. Leasing, buying, and the cost of capital services. *Journal of Finance* June: 761-786.

Modigliani, F. and M.H. Miller. 1973. Corporate income taxes and the cost of capital: a correction. *American Economic Review* June: 433-443.

Myers, S.C. 1977. Determinants of corporate borrowing. *Journal of Financial Economics* November: 147-175.

Myers, S.C., D.A. Dill and A.J. Bautista. 1976. Valuation of financial lease contracts. *Journal of Finance* June: 799-819.

Packham, R.E. 1975. An analysis of the risk or leveraged leasing. *Journal of Commercial Bank Lending* March: 2-29.

Parrish, K.M. 1983. International leasing. In *The International Banking Handbook*, ed. W.H. Baughn and D.R. Mandich: 173-82. Homewood Illinois: Dow Jones-Irwin.

Perg, W.F. 1978. Leveraged leasing: the problem of changing leverage. *Financial Management* Autumn: 47-51.

Phillips, P.F.J. 1985. Asset structure, political risk and the multinational firm: evidence from Mitterand's election. Paper presented at *The Annual Meeting of Eastern Finance Association*. Dallas, Texas.

Shanno, D.F. and R.L. Weil. 1976. The separate phases method of accounting for leveraged leases: properties of the allocating rate and an algorithm for finding it. *Journal of Accounting Research* Autumn: 348-356.

Smith, B.D. 1982. Planning models in the leasing industry. *OMEGA* 10, no. 4: 345-351.

Smith, P.R. 1973. A straightforward approach to leveraged leasing. *Journal of Commercial Bank Lending* July: 40-47.

Steele, A. 1984. Different equation solutions to the valuation of lease contracts. *Journal of Financial and Quantitative Analysis* September: 311-328.

Weingartner, H.M. 1987. Leasing, asset lives and uncertainty: guides to decision making. *Financial Management* Summer: 5-12.

Weston, J.F. and T.E. Copeland. 1986. *Managerial Finance*. New York: The Dryden Press.

Appendix 11.A Calculation of the PV of ITS of the debts supported by a leasing project

I. Calculation of the PV of ITS of the debt supported by the prospective DTS

First, let's calculate the debt supported by the prospective DTS. In period *1*, the debt supported by the DTS, S_1, is:

$$S_1 = \mu^d D_1{}^h T^h \qquad\qquad\qquad [11.A1]$$

Where: μ^d is the fraction of the value of the DTS that is added to the firm's debt capacity.

In period *2*, the debt supported covers two parts: the debt supported by the DTS in period *2*; and the debt supported by the interest tax shield of the debt supported due to the DTS in period *1*. Let μ^i be the fraction of the value of the interest tax shield of the debts supported that is added to the firm's debt capacity. Assume that the debts supported by a leasing project have the same risk characteristics as the normal debts, *r* to be the interest rate of the debts supported (of course, of the normal debts), and $S_1 = S_2/(1+r)$, then:

$$S_2 = \mu^d D_2{}^h T^h + \mu^i r T^h S_1 = \mu^d D_2{}^h T^h + \mu^i r T^h S_2/(1+r) \qquad [11.A2]$$

Certainly:

$$S_2 = \frac{\mu^d D_2{}^h T^h (1+r)}{[1+r(1-\mu^i T^h)]} \qquad\qquad\qquad [11.A3]$$

Similarly,

$$S_3 = \mu^d D_3{}^h T^h + \mu^i r T^h S_2 = \mu^d D_3{}^h T^h + \mu^i r T^h S_3/(1+r) \qquad [11.A4]$$

$$S_3 = \frac{\mu^d D_3{}^h T^h(1+r)}{[1+r(1-\mu^i T^h)]} \qquad [11.A5]$$

For S_n $(n > 1)$,

$$S_n = \mu^d D_n{}^h T^h + \mu^i r T^h S_{n-1} = \mu^d D_n{}^h T^h + \mu^i r T^h S_n/(1+r) \qquad [11.A6]$$

$$S_n = \frac{\mu^d D_n{}^h T^h(1+r)}{[1+r(1-\mu^i T^h)]} \qquad [11.A7]$$

Note that S is the debts that are supported by the prospective DTS and the ITS associated with the debts supported in the previous period.

Secondly, calculate the present value of ITS resulted from the debts supported. If K_s is the discount rate for discounting this cash flow, then:

$$PV\ (ITS_1) = T^h r(\mu^d D_1{}^h T^h)/(1+K_s) \qquad [11.A8]$$

$$PV\ (ITS_2) = T^h r\{(\mu^d D_2{}^h T^h)(1+r)/[1+r(1-\mu^i T^h)]\}/(1+K_s)^2 \quad [11.A9]$$

$$PV\ (ITS_3) = T^h r\{[(\mu^d D_3{}^h T^h)(1+r)/[1+r(1-\mu^i T^h)]\}/(1+K_s)^3 \qquad [11.A10]$$

$$\begin{matrix} \vdots & \vdots & \vdots & \vdots \\ \vdots & \vdots & \vdots & \vdots \end{matrix}$$

$$PV\ (ITS_n) = T^h r\{[(\mu^d D_n{}^h T^h)(1+r)/[1+r(1-\mu^i T^h)]\}/(1+K_s)^n \qquad [11.A11]$$

Summing up $(n > 1)$:

$$\sum_{i=1}^{n} PV\ (ITS_i) = \frac{T^h r(1+r)}{[1+r(1-\mu^i T^h)]} \sum_{i=1}^{n} \frac{\mu^d D_i{}^h T^h}{(1+K_s)^i} \qquad [11.A12]$$

II. Calculation of the PV of ITS of the debts supported by the lessee's commitment of lease payments

The procedure of calculation of the present value of ITS due to the debt supported by the lessee's commitment of lease payments is the same as the calculation of the above case. However, we start from the last period of the lease, n.

In period n, the debt supported (P_n) contains two parts: the debt supported by the after-tax lease payment in period n,[31] and debt supported by the ITS of the debt supported by the lease payments previously. Let μ^L be the fraction of the value of the after-tax lease payments that is added to the firm's debt capacity. Again, μ^i is the fraction of the value of the ITS of the debts supported that is added to the firm's debt capacity, and assume that the debts supported by a leasing project have the same characteristics as the normal debts, r to be the interest rate of the normal debts, and $P_{n-1} = P_n/(1+r)$, where $n > 1$, then:

$$P_n = \mu^L[Q_nL_n(1-T^h)] + \mu^iT^hrP_{n-1}$$

$$= \mu^L[Q_nL_n(1-T^h)] + \mu^iT^hrP_n/(1+r) \qquad [11.A13]$$

From Eq.[11.A13], P_n can be known:

$$P_n = \frac{\mu^L[Q_nL_n(1-T^h)](1+r)}{[1+r(1-\mu^iT^h)]} \qquad [11.A14]$$

In the period $n-1$,

$$P_{n-1} = \mu^L[Q_{n-1}L_{n-1}(1-T)] + \mu^iT^hrP_{n-2}$$

$$= \mu^L[Q_{n-1}L_{n-1}(1-T)] + \mu^iT^hrP_{n-1}/(1+r) \qquad [11.A15]$$

So:

---

[31] Note the after-tax lease payment in period n is zero if the lessor requires the first payments be paid in advance. In this case, the debt supported by the after-tax lease payment in period n is also zero.

$$P_{n-1} = \frac{\mu^L[Q_{n-1}L_{n-1}(1-T^h)](1+r)}{[1+r(1-\mu^iT^h)]}$$ [11.A16]

Similarly,

$$P_2 = \mu^L[Q_2L_2(1-T)] + \mu^iT^hrP_1$$

$$= \mu^L[Q_2L_2(1-T)] + \mu^iT^hrP_2/(1+r)$$ [11.A17]

So:

$$P_2 = \frac{\mu^L[Q_2L_2(1-T^h)](1+r)}{[1+r(1-\mu^iT^h)]}$$ [11.A18]

Clearly:

$$P_1 = \mu^L[Q_1L_1(1-T)]$$ [11.A19]

Now, calculate the present value of ITS due to the debts supported. If K_p is the discount rate for discounting this cash flow, then:

$$PV\,(ITS_1) = T^hr\{\mu^L[Q_1L_1(1-T)]\}/(1+K_p)$$ [11.A20]

$$PV\,(ITS_2) = T^hr\{\mu^L[Q_2L_2(1-T)](1+r)/[1+r(1-\mu^iT^h)]\}/(1+K_p)^2$$ [11.A21]

$$PV\,(ITS_3) = T^hr\{\mu^L[Q_3L_3(1-T)](1+r)/[1+r(1-\mu^iT^h)]\}/(1+K_p)^3$$ [11.A22]

$$\vdots \quad \vdots \quad \vdots \quad \vdots$$
$$\vdots \quad \vdots \quad \vdots \quad \vdots$$

$$PV\,(ITS_n) = T^hr\{\mu^L[Q_nL_n(1-T)](1+r)/[1+r(1-\mu^iT^h)]\}/(1+K_p)^n$$ [11.A23]

Summing up:

$$\sum_{i=1}^{n} PV\ (ITS_i) = \frac{T^h r(1+r)}{[1+r(1-\mu^i T^h)]} \sum_{i=1}^{n} \frac{\mu^L Q_i L_i (1-T^h)}{(1+K_p)^i} \qquad [11.A24]$$

III. Calculation of the PV of ITS of the debts supported by a lease

Let Φ be a coefficient, and define $\Phi = [T^h r(1+r)]/[1+r(1-\mu^i T^h)]$, and put Eq.[11.A12] and Eq.[11.A24] together, then we obtain:

$$PV = \Phi \sum_{i=1}^{n} [\frac{\mu^d D_i^h T^h}{(1+K_s)^i} + \frac{\mu^L Q_i L_i (1-T^h)}{(1+K_p)^i}] \qquad [11.A25]$$

12 International sale-and-leaseback

Why do firms sell and leaseback?

A sale-and-leaseback is a particular form of financing. Under sale-and-leaseback deals, companies sell fixed assets, such as buildings, to a financial institution or other purchaser, thereby removing the asset's value and any associated liabilities, such as mortgages, from their balance sheets. The purchaser then lease the asset back to the company so that it can go on using it. In a sale-and-leaseback, a firm sells an asset it owns to another party and simultaneously leases the asset back from the new owner. The lessee receives funds in the amount of the current market value of the asset while retaining the use of the asset as an input to the firm's productive activities. Generally, the sale-and-leaseback is a long-established means for a company to obtain an immediate cash value for an asset, improve its balance sheet and still retain the use of that asset in its business. Conceptually, an international sale-and-leaseback is mostly the same as a domestic sale-and-leaseback except that the new owner is a foreigner.

An international sale-and-leaseback, or more precisely an export sale-and-leaseback can be defined as a domestic asset (equipment or real estate) is sold to a foreign institution, which in turn leases the asset back to the seller. In economic terms, however, such transactions are a form of debt financing (Slovin *et al.* 1990, p.290).

Aircraft leasing accounts for the majority of sale-and-leaseback transactions, with close to 25% of all planes leased. Every US, and most Asian and European airlines are involved in some form of sale-and-leaseback arrangement.[1] Other sale-and-leaseback transactions involve equipment, capital assets and land. More recently, many hospitals and universities have entered into sale-and-leasebacks to gain access to much-needed funds. In the past few years a number of hospitals in the UK, USA and Canada entered into sale-and-leasebacks involving medical equipment.

Why do firms sell and leaseback? The most common is that the lessee has ordered and paid for assets before the decision is made to obtain lease finance. Even if the assets have not been paid for it might not be practical to obtain the supplier's agreement for the order to be altered in favour of the leasing company.

Second, a sale-and-leaseback of a major asset is the economic equivalent to the issuance of a collateralised bond or a mortgage, except that title to the asset is transferred to a buyer. Slovin *et al.* (1990) report that there are positive and significant effects on shareholder wealth upon announcement of sale-and-leasebacks by non-financial firms.[2] The empirical results indicate that sale-and-leasebacks enhance the lessee's value by reducing expected taxes but have no significant effects on lessors. Slovin, *et al.* (1990) report that announcements of sale-and-leasebacks of major structures by non-financial firms significantly increase shareholder wealth of lessees by 0.85%, because of a reduction in the present value of expected taxes.

Third, a sale-and-leaseback may provide attractive benefits to both the seller/lessee and the buyer/lessor. The seller usually receives 100% of the value of the asset while retaining its full use during the term of the lease. The buyer receives an investment asset and all of the financial and tax benefits associated with the asset ownership.

Fourth, the most obvious motivation for a firm to sell and leaseback its assets is to generate cash to finance a business expansion or capital acquisition. Cash provided in this manner would be available to produce returns consistent with those generated by the mainstream business, generally far higher than if left as assets. The survey by El-Zayaty (1986) show that financially troubled firms tend to take the sale-and-leaseback action to avoid bankruptcy.

---

[1] See *The Japan Economic Journal*, April 13, 1991, p.10.
[2] In contrast, Slovin, *et al.* (1991) find that sale and leasebacks by banks have a significantly negative effect on shareholder wealth similar to announcements of seasoned common stock by bank holding companies. This difference is partly because capital regulation influences the market's interpretation of bank managerial announcement.

Fifth, a sale-and-leaseback may provide an opportunity for the seller/lessee to establish an attractive lease arrangement with rental rate and lease term tailored to meet some other business requirements.

In the literature, it has been debated whether a sale-and-leaseback is one or two transactions since 1974 when the FASB published "Discussion Memorandum on Accounting for Leases". In my view, any sale-and-leaseback arrangement should generally be considered as one transaction since this is merely a method to raise funds by offering the asset/equipment as collateral and at the same time retaining asset/equipment rights. Asset sales are a type of corporate control event, whereas sale-and-leaseback transactions are, in effect, a form of financing. In some cases, however, when the lessor/buyer assumes all the risks of ownership and the lessee/seller leases back the assets for a transitional period which is significantly less than the life of the asset leased with no renewal options, the transaction may likewise be accounted for as two independent transactions. In normal cases, sale-and-leaseback should not be accounted for as two independent transactions.

How to structure an international sale-and-leaseback

An international sale-and-leaseback of assets and real estate can be structured in several ways, depending on the objectives of corporate management. Normally, the objective would be to generate the maximum amount of cash with the leaseback rate determined by current market rental rates for a comparable facility. In some cases, companies may elect to have either a higher or lower lease rate and the selling price of the asset or property is adjusted to reflect the variance from current market conditions. In other cases, the objective is to avoid financing difficulties, or to take advantage of legal, and tax systems. It is also possible to use a sale-and-leaseback to hedge foreign exchange risk, to diversify the firm's portfolio of capital, or to restructure the firm's capital structure and balance sheet.

When considering a sale-and-leaseback, the required rate of return of the transaction depends on: the sale price of the asset, the term of leaseback, the financial strength of the tenant leasing back the asset or property, the residual value of the asset at the end of the leaseback term, and so on.

There are many factors to consider in structuring an international sale-and-leaseback. However, around the world no country so far has set formal legal rules governing the sale-and-leaseback transactions. In most cases, accounting treatments are the main reference of determining a sale-and-leaseback for tax purposes by tax authorities, although there is a difference in determining the sale-and-leasebacks between from an accounting point of view and from a legal point of view. Therefore, understanding the accounting treatment is of great importance to structure an international sale-and-leaseback. In this chapter I will focus on major accounting considerations involved in a sale-and-leaseback.

Although there are also no accounting standards on international sale-and-leasebacks, most countries use accounting standards for domestic sale-and-leasebacks to treat international cases. The FASB in May 1988 issued Statement of Financial Accounting Standards No.98 "Accounting for Leases: Sale-Leaseback Transactions Involving Real Estate, Sales-Type Leases of Real Estate, Definition of the Lease Term, Initial Direct Costs of Direct Financing Leases" (FASB No.98). This statement establishes new reporting rules for sale-and-leaseback transactions, including real estate sale-and-leasebacks with equipment such as commercial office building, manufacturing facilities and refineries. The provisions of FASB No.98 that address sale-leaseback transactions are based on the view that those transactions should qualify for sales recognition before it is appropriate for the seller-lessee to use sale-leaseback accounting. However, the Board noted that most sale-leasebacks are entered into as a means of financing, for tax reasons, or both and that the terms of the sale and the terms of the leaseback are usually negotiated as a package. Because of this interdependence of terms, no means could be identified for separating the sale and the leaseback that would be both practicable and objective (paragraph 107, FASB No.13). The new rules impose restrictive tests for recognising sales, and then lengthen lease terms. According to the FASB No.98, a sale-leaseback transaction must include all of the following:

a) A normal leaseback which is defined as a lessee-lessor relationship that involves the active use of the property by the seller-lessee in consideration for payment of rent, including contingent rentals that are based on the future operations of the seller-lessee;

b) Payment terms and provisions that adequately demonstrate the buyer-lessor's initial and continuing investment in the property;

c) Payment terms and provisions that transfer all of the other risks and rewards of ownership. There must be no continuing seller-lessee involvement other than through a normal leaseback.

There are some conditions or provisions that may preclude transactions qualifying for sale-leaseback accounting under FASB No.98. We summarise them as follows:

- There is an option to repurchase the asset or property, even if the option price equals the asset's or property's fair value at the date the option is exercised;
- The seller-lessee has to repurchase the asset or property, or the buyer-lessor can compel such a repurchase at any future time;
- The seller-lessee guarantees the buyer-lessor's investment or a return on that investment for a limited or extended period of time;
- The seller-lessee compensates the buyer-lessor for a decline in the asset or property's fair value;
- The seller-lessee provides non-recourse financing to the buyer-lessor for all or part of the sales price;
- The seller-lessee provides recourse financing in which the only collateral is the asset or property sold;
- The seller-lessee remains obliged on existing debt related to the asset or property;
- The seller-lessee provides collateral to lenders on behalf of the buyer-lessor other than the asset or property directly involved;
- The seller-lessee (or a party related to the seller-lessee) guarantees the buyer-lessor's debt;
- A related party to the seller-lessee guarantees a return of or on the buyer-lessor's investment;
- The seller-lessee's rental payments are contingent on some level of future operations by the buyer-lessor;
- The seller-lessee enters into a sale-leaseback transaction involving asset or property improvements or integral equipment without leasing the underlying land to the buyer-lessor;
- The buyer-lessor is obligated to share with the seller-lessee any portion of the appreciation of the asset of property;
- The seller-lessee is allowed to participate in the buyer-lessor's future profits or the appreciation of the asset of property.

Under any of the above cases of continuing involvement, the transaction must be reported either as a financing[3] or by the deposit method.[4] A sale-leaseback transaction that qualifies for sales recognition is accounted for using sale-leaseback accounting by the seller-lessee whether the leaseback is classified as a capital lease or an operating lease in accordance with FASB No.13. In other words, sale-and-leasebacks must be classified as operating leases or finance leases. Where an operating lease results and the sale is for fair value, any profit arising from a sale is recognised at that point of time. Any profit arising from a finance lease is recognised over the period of the lease. In addition, FASB No.98 requires the seller-lessee to describe in the notes the sale-leaseback transaction, including future commitments, obligations, and provisions or circumstances resulting in continuing involvement with the asset or property by the seller-lessee.

Financially, a sale and leaseback of an asset or equipment may be viewed as a way of using a valuable asset to raise finance without losing control of it altogether. There are some tax advantages attached to the transaction. In the UK, Sections 75 and 76 of the Capital Allowances Act 1990 can be applied to a sale and leaseback between companies whether or not the parties are connected. Essentially, the amount which the buyer can bring into his capital allowance pool is limited to the disposal value which the seller has recognised in his own capital allowances computation, preventing a tax-free uplift. If the seller is not within the capital allowances system in respect of the asset, then the limitation is by reference to the lowest of market value, the capital cost of the asset to the seller, or the capital cost of the asset to any person connected to the seller. The rules, which contain a number of detailed amplifications and exceptions, also apply to assignments of hire purchase and conditional sale contracts. In commercial terms, the main effect of the legislation is to prevent the use of leasing to achieve a step-up in the amount on which capital allowances are being claimed on existing asset or equipment.

Sale and leaseback transactions have been the subject of extensive debate in legal literature and of conflicting judicial decisions. The very structure of

---

[3] Under this accounting, the asset appears in the balance sheet and is depreciated. Sale proceeds are reported as a liability. Lease payments, less a portion considered to be interest expense, decrease the liability and collections of principal and interest on the buyer-lessor's note increase the liability.

[4] Under this method, any down payment and payments of principal and interest are reported as a deposit liability. Lease payments decrease this liability and collections of principal and interest on the buyer-lessor's note increase it. The asset is carried in the seller-lessee's balance sheet and is depreciated.

the transaction emphasises its purposes, consisting in the injection of fresh funds into the lessee and the transfer to the lessor of title to the lessee's assets in what may be regarded as a provision of security. In other words, a sale and leaseback lends to being construed as a loan to the lessee by the lessor, secured by the transfer of the lessee's assets and repaid over the term of the lease.

Recently, the Financial Reporting Review Panel in the UK, an investigative sister body of the Accounting standards Board signalled that they would not allow sale and leaseback transactions to flatter the performance of companies. This indicates that the authorities are aware of the advantages provided by a sale-and-leaseback and the transaction can be used to improve the balance sheet position. Therefore, it is anticipated that new rules will impose on the transaction to reduce the effects on the performance and balance sheet of the company that uses a sale-and-leaseback.

Conclusion

There may be a number of reasons why sale and leaseback transactions are entered into. Amongst the other financial reasons are: 1) the transaction may provide working capital for the business of the lessee; 2) the transaction may generate a book profit where the fair market value of an asset exceeds the book value in the lessee's account; 3) where the original purchase of the leased asset was financed either from cash resources or short-term funds and the needs of the lessee's business indicate that medium- or long-term finance would better meet financial planning targets; and 4) where lease finance would produce a lower rate of interest than is being presently paid by the lessee under existing finance for the purchase of the leased asset.

Generally, there are no legal rules governing the structure of the transactions. Accounting treatments are the most important considerations in structuring a sale-and leaseback. This chapter has provided a number of accounting issues involved in sale-and-leasebacks. However, the accounting rules are under scrutiny by the authorities in many countries, and some advantages of sale-and-leasebacks may be lost.

Reference

EI-Zayaty, A.I. 1986. *Business Failure Prediction: An Analysis of Type II Prediction Errors*. PhD Dissertation, City University of New York.

Financial Accounting Standards Board (FASB). 1988. *Statement of Financial Accounting Standards No.98: Accounting for Leases: Sale-Leaseback Transactions Involving Real Estate, Sales-Type Leases of Real Estate, Definition of the Lease Term, Initial Direct Costs of Direct Financial Leases*. Stamford, CT.

Slovin, M.B., M.E. Sushka and J.A. Polonchek. 1990. Corporate sale-and-leasebacks and shareholder wealth. *The Journal of Finance* March: 389-299.

Slovin, M.B., M.E. Sushka and J.A. Polonchek. 1991. Restructuring transactions by bank holding companies: the valuation effects of sale-and-leasebacks and divestitures. *Journal of Banking and Finance* April: 237-255.

13 Leasing in emerging markets: eastern Europe and China

Introduction

Leasing as a financing tool was not used in China and eastern Europe[1] before their economic reforms as the funds for capital construction were provided mainly by the State government and assets/equipment acquired were owned by the State. During the transition periods, leasing has been recognised as a valuable financing tool to companies in these economies.

Although leasing is one of the most growing areas in eastern Europe and China, research has been exceptionally inadequate. Researches in the area are mostly concerned with individual country studies. For example, Dipchand (1993) only describes some leasing companies and leasing development in China. Gao (1995) only studies leasing and its problems in Poland. Although Gao and Herbert (1996) provide a comparison of leasing between the Czech Republic, Hungary and Poland, their research is limited to only examine three closely related countries in central Europe.

This chapter aims to identify the development of leasing in the transitional economies (China and eastern Europe) and its financial function to the economic reforms. Leasing itself is currently undergoing a period of transition where many new laws and regulations have been passed to promote leasing as a valuable financing tool for companies in these countries which want to modern their outdated equipment.

---

[1] In this paper, countries in central Europe are also categorised as eastern European countries for the political and economic grouping rather than the geographical separation.

Leasing in China: industry, markets, regulatory developments and accounting for leases

China's recent history of economic expansion is unique among developing countries, evidenced by the around 10% GDP growth rate annually between 1980 to 1997. Even in 1998 with effects of the Asian financial crisis, China managed to achieve 7.8% GDP growth. The economic reforms and industrial expansions in Chinas have resulted in a growing demand for capital investment. Although the establishment of stock markets in Shenzhen and Shanghai which provides an effective channel of finance, demands for capital finance are extremely enormous as China is a huge and one of the fastest developing countries with 1.2 billion population.

Since 1979 when China started its open door policy and began economic reforms, leasing has increasingly been used in financing investment projects and productive facilities, as well as in financing the purchase of aircraft and large transportation equipment. The leasing industry has since continued to grow in line with the overall development of the Chinese economy.

Industry and markets

From 1978 to the present, the political and economic environment in China has drastically changed. In 1978, the Chinese government decided to implement political and economic reform. It began to adopt a market economy and an open door policy to the world. Accordingly, the mono-banking and financial system was gradually dismantled. The reform in the financial services was marked by the restoration of the state-owned banks. In February 1979, the Agricultural Bank of China was restored, and served as a specialised bank handling rural financial affairs. In the same manner, the State Council, decided to expand the authority of the Bank of China (BOC) and separated it from the People's Bank of China. It was made to focus on foreign exchange, international settlements and foreign trade.

At the same time, non-banking financial bodies have also grown at a relatively rapid pace, eventually completing the transition from a highly unified banking economy to a diversified finance environment where various financial institutions exist. At present, apart from the 4 specialised state banks, there are more than 10 regional and national commercial banks, 12 insurance companies, about 400 financial and trust companies, over 60 financial leasing companies, 59,000 rural credit cooperatives and over 5,000 urban credit cooperatives. Aside from these, foreign banks and other financial institutions from over 15 countries around the world have secured a foothold in China. Many of them have opened branches in Shanghai and Guangzhou, and representative offices in many parts of China.

The Chinese leasing industry first took root in 1980. In January 1980, the first leasing company in China, China Orient Leasing Co. was established as a joint venture involving Japan Oriental Leasing, China International Trust and Investment Corporation, and Peking Machine and Electric Equipment Corp. This joint-venture leasing company concentrated on the financing of export-oriented industries to ensure that hard currency earnings would be available to meet lease obligations. Within a year, the first state-owned leasing company (China Leasing Co. Ltd.) was established in 1981. By the end of 1994, there were 63 Chinese enterprises specialising in the leasing business, including 33 Sino-Foreign Equity Joint Ventures. Besides the specialist leasing companies, some 400 other institutions (such as banks and finance companies) are presently engaged in leasing as a part of their business (World-Leasing-Yearbook 1997 p.133). Leasing is currently an important channel through which Chinese enterprise can acquire complex fixed assets when needed, and it is an important instrument of financing (Fang and Tang 1991, p.86). According to World Leasing Yearbook (1997), the leasing industry attracted over US$15 billion of foreign capital to the Chinese economy from 1979 to 1994 (p.133). The Chinese leasing industry is now at its initial stage of development and is trying to find out a way of its own (Gao 1991, p.31).

The Chinese leasing market is a product of the rapid economic growth that resulted from the open-door policy of 1979. The current economic development in China is summarised in Table 13.1. The leasing industry in China has continued to see further growth in line with the overall development of the Chinese economy, and the role of leasing has been recognised by the Chinese government.

However, leasing is still small scale business in China. Leasing represents less than 4% of the capital expenditure in China compared with an average figure of 15% for the rest of World. Comparing with other transitional economies in eastern Europe as shown in Table 13.2. The Chinese leasing industry also lags far behind the industries of the Czech Republic, Hungary, Slovenia and Slovak in terms of the market penetration (i.e., capital expenditure through leasing). Obviously, the Chinese leasing market has much further to grow. Current lease transactions in China, similar to those in Western countries, can be separated into two categories: an operating lease, and a financing lease (Fang and Tang 1991, p.86). However, financial leasing is the predominant leasing form (Gao 1991, p.31). Leasing contract ranges from 3 years to 10 years with fixed rental payments annually. Recently, operating leasing has gained popularity in the leasing of aircraft, computers, office equipment and consumer goods.

Table 13.1 China: selected economic indicators

	1993	1994	1995	1996[1]
	In per cent			
Domestic economy				
Change in real GDP	13.5	12.6	10.5	9.7
Change in retail prices (period average)	13.0	21.7	14.8	6.1
	In billions of U.S. dollars[2]			
External economy				
Exports	75.9	102.6	128.1	128.5
Imports	-86.3	-95.3	-110.1	-114.6
Current account balance[3]	-11.9	7.7	1.6	3.9
Direct investment	23.1	31.8	33.8	38.8
Portfolio investment	3.0	3.5	0.8	2.4
State gross official reserves[4]	23.0	53.5	76.0	107.7
Current account balance (in per cent of GDP)	-2.7	1.4	0.2	0.5
External debt	84.4	95.0	106.6	116.2
Debt service (in per cent of exports of goods and nonfactor services)	12.6	11.6	10.6	10.9
Change in real effective exchange rate (in per cent)[5]	-1.90	9.01	5.34	4.95
	In per cent of GDP[2]			
Financial variables				
Overall budgetary balance[6]	-2.0	-1.6	-1.7	-1.5
Gross national saving	40.6	42.6	41.1	42.9
Gross domestic investment	43.3	41.2	40.8	42.4
Change in broad money (in per cent)[7]	24.0	34.5	29.5	25.3
Interest rate (in per cent; one-year time deposits, year-end)	10.98	10.98	10.98	7.47[8]

Notes: [1]Fund staff estimates; [2]Unless otherwise noted; [3]Series has breaks in 1995 and 1996 owing to changes in the coverage of services items; [4]Includes gold, SDR holdings, and reserve position in the Fund; [5]December averages; [6]Central and local governments; [7]End of period; banking survey. Owing to break in the series in 1993, growth rates for that year are not available and monetary survey data (broadly similar) are reported instead; [8]End-March 1997.

Source: *IMF Annual Report, 1997.*

Table 13.2 Volume, growth and market penetration of leasing in transition economies (1995)

Country	Annual volume (US$ bn)	% growth (1994-1995)	% Market penetration
China	1.50	37.6	3.5*
Czech Republic	1.30	10.2	16.0
Hungary	0.69	-23.5	15.5
Poland	0.67	99.8	4.5
Slovak	0.22	138.7	8.2
Slovenia	0.19	119.3	11.3
Russia	0.20	n/a	n/a
Asia	*104.8*	*5.6*	*6.0**
Worldwide	*409.1*	*14.8*	*15.0**

Source: *World Leasing Yearbook*, 1997, p.3.
* Author's estimate.

Law and tax regulation

It is argued that the economic reform programme would no succeed unless accompanied by complementary regulation, tax and accounting reforms. Currently, China is making fundamental changes to its regulatory, tax and accounting systems. The changes in these systems are always accompanied with some problems. For example, a number of legislation have been hastily drafted and passed by the People's Congress and the government. As a result, it is often incomplete, ambiguous or at least open to interpretation. Moreover, despite China's enormous strides in introducing new legislation, China's legal system continues to develop within the context of a planned economy and central bureaucracy. Internal politics, policy considerations and traditional influences are often dominant factors operating behind the law. In many respects, the practical application of law in China actually begins not with the written law but with a complex network of informal systems operating beneath the formal legal one.[2]

---

[2] In leasing business, a network of informal systems (e.g., *GuanXi*: personnel relationship) is extremely essential to securing a lease contract between a lessor and a lessee. One of the

China's Ministry of Foreign Trade and Economic Co-operation (MOFTEC) is responsible for the licensing of foreign joint ventures in China, including leasing joint ventures, and external trade in general. There is no specific leasing law in China at the present time, although this will probably change in the very near future. Leasing transactions are currently governed by applicable portions of the three existing major contract laws, which at most reflect a traditional rental orientation: the Law on Economic Contracts (1981, amended 1993), the Law on Economic Contracts Concerning Foreign Interests (1985) and the Law on Technology Contracts (1987). China is currently in the process of drafting a new law on economic contracts which will replace these three laws with a single, unified contract law. This new law will most likely contain a section specifically addressing financial leasing. The rather limited existing coverage of traditional rental contracts is also likely to be expanded. Although work on the new contract law has been going on for some time, its official promulgation is not expected until sometime in 1999.

There are eight articles on the subject of civil aircraft leasing in China's Civil Aviation Law which came into effect on March 1, 1996. Apart from the Civil Aviation Law, there is no specific legal definition of a lease, nor of the difference between an operating and a finance lease under Chinese law. Leases are generally treated as a type of economic contracts under Chinese laws. Also, Chinese law provides that in the case of foreign economic contracts, in respect of matters which are not covered by Chinese law, international practice may apply. As a result, the concept of a lease under Chinese law is more or less similar to the internationally recognised concept (i.e., a contract of letting in which one party is granted the possession and use of asset/equipment in return for the payment of rent). Chinese law does not specify in detail the terms which leases are required to have. There are no standard forms of lease contracts, and the contacting parties are generally free to specify such terms as they wish and these will be upheld by a Chinese court providing that they do not otherwise conflict with Chinese law or fundamental principles.

Leasing companies in China are generally susceptible to the following taxes:[3]

---

interviewees comments that "No *GuanXi*, No business; No business, No invitation for everything, No life."

[3] For details, see World Leasing Yearbook 1997, pp.136-137.

(a) *Income tax.* Chinese leasing companies are generally required to pay tax at the rate of 35% on their income derived from the leasing business. Income is divided into two distinct categories: i) profit margin; and ii) rental income. A leasing company which has no affiliation with a financial institution will be required to pay tax on its profit margin whilst one which is so affiliated will be taxed on its total rental income;

(b) *Business tax.* The business tax is a turnover tax. Chinese leasing companies pay a business tax (about 5%) on their leasing activity;

(c) *Import duty.* All equipment imported into China for utilisation by Chinese lessees will generally bear import duty, the level of tariff depending on the type of equipment. As China moves towards GATT and tries to join WTO, there are likely to be changes in the current regulations relating to the levying, and amount, of import duty;

(d) *Withholding tax.* Lease payments made by a Chinese lessee to a foreign lessor incurred withholding tax (also called, rental income tax).[4] The Chinese Ministry of Finance (MOF) may also grant an exemption from rental income tax in certain cases, such as with aircraft and rolling stock, or where the asset will be used as an investment by a foreign investor in an equity joint venture;

(e) *Stamp duty.* Leased documents are subject to Chinese stamp duty, at the rate of 0.1% of the leasing fee for operating leases and possibly 0.005% for financial leases. However, the State Tax Bureau may grant a reduction or exemption in certain cases. In the case of aircraft leases in particular, a stamp duty exemption is invariably granted.

China has a unique dual licensing system: 1) domestic leasing companies are licensed by the central bank, the People's Bank of China, while 2) foreign joint venture leasing companies are licensed by the MOFTEC. As a result, domestic Chinese leasing companies are supervised as a non-bank financial institution, while foreign joint ventures, although licensed, are essentially unsupervised. Also foreign joint ventures have free access to foreign exchange, in part as a result of being under the preview of MOFTEC, domestic lease companies have limited foreign exchange access. Although

---

[4] The rate was normally 20% until the end of 1995 when the rate was reduced to 10% by the Chinese tax authorities in order to attract foreign investment and accelerate economic development. However, this may be reduced in the case where China has a double tax treaty with the foreign country in question.

China was a major participant in the drafting process of the Unidroit Convention on International Financial Leasing, it has yet to ratify it.

Accounting for leases

Accounting in China is very much influenced by the socio-economic environment in which enterprises operate, and being a centrally controlled economy, accounting practices in China differ to a considerable extent from those of western countries (Tang, *et al.* 1995). However, China is moving towards the adoption of Western style accounting standards. Chinese enterprises were regulated generally by "Accounting Standards for Enterprises" promulgated on November 16, 1992 and became effective on 1 July 1993. The Accounting Standards introduce major changes to the traditional accounting practices in China. For instance, the standards bring changes in the function of accounting and address the needs of different users of accounting information. Traditionally, accounting in China was used to provide information for the central government for decision-making in macro-economic control. The new standards broaden the user groups of accounting information to include external users, such as investors and creditors, and internal users such as managers.

Chinese accounting treatments for lease are quite close to those stipulated in International Accounting Standards (IAS) No.17, and leases are required to be separated between an operating lease and a capital lease. The Chinese accounting standards are applicable to all leasing firms and lessees in China, regardless specific types of ownership and industries. These provide for assets acquired pursuant to a finance lease to be reflected in the lessee's balance sheet as though they were the owner thereof (the position was formerly unclear). Depreciation is to be calculated by reference to original cost, estimated net residual value (ENRV) and on the basis of an estimated useful life or workload method. In the case of a finance lease the regulation provides that "original cost", for the purposes of calculating depreciation, will be the cost as set out in the lease, plus expenses payable by the lessee (freight, insurance, tax etc.). If the contract price for the asset includes interest and commission then these are deducted from the original cost. The ENRV should not generally be less than 10% of the original cost and the straight-line method is generally to be used, unless unsuitable.

According to the accounting reform plan, the next phase of the reforms will be the establishment of a full set of accounting standards covering operational aspects of business activities. The Ministry of Finance plans to complete this task in about three years (Tang *et al.* 1995). However, the establishment of standards of accounting for leases is not on the agenda.[5] This has caused a great concern to the Chinese leasing industry and many foreign leasing companies. It has been argued that the establishment of accounting standards for leases is important to the future development of China's leasing market and the internalisation of the Chinese leasing industry.

Problems and future challenges

China's desire to "catch up" with the West in economy is beyond doubt, and some success has been achieved, albeit not as much as the Chinese themselves would have liked. Leasing as a financial instrument has been practised and the leasing industry has emerged in China since 1978. Leasing has brought finance and investment into China, even if not much, comparing with the potential needs and the huge market and with other reforming countries in eastern Europe. Over the last few years, there were some success in developing the leasing industry and the market in China such as the formulation of leasing companies, the growth of both domestic leasing and international aircraft leasing. Nevertheless, the leasing industry is till young and the market is underdeveloped in many aspects, particularly in real estate leasing market and operating leasing market. The major problems facing the leasing industry in China are the lack of finance and capital investment and of appropriate legislation protecting the industry. Business relies much on personal relationship and informal network, and there is a poor information flow system. The major problems are summarised as follows:[6]

1. There is a lack of management and personal experiences in the leasing business. To many managers and businessmen, the understanding of leasing and experiences in leasing are very limited. In many aspects, the traditional views of the priority of owning assets (the ownership) still prevent the development of leasing.
2. There are serious bad debts problems resulting from the "triangle debts" situation. Bad debts problems occurred with the economic problems and the failure of macro-control has seriously affected leasing business. In many cases, lessees are facing difficulty to pay the rentals on schedule. The delay of rental payments by lessees makes lessors impossible to finance

---

[5] Aiken, *et al.* (1995) list 18 standards that are on schedule to be established soon. Accounting for leases is not in the list.
[6] These problems are based on interviews with Chinese managers of both lessors and lessees.

and borrow further so the market is restrained. Currently, the closure of many non-bank financial institutions including investment trusts has financial impacts on leasing companies as some of them are subsidiaries of these institutions and trusts.

3. There is inconsistent governmental policy in finance and fiscal policies. China is still centrally controlled state where the central government from time to time imposes policies and regulation to local government and state-owned enterprises. Many leasing companies are either state-owned, or a joint venture with a Chinese state-owned enterprise, thus they are often interfered with directly or indirectly by the government.

4. The legal position on ownership of land, building and assets/equipment is unclear. In addition, the lack of leasing regulations gives rise to questions as to a lessor's security in the asset and building, in particular in joint venture leasing firms.

5. The flow of information on the business in the domestic leasing market is poor. As a result, lessors have to take extraordinary and costly promotional approaches to attract business. However, potential lessees may not have information that would enable them to "shop around" for better deals (Dipchand, 1993). Informal network and relationship dominate the business and contracts.

6. The absence of sufficiently long-term finance, tax incentives and the ambiguous legal positions on ownership of land lead to the underdevelopment of the property leasing market.

Leasing in eastern Europe: markets, industry and regulatory developments

The transition of the national economy is spreading throughout eastern Europe. The impact of the economic transition is remarkably obvious and far-reaching. Apparently, the economic transition from a centrally-planned to a system of market economy must be undertaken against a background of sever economic, social and political problems. For instance, large parts of the economic infrastructure in these transitional economies in eastern Europe are obsolete and their levels of productivity are well below international standards. The economic development and restructuring have put a great demand for financing and investment in these countries, of which they have been severely short for some time.

Leasing has already proved its suitability both for investments and for covering private needs in eastern Europe. Given the continued security of funds and the notorious lack of capital of most new private enterprises, small and medium sized companies, leasing is obviously an extraordinarily suitable finance option for them. With leasing they may be able to overcome the current difficulties in obtaining loan security. In many countries, managers have already realised the advantages of leasing in handling their cash flows and in providing a tax efficient alternative form of financing. The advantages of leasing have brought about great demand for leasing services in eastern Europe. Leasing services are now offered by a number of local companies. Almost all companies with a remarkable position in the market (e.g. in the Czech leasing market) are independent leasing firms, banks and their subsidiaries. Many foreign banks and leasing companies have entered the leasing market in eastern Europe. Some of them were established as joint ventures with local entities.

Table 13.3 Volume, growth and market penetration of leasing in eastern Europe

| Country | Annual volume (US$ bn) (growth %) | | | | | Market penetration (1995) |
	1991	1992 (%)	1993 (%)	1994 (%)	1995 (%)	
Czech	0.25	0.60 (140.0)	0.65 (8.3)	1.04 (60.0)	1.30 (25.0)	**16.0%**
Hungary	0.18	0.67 (272.0)	0.73 (9.0)	1.06 (45.2)	0.69 (-34.9)	**15.5%**
Poland	0.07	0.10 (42.9)	0.12 (20.0)	0.25 (108.3)	0.67 (168.0)	**4.5%**
Slovak	n/a	n/a	n/a	0.11 (16.6)	0.22 (100.0)	**8.2%**
Slovenia	n/a	n/a	n/a	0.11 (10.0)	0.19 (72.7)	**11.3%**
Russia	n/a	n/a	n/a	n/a	0.20 (n/a)	**1.0%**

Source: *Leaseurope Reports, Leasing Associations' Reports, World Leasing Yearbooks.*

The emergence of the debt problem and the underdeveloped capital markets have made leasing an attractive and valuable tool to coping with financing and investment problems in these countries. Leasing has been developed rapidly in those countries in the last few years.[7] Table 13.3 provides a general picture of leasing in some east European countries. Investment through

---

[7] Leasing in these countries is not treated just as a method of financing, but also as an important mechanism of economic reforms (Gao, 1994, pp.2-3). In this book, leasing only refers to lease financing.

leasing in the Czech Republic and Hungary has passed an average figure of about 15 per cent for the world (see Table 13.3).

Analysing the type of assets acquired by leasing it appears some difference among those countries, as shown in Table 13.4. Generally, apart from Russia, all other selected countries financed through leasing over 60 per cent of commercial vehicle and cars.[8] This is much higher than the developed market average, and early focus on cars and commercial vehicles is typical of young leasing markets, as barriers to entry are few, cars represent good security, and have a good second-hand market value.

Table 13.4 New assets acquired through leasing in eastern Europe by asset type in 1995 (ECU million)

Country	Machinery & Industrial Equipment (%)	Computers & Business Machines (%)	Commercial Vehicles (%)	Cars (%)	Ships Aircraft Railcars (%)	Other (%)	Total
Czech	166 (18.9)	50 (5.7)	129 (14.7)	489 (55.8)	5 (0.0)	38 (4.3)	877
Hungary	55 (18.3)	12 (4.0)	75 (24.9)	159 (52.8)	0 (0.0)	0 (0.0)	301
Poland	93 (24.2)	59 (15.3)	181 (47.0)	52 (13.5)	0 (0.0)	0 (0.0)	385
Slovakia	25 (16.2)	23 (14.9)	23 (14.9)	81 (52.6)	0 (0.0)	2 (1.3)	154
Slovenia	13 (12.8)	4 (3.9)	27 (26.5)	54 (52.9)	0 (0.0)	4 (3.9)	102
Russia	2 (11.1)	6 (33.3)	1 (5.6)	3 (16.7)	0 (0.0)	6 (33.3)	18

Source: *World Leasing Yearbook, 1997.*

The Czech Republic

In 1991 when the Czech leasing association was established by six companies, the extent of moveable assets leased by the members amounted to 182 million ECU. In the following year the amount reached 452 million. In 1995 the amount of new moveable assets leased by members of the Czech leasing association rose further to 877 million ECU. The biggest portion of leasing market belongs to car leasing representing 56% of the leasing

---

[8] In Poland, however, since April 1994 there is no passenger car leasing due to the restrictions which have been created by the Ministry of Finance. Passenger cars are seen by the Ministry as having no economic use in the development of companies and should not be treated as an investment.

business. The second position is taken by leasing of machinery with 6%, then others with 4% and in the last position leasing of ships, aircraft and railway rolling stock with 1%. In the Czech Republic there are now around 50 leasing companies with almost 80-90% of the business financing for private sector companies. About two dozen foreign banks and leasing companies have entered the market. The range of products covered includes machinery for factories, real estate, medical equipment, cash registers and cars and trucks. In 1993, a new tax law required the duration of a leasing contract to be at least three years. This enables a lessor to utilise all advantages that leasing can offer.

The current major problem to the development of leasing in the Republic is the lack of medium and long-term financing available to leasing companies. The treatment in the Czech taxation law is slightly preferential or neutral to leasing business. The most important taxation issue in dealing with leasing is the distinction between operating and financial leases. Ownership of a leased asset has to be passed to the lessee in a financial lease, according to the Czech taxation law. The period of any financial lease has to be longer than one fifth of the depreciation period of the leased asset or at least 3 years. Leasing payments are subject to VAT, with, in most cases the standard VAT rate of 22% applies. As to the taxation treatment of a financial cross-border lease into the Czech Republic, only a 1% withholding tax is applied on the lease payments of a Czech lessee to a foreign lessor. Conversely a 25% withholding tax applies to operating leases with foreign lessors. These withholding taxes can generally be taken as a tax credit in the home country of the foreign lessor. In a cross-border lease, both financial and operational, the lessee may defer the payment of customs duties and VAT on the imported asset.[9]

Equipment leasing in the Czech Republic is regulated, to a very limited extent by: 1) the general provision on leasing contained in the Civil Code; 2) special provisions covering leasing for business purposes contained in the Civil Code; and 3) special provisions dealing with the leasing of a means of transport and with the purchase of leased assets, contained in the Commercial Code. The Commercial Code is the main act relevant to leasing as it is this Code which primarily governs business activities and relations generally. A substantial amendment to the Civil Code and a new Commercial Code came

---

[9] This is done through the application of the so-called temporary use regime under the Czech customs laws, which allows qualifying importers to postpone payment of customers duties and VAT for up to 34 months.

into force on January 1, 1992. Furthermore, the entire taxation regime in the country has been substantially revised; a new regime came into force on January 1, 1993 but this itself was amended in July 1993. Tax treatment differs depending, broadly, on whether the lessee is to buy the asset at the end of the lease term. If the lessee is not to buy the asset, there is a choice of claiming straight-line or accelerated depreciation under the normal rules. Under these rules, the allowance for the first year is effectively half the normal allowance. If the lessee is to buy the asset, special rules can enable the lessor to claim faster tax depreciation. Leases do then have to meet certain conditions in order for a business lessee to claim deductions for rent.

Accounting is based on the legal approach in the Czech republic. The methodology of accounting for leases is very similar among others to that of France and Italy. The leased assets are not included as assets on the balance sheet and they are registered separately and treated as off-balance sheet items. There are no requirements to separate leases between financial and operating leases. All leases are treated as operating leases from the accounting perspective. However, the lessee is obliged to include their obligations resulting from any leasing contract in the end note to the balance sheet.

The major problem facing the Czech leasing industry is scarcity in financial resources. It is generally difficult or even impossible for independent leasing companies to obtain credit due to the fundamental problems in the banking sector of lending policy. At present, only leasing subsidiaries of banks and holdings may be able to secure credit resources for financing their leasing activities. In response to the current limits of the credit market, a growing number of leasing companies are seeking more accessible sources of financing available domestically and internationally. Many of them are being refinanced through forfaiting.[10] For instance, more than 80 Czech based leasing companies are involved in a forfaiting programme offered by Investicni a Postoni Banka.

Hungary

The vast majority of Hungarian leasing companies were established following the approval of the Corporate Law in 1988. The expansion of domestic leasing in the last few years resulted from that domestic bank loans were too

---

[10] For forfaiting, see: Dufey and Giddy (1981); Euromoney (1988); and Ripley (1996).

expensive, and hard to raise especially over 12 months. There are two principle types of leasing in Hungary: domestic and import (cross-border) leasing, which have developed with different characteristics. Most leasing agreements mean transactions in the form of finance leasing, although operating leasing is slowly gaining ground. Leasing companies normally finance 18% of their leasing transactions from bank loans, 38% from other sources and 44% from their own capital. Leasing covers a range of products from machinery to consumer goods. However, it is difficult to measure the role of leasing in the Hungarian economy due to the problem that statistics do not cover companies of less than 50 employees. Most leasing companies and their clients belong to this group. The prospects of leasing in the past few years have been determined by the shrinking level of investments. The lack of finance and investment is the main problem facing the Hungarian leasing industry.

The legal framework for leasing can be found from Decrees of the Ministry of Finance since 1970. The Association Law, which came into force on January 1, 1989, modernised Hungary's old business law by replacing the Corporate Law chapters of the 1875 Merchant Code as well as the 1930 Act on limited liability companies. The Association Law is, to a great extent, modelled on German corporate law. It recognises the basic forms of business formation such as general partnership, limited partnership, joint venture, limited liability company, and share holding company. The majority of Hungarian leasing companies were established in the form of limited liability company which requires the minimum capital of *Forints* 1 million. In Hungary, in the early years there was a keen demand for the so-called prompt leasing, which offered full tax deduction to the lessee at the lowest cost, since the total leasing fee (paid by the lessee in one lump sum at the very beginning of the leasing term) could be written off in one lump sum as expenses. The Corporate Tax Law and the Accounting Law, both enacted in January 1992, put an end to this type of business. The Corporate Tax Law defines leasing as: "transfer of products under a lease contract for a determined, minimum period of 365 days". The accounting law stipulates that "should the lessee charge more than 36% (in the case of real estate leasing 13%) of the total net leasing fee to expenses in one calendar year, he is obliged to increase his pre-tax profit with the surplus". The Accounting Law prescribes furthermore that companies such as limited liability companies, and joint stock companies may charge the net leasing fee to expenses only in proportion to the time elapsed from the leasing term (i.e., 3% in a month) without increasing their pre-tax profit. Nevertheless these companies are entitled to mark off their expenses temporally, therefore a leasing term of minimum 34 months allows full tax deduction for them irrespective of the actual payments. The above changes in the regulations have resulted in a diversity of leasing deals and to the strengthening of lease financing and risk assessment side.

Poland[11]

Leasing is small scale business in Poland, although there is about 100 leasing companies operated in the Polish market. Seven big leasing companies belong to banks and they control about 65% of the market. The 1995 figure by the Polish Leasing Association represents only 4.5% of the annual capital expenditure in Poland. Generally, the Polish leasing industry has also lagged far behind other transition economies, Hungary and Czech Republic, in terms of both the leasing volume and the market penetration. Leases in Poland have been written for the provision of cars (mainly non-passage cars), trucks, computers, industrial/construction equipment and others such as fax machines. Statistics for 1995 indicate that the great majority of lease contracts, 80% have a maximum lease period of two years, 20% of them have a lease period of three to five years, and that lease contracts of over five years are exceptional. All lease transactions are finance leases although they are not comparable with western style leases. Lack of competition, and the fact that the lease does not appear on the lessee's balance sheet and that the level of gearing is generally unknown militates against the development of operating leases.

Civil Code in Poland comprehensively encapsulates the conditions of most commercial transactions, with leasing being a notable exception. Leasing operates more within the framework of general legal and regulatory principles which may not mention leasing by name. Usually, a distinction is made between leasing and sale on instalment. With the latter, title passes automatically with the final payment, whereas with leasing the lessee is granted the first right to buy the asset at the end of the lease term. Until 1993 only the legal owner of an asset capitalised and depreciated leased assets. Lessees did not capitalise assets except in certain privatisation cases. For taxation purposes a deduction was allowed to the lessor equal to the depreciation charge. Rentals were taxed as lessor's income at 40 per cent.

---

[11] For the details of leasing, and its legal and accounting treatments in Poland, see Gao (1995).

The lessee could deduct the full lease payment for taxation purposes. In 1993, the Ministry of Finance issued important new regulations affecting the definitions of operating and finance leasing, their consequent accounting and tax treatments, and special restrictions on the depreciation and tax-deductibility of lease rentals pertaining to passenger cars. The new regulations defined two separate treatments, one for operating leases defined as any rental, hire or similar agreement meeting specified criteria such as lease term to depreciation periods, but most importantly giving only the option to buy.[12] Operating lease rentals are taxable income for the lessor and a tax deductible expense for the lessee.[13] The lessor is the owner of the asset and depreciates it for tax purposes as well as deducting interest costs from tax. VAT is chargeable on the whole of the lease rental and may be reclaimed, except in the case of passenger cars. Finance leases, which are transactions not meeting the operating lease criteria, mainly by offering a firm purchases option, are treated as assets of the lessee and are tax-depreciated by the lessee. The lessee may also expense the interest element of the rental. The lessor records only the interest portion of the lease rental as taxable income against which it can offset its interest expense. Leased equipment remains the property of the lessor until the lease ends.

Slovakia

A significant number of new banks and leasing companies have opened since 1990 in Slovakia, mainly private sector banks and financial institutions, some with foreign participation. In the banking sector, for example, by the end of 1996, 25 new private banks accounted for 43 per cent of the assets in the banking system, while the 5 remaining state-owned banks accounted for the remaining 57 per cent. In Slovakia, the consistently high budget and current account deficits have been financed increasingly by short-term and foreign borrowing. The Slovak central bank has been forced to impose high real interest rates, and the increasing burden of servicing domestic debt has forced Slovak companies and banks to finance their operations and investment needs abroad and use non-traditional means. Leasing has been recognised in

---

[12] This is different from the operating leases defined in the USA, UK, and many other western countries where operating leases do not offer buy option.

[13] Except for the case of passenger cars. In the case of passenger cars the lessee may only deduct the running costs of the vehicle relative to the actual mileage, and not the whole of the lease rental.

Slovakia as a most effective means to finance the projects and to attractive foreign investment. However, real information on leasing and its development in regulation and accounting treatment is unknown. Generally speaking, many operating and accounting treatment issues are more or less similar to the Czech republic as it was used to be part of the federation. The accounting treatment for leases in Slovakia is the same as in the Czech Republic as the Accountancy Act which was approved by the Federal Assembly of the Czech and Slovak Federal Republic on 12 December 1991 still applies to companies in the Slovak Republic. The Act does not mention leases and cover any details of treatments of rented assets or equipment.

Russia

The process of radical economic reform towards a more open and market orientated economy has been underway in Russia since January 1992. Leasing has been recognised as playing a large part in Russia's transformation to a market economy with predictions of business turnover between \$5-10 billion by the year 2005, despite leasing is presently a very small business in Russia. In 1996, leasing transactions are estimated to comprise only about 1% of the total expenditures for new equipment acquired in Russia. Due to the Russian banks' inability to supply funds, leasing is an attractive tool for small growing companies looking for new technology and equipment in order to compete actively within the new economy. The costs of lease payments, including built-in finance charges, and are fully deductible for Russian lessees, while interest payments on loans are not. Accelerated depreciation of leased assets is allowed under Russian law at a rate three times faster than straight line. Russian leasing companies are mostly subsidiaries of Russian banks or industrial groups. The clients of Russian leasing companies are almost exclusively customers of their controlling shareholders or their controlling shareholders themselves. Russian corporate-controlled leasing companies are mainly used as a means of distributing particular items of equipment to affiliated companies rather than providing cash financing. Currently, the reform of Russia's business environment which is essential to the growth of the leasing industry has been neglected. Poor regulation and an inadequate legal system are stifling the creation of new leasing companies and inward leasing investment.

Generally speaking, leasing industries in eastern Europe are immature and the markets are underdeveloped. However, measuring the size of leasing markets and performance of leasing companies in eastern Europe is more of an art than a science. Accounting standards vary across and within countries and balance sheets do not always present the full financial picture of companies. Statistics do not cover small companies that most leasing companies and their clients belong to.

Conclusion

Leasing as an alternative means of financing has been introduced into and developed in both China and eastern Europe, though it is a small scale business. Over the last few years, there were some successful developments of leasing in those economies. For example, almost all countries have established their leasing associations and attempted to attracted foreign leasing companies to invest in their markets. Aircraft leasing has been used to financed their aviation industry (particular in China). The period of complete dominance of a simple financial lease on the markets is over. Operating leases have increasingly played a role in the economies. The scale of additional services is also growing. Market pressure is gradually leading to taking over of residential value risks by leasing companies. Credit risk of both customers and suppliers is being verified with greater care. A remarkable concentration and specialisation is occurring in the area of leasing supply. It is expected that in the future the markets in these economies will consolidate in the hands of a few strongest leasing companies.

The major common problems facing the leasing industries in all transition economies are the lack of finance and capital investments and of appropriate legislation protecting the leasing industry and business. As a result, the majority of leasing players are small and financially dependent on their parent companies or other partners. However, joint venture leasing companies are often confronted with the following, often seemingly in-solvable issues:

- credit assessment and due diligence problems and lack of reliable, verifiable historical information;
- poor or non-existed database and market information needed to make reliable forecasts of expected cash flows from operations and route networks;
- assessment of non-transparent cost-bases;
- structural weaknesses of the domestic banking and financial sectors.

It has been known that structural weaknesses of the domestic banking and financial sectors were a main cause of the east Asian financial collapse due to their immature markets and weak institutional structure. To the leasing industries in transition economies, they are especially vulnerable to such external shocks and pressures. The future development of leasing will depend on the general economic reform and particularly on the banking and financial services reforms. Supports from banks and government policies (e.g., tax provision) will be the key for the leasing industry to expand their market share and overcome the financing difficulty. The potential areas for further growth will be the property lease and high-tech operating lease. Internationalisation of the leasing industry will be paralleled with the development of cross-border leasing. However, it is impossible to harmonise the legal and accounting treatments of leases in a short run as the transition economies have their own political and economic agenda which will delineate the future legal and accounting systems.

The flow of private capital to the transition economies of eastern Europe and the former Soviet Union has reflected the trends from official funding, FDI, non-guaranteed debt, dedicated equity funds to direct local stock and money market investments (Lankes and Stern 1997). The level and quality of private capital flows depends crucially on perceptions of risks and returns. These, in turn, depend not only on basic endowments and opportunities, but also on the ability to respond to opportunities in an effective, market-oriented fashion, or more generally, the 'investment climate' in recipient countries. International leasing investors in emerging markets follow the similar pattern. There is evidence that these investors are recently turning to eastern Europe as a bulwark against concerns over Asia and Latin America, and the region's links with western Europe. Most of these countries have controlled inflation and lowered interest rates, and great demand for updating their enterprises' equipment. However, future financial sector problems and unstable political systems in eastern Europe could hit the confidence of international leasing investors.

Reference

Aiken, M., W. Lu and X.D. Ji. 1995. The new accounting standard in China: a critical analysis. In *Perspectives on Accounting and Finance in China*, ed. J. Blake and S.S. Gao. London: Routledge: 159-177.

Dipchand, C.R. 1993. Leasing is gaining popularity in China. *Working Paper No. 12.* Centre for International Business Studies, Dalhousie University, Halifax, Nova Scotia, Canada.

Dufey, G. and I.H. Giddy. 1981. Innovation in the international financial markets. *Journal of International Business Studies:* 33-51.

Euromoney. 1988. Forfaiting: changing the face of trade. *Euromoney (Supplement)* February: 1-29.

Fang, Z. and Y. Tang. 1991. Recent accounting developments in China: an increasing internationalization. *The International Journal of Accounting* 26: 85-103.

Gao, S.S. 1991. Economic and Financial System Reforms in the People's Republic of China. *Report 9107/ACC,* Rotterdam: Centre for Research in Business Economics, Erasmus University Rotterdam.

Gao, S.S. 1994. The development of lease financing in China: market, regulations, taxes and accounting. Paper presented at *The Annual Conference of the Chinese Economics Association (UK).* London.

Gao, S.S. 1995. Leasing in Poland: privatisation, financing and current problems. *European Business Review* no. 5: 31-40.

Gao, S.S. and W. Herbert. 1996. Leasing finance in emerging markets: an eastern European study. *Managerial Finance* 22, no. 12: 39-53.

IASC. 1982. *International Accounting Standards (IAS) No.17: Accounting for Leases,* International Accounting Standards Committee.

Lankes, H.P. and N.H. Stern. 1997. Capital flows to eastern Europe and the former Soviet Union. *EBRD Working Paper No.27* February.

Ripley, A. 1996. *Forfaiting for Exporters: Practical Solutions for Global Trade Finance.* London: International Thomson Business Press.

Tang, Y.W., B.J. Cooper and P. Leung. 1995. Accounting in China: developments and opportunities. In *Perspectives on Accounting and Finance in China,* ed. J. Blake and S. S. Gao. London: Routledge: 23-37.

World Leasing Yearbook. 1997. London: Euromoney Publication.

14 Conclusions

Summary and conclusions

Although the leasing industry has come of age, international leasing is quite new to business, particularly in many emerging economies. Even in the west developed countries, cross-border leasing has not been fully explored and is underdeveloped in many areas due to its complexity, high risks involved, and the frequent changes of tax and accounting rules. Many banks and financial services firms do not have the skills and experience to enter this type of business.

Especially, international leasing has not been paid much attention in the academic world. Very few academic research books and papers on the subject can be found. This book is a study of international leasing with a special focus on its strategy and decision. The objective of this book, as described in Chapter 1, is to systematically investigate international leasing with a special focus on its strategy and decision aspects. The scope of this book, however, not only covers these two aspects, but also deals with more wider aspects relating to its marketing, investment, financing, taxation and risk areas.

In *Chapter 1*, an overview of the world leasing market is presented for the purpose of identifying the academic challenges and the objective of this book. From a general overview of the world leasing market, it is concluded that leasing has established itself as an important form of financing in developed countries and recently expanded considerably in developing countries, and international leasing has gradually spread through nations and increasingly become an important means of investment and financing. However, academic research on international leasing is very limited. Many modern economics and finance theories have not been applied to international leasing. Clearly, there is a gap between international leasing practices and academic research.

Chapter 2 is concerned with the theory of leasing. The concept of leasing is discussed with a review of the literature. My own definitions of "lease" and "leasing" are presented, and four main characteristics of leasing are discussed. A lease is a contract essentially stipulating the separation of ownership of an asset and the right to use it; the user (lessee) will obtain the right to use the asset in exchange for promising to make a series of payments to the owner during a certain period of time that generally corresponds with the useful life of the asset. Leasing is a process of setting up a transaction wherein the owner (lessor) passes the possession and the right to use the asset to the user (lessee) in return for payments made by the user (lessee) for a certain period of time that generally corresponds with the asset's useful life. This chapter also discusses the advantages of leasing. Although leasing offers a number of unique operating and financial advantages, research has also shown some controversies for some of the advantages usually mentioned in leasing books.

Chapter 3 is concerned with the theory of international leasing. The concept of international leasing has not been well defined in the literature. I define international leasing as a process of setting up a transaction wherein the use of an asset is transferred directly or indirectly from the owner (lessor) in one legal jurisdiction to the user (lessee) in another without changing ownership of that asset within a certain period of time that generally corresponds with the useful life of that asset, and the user obtains the right to use that asset in exchange for paying a series of rental charges to the owner or the lessor. A comparison of international and domestic leasing is made in a table. In this chapter, I also discuss types of international leasing by reviewing the literature and deliberating the criteria of classification. Using various criteria, I divide international leasing from the lessor's and lessee's points of view into export/import leasing versus investment/financing leasing; currency leasing versus barter leasing; tax-oriented leasing versus non-tax-oriented leasing; capital/finance leasing versus operating leasing; direct leasing versus leveraged leasing. In addition, the structure of international leasing, and the forms of international leasing transactions are described. There are generally five segments of international lessors composed of financial institution lessors, independent lessors, captives, joint venture leasing companies, and state-owned leasing companies. In terms of forms of international leasing transactions, there are broadly four basic types: a direct two-country cross-border leasing transaction; a direct three-country international leasing transaction; an international leveraged leasing transaction; and an international wrap leasing transaction.

In *Chapter 4*, the relation between international trade and international leasing is discussed. After a discussion of the current trade environment, it is argued that a favourable climate of international trade will provide potential opportunities for the development of international leasing, whereas the growth of international leasing will promote international trade. The main routes of leasing promoting exports are presented in this chapter. Chapter 4 also explores a new concept of "counterleasing" and discusses international leasing in the balance of payments. Counterleasing refers to a variety of unconventional international leasing transactions which directly or indirectly link exchange of the use of goods or assets in an attempt to pass over currency transactions, and it consists of four main forms: barterleasing, counterlease, lease-back and lease-offset.

In *Chapter 5*, the relation between international finance and international leasing is discussed with a special focus on the international finance environment, the foreign exchange market and hedge strategies. It is concluded that the changing financial environment, mainly represented in the current deregulation and liberalisation of international financial markets has created new problems and challenges to international leasing. The increasing globalisation of leasing requires the leasing industry to adapt the change of the new environments and accordingly to change their strategies.

Chapter 6 addresses the issue of international leasing investment. It is argued that international leasing is an important form of international investment in equipment and facilities, and international leasing investment is expected to play a certain role in global investment in the future. International leasing investment means that a lessor (an investor) leases an asset to a foreign firm, institution, or government organisation in order to earn a return in the form of net rentals or other forms of capital gains. A comparison between portfolio investment, direct investment and leasing investment is made with a view to exploring the characteristics of leasing investment. This chapter also discusses political risks of foreign leasing investment.

Chapter 7 examines leasing as a device of international marketing. The special role played by leasing in international marketing is due to the fact that leasing not only distributes assets to customers, but also provides customers financing services. The provision of financing makes leasing a preferred marketing channel for many exporters. This chapter also discusses international leasing market segments, marketing research and international lease pricing. Leasing marketing research is a systematic gathering, recording, and analysing of data about leasing marketing problems, and it facilitates leasing decision making.

Chapter 8 is concerned with the principles, techniques and factors of international leasing analysis. The principles and rules include: the principle of maximisation of shareholders' wealth; the risk and tradeoff; the four-step decision rule; the value-additivity principle; and considering quantitative and non-quantitative factors. This chapter also introduces some financial theories and decision-making techniques with a particular focus on their interpretation and application in international leasing. Among others, they are present value and net present value, the risk-adjusted discount rate technique, option theory, the sensitivity analysis technique, and the risk ranking technique. Furthermore, this chapter analyses a number of factors that may influence international leasing strategy-planning and decision-making. Factors include cash flows, discount rates, risks, foreign exchange rates and risks, inflation, taxes, import and stamp duties.

Chapter 9 specially focuses on the double-dip issue of international leasing analysis. One of the main advantages of cross-border leasing is the tax savings through structuring a double-dip transaction in which both the lessor and the lessee are qualified in their own tax system as the owner for tax purposes given to the leased asset. This chapter examines the financial advantages of double-dip leasing by developing an evaluation model. It is also mentioned in this chapter that there is an increasing difficulty to design a double-dip transaction as most tax authorities recently take extraordinary measures to prevent the tax advantages to international leasing.

Chapter 10 deals particularly with the strategy and decision of international leasing from the lessee's point of view. In this chapter several international leasing decision models are built according to the basic principles, techniques and factors discussed in Chapter 8. Why do firms lease overseas? The reasons differ considerably from lessee to lessee, and from country to country. Broadly speaking, international leasing has the following main advantages: it may be the cheapest (or only) way to obtain the use of assets due to import (or export) controls, the existence of patent rights, or other constraints; it may offer an additional foreign source of finance; it may provide lessees worldwide with a steady supply of long-term financing during the period of credit scarcity and interest-rate volatility; it may take advantage of tax differences between countries of a lessee and a lessor; it may provide investors with diversification benefits; it may reduce political risks of a lessee; it can be used to take advantage of different accounting or legal treatments among countries; and it may lower other costs of acquiring the use of assets. After discussing the advantages of international leasing, this chapter considers theoretical considerations of international leasing strategies and decisions from a lessee's perspective. Mainly, it discusses passive and active strategies and decisions, underlying decision roles, asymmetrical tax incentives, and capital structure of a lessee. It explores in a general way the strategies and decisions of a lessee, including the lease vs. make decision, the lease payments decision, and the operating leasing decision. Further, it concentrates on international financial leasing decisions and strategies. The decision process is presented. Generally, a lessee should first make a "passive decision" assuming that leasing is a normal financial leasing case in which the lessee is unable to obtain depreciation tax shields. If the adjusted present value of a leasing project at this case is positive, this project should be undertaken. If the adjusted present value is negative, the lessee should further consider an "active decision" specially focusing on a double-dip leasing case. If the adjusted present value under a double-dip case is still negative, the project should be rejected, whereas if it is positive, then the project should be undertaken. This chapter further discusses evaluation models. After this, this chapter focuses on the international lease vs. import decision by developing a decision-making model. The model is derived from the objective of maximising the equilibrium market value of the firm taking interactions of capital budgeting decision, financing decision and other variables into account.

Chapter 11 addresses the strategy and decision of international leasing from the lessor's perspective. Traditional analysis of leasing has focused almost exclusively on the problem of a lessee, the user of the equipment, and very little has been written on lease analysis from a lessor's point of view. Two factors are of utmost importance in decision-making with respect to international leasing from the lessor's point of view: the timing and size of cash flow, and the appropriate discount rate. The discount rate used in decision-making should contain a risk premium reflecting both the gains from international diversification, and exchange risks and costs associated with international transactions. Following a discussion of general considerations, this chapter addresses common strategies and basic models available for an international leasing company. One common strategy is to establish leasing ventures within the domestic markets of foreign countries. This chapter is particularly concerned with international leasing financial decisions from the lessor's point of view examining three major types of international leasing: international financial leasing, international leveraged leasing, and international operating leasing. First, financial decisions of international financial leasing are addressed with emphasis on model-designing by way of expanding the Lessard model. In terms of the discount rates in the model, it suggests to use the risk ranking method, and shows how it could be done with a hypothetical example. Second, financial decisions of international leveraged leasing are investigated. International leveraged leasing is a relatively complex financial instrument, currently gaining in popularity in financing large and expensive assets. An international leveraged lease is a multi-party/nation financial leasing agreement in which the lessor borrows from a third party lender a substantial portion of the purchase price of the asset. The debt instrument provides for a non-recourse loan by the lender to the lessor who, in turn, leases the asset to the foreign lessee. A number of evaluation models including the sinking fund method/model, the separate phases model, the averaged growth rate model, the internal rate of return model, the net present value model, the net terminal value model, and the mixed integer linear programming model are compared. Third, financial decisions of international operating leasing are analysed laying emphasis on designing financial models of international operating leasing. International operating leasing is a lease transaction that is short-term and cancellable during the lease contract period at the option of a foreign lessee. From the lessor's point of view, international operating leasing is riskier than financial leasing. This is because the cost of a leased asset under an operating lease is not wholly recovered by the lessor out of the rentals receivable during the non-cancellable period that is normally significantly shorter than the estimated useful life of the asset. In fact, international operating leasing is a flexible and increasingly popular financing instrument, but the related literature is very scarce. The Copeland and Weston model was traditionally regarded as a basic model for the evaluation of an operating lease. In this chapter, an alternative analysis is presented by way of splitting the value of an operating lease into two elements: one element is merely used to cover those items relating to depreciation tax shields, investment tax credits, and interest tax savings of debts supported by the obtaining of depreciation tax shields; and the other element is merely used to refer terms that depend on the lessee's cancellation of the lease contract. This separation enables analysts to concentrate on the items that are closely related to the lessee's cancellation.

Chapter 12 briefly discusses international sale-and-leaseback transactions with a special focus on the issue of why firms sell and leaseback, and the conditions to structure an international sale-and-leaseback from the accounting point of view.

Chapter 13 studies leasing in emerging markets with a focus on China and eastern Europe. It examines the development of leasing in the transition economics and its financial functions to the economic reforms in these countries. Leasing as an alternative means of financing has been introduced into and developed in both China and eastern Europe, though it is small scale business. In this chapter, the leasing industries in China, the Czech Republic, Hungary, Poland, Slovakia, Russia and its legal and accounting aspects are studied. The major problems facing the leasing industries in all transition economies are the lack of finance and capital investments, and of appropriate legislation protecting the leasing industry and business. As a result, the majority of leasing players in these markets are small and financially dependent on their parent companies.

Areas for further research

In this final section I shall touch upon some of the questions that have not been fully addressed or solved in this book. The questions are mainly related to the empirical research and the application of new theories. As mentioned previously, empirical data about international leasing are very scarce, and official publications of financial information do not give the whole picture of international leasing transactions. It will be very interesting and useful if we can empirically identify, if the data would be available, the relationship between international leasing and international trade. Also, it will be valuable to the development of financial theories if the impact of international leasing on the value of the firm can be measured empirically.

An understanding of the global environmental and cultural context of leasing, and of the impact of international forces for change, is instructive in providing the rationale and inspiration for a variety of important challenges for international leasing researchers. In this context, an attempt is made here to identify some important leasing research issues which would seem worthy of attention and future investigation.

We do know that multinational and diversified companies must take international leasing into account when developing and setting policies regarding the capital structure, financing, investment, marketing, evaluation and management of their subsidiaries. But, we don't know how they do it in practice. In fact, the ways of treating international leasing in designing business strategies and making decisions differ from company to company, and from country to country. However, an international comparison and classification should be made in order to know how multinational companies take account of international leasing in their decision making and strategy formulation. This is an area we hope to research further.

Along with the changing strategies and organisation of international leasing corporations there are a range of issues concerning the design, implementation and use of control systems, and criteria for performance evaluation, with the goal of not only matching or incorporating the national culture of foreign subsidiaries but also promoting overall co-ordination of leasing business. To what extent and with what effect are international leasing corporations adapting their systems to cope with changing organisational structures in the context of asset/equipment-focus consolidation and global diversification?

Theoretical arguments for the use of international leasing have been set forth in the literature. However, empirical studies indicate the complexities of leasing evaluation and decision-making, and find that many practitioners have to some extent been defeated by the complexities. There is a question left to be answered. How to narrow the gap between the theoretical arguments for the use of international leasing and the practical difficulties of doing international leasing business? Whether or not our theoretical evaluation models are simplified enough to be used to determine the cost of overseas leasing of assets, and to discover the advantages of leasing over other financing instruments.

From the business point of view, the future and success of individual lessors will depend more and more on their ability to come up with new structures and products, and on their marketing abilities. Lessors will also have to consider more carefully the role of leasing in the financial community. If lessors believe that their main role in the future will be the creation of assets rather than be the providers of money, how do they change their existing operation strategies?[1] Indeed, lessors will have to acquire even more specialist knowledge of the assets they provide in order to give the customer the added-value benefits. In this sense, the further research should focus not only on financing aspects of leasing, but also on assets and products management of leasing. However, assets and products management research

---

[1] Although there are currently two main types of lessors: lessors/manufacturers and lessors/financiers which are considered as "providers of money", the role of the latter type may have to shift in the future from traditional financial leasing approaches to approaches that are directly related to assets and asset creation activities.

will require the researchers to have more specialist knowledge of particular assets. This is a challenge facing leasing researchers.

The capital structure of a firm has an important impact on its profitability and stability. While a high proportion of debt may make a company very profitable as it is growing, it also increases the probability of bankruptcy and ruin especially if that growth slows down or temporarily becomes negative. Leasing as a kind of loan, being a long/medium-term debt to a lessee does influence the capital structure of the lessee. How to make the choice between leasing capital assets or buying them is essential to the success of the lessee. International leasing is gaining popularity around the world which is the result of the development of international financing markets and the global economy. In this connection, the global leasing community is also being forced to consider the regulatory changes affecting environmental and product liability. Among the questions to be asked in respect of regulation are: should there be some sort of international institutes to regulate the international leasing community, particularly with the internationalisation of leasing? Who should regulate leasing in the individual countries and what should be the role of the leasing associations? No doubt, leasing legislation will be a prospective target of the authorities around the world. Therefore, research on regulatory factors influencing international leasing, and the legal and tax harmonisation will be one of the main research areas in the future.

Political developments, economic and financial reforms in eastern Europe have revealed an enormous requirement for new investment in capital equipment. The impact of this requirement provokes a rethinking of the use and application of international leasing. However, without sound research into the system of eastern Europe, it will not be easy for both the east Europeans and western lessors to develop leasing business there. Therefore, to examine the possibility and the ways of developing leasing finance in eastern Europe is expected to be put on the research agenda.

Business capabilities and objectives differ from lessor to lessor for a variety of reasons. In order to profit in the highly competitive leasing business, companies have to develop financial and product niches. The Asian crises in 1997 and the crisis in eastern Europe and Latin America in 1998 all added to international leasing companies' fear for overseas leasing market and falling returns. However, it will take some time to overcome the difficulty, particularly in south eastern Asia as many companies are tightening their investment in equipment and overseas import. Market competition for industrial equipment and high-tech assets export has been intensive, and more flexible financing mechanism has been required to attract customers.

International leasing companies need to examine the opportunity for innovation and new products. Traditional leasing, supplemented with other approaches of marketing will add value to equipment and assets. Services attached to the leased equipment and assets will be an important bargain for overseas customers. In an age of increasing globalisation, internationalisation and sophistication, this expectation is becoming more obvious.

1999 marks the beginning of a new era within the financial services and leasing world. The convergence of eleven national currencies into one has been an issue at the forefront of everyone's thoughts in recent years. What will be the impact of single currency on international leasing in the future? No doubt, tax advantages will disappear gradually, and single accounting treatment derived from international accounting standards has bee proposed to replace national practices within the members of EU countries which will, on the one hand, demolish the off-balance benefits which are available in some countries particularly to operating leases. On the other hand, however, this will provide an opportunity to open leasing market for cross-border activities in the future. Non-tax international leasing will expectedly be the mainstream of the business.

To conclude, the 1980s were the decade of domestic leasing. The 1990s and especially the next century will be the era of international leasing and the globalisation of leasing business and markets.

For Product Safety Concerns and Information please contact our EU
representative GPSR@taylorandfrancis.com Taylor & Francis Verlag GmbH,
Kaufingerstraße 24, 80331 München, Germany

Printed and bound by CPI Group (UK) Ltd, Croydon, CR0 4YY

08/05/2025

01864366-0009